# AutoCAD:
# A Concise Guide to Commands and Features

### Ronald W. Leigh

VENTANA
PRESS

**AutoCAD: A Concise Guide to Commands and Features**
Copyright © 1989 by Ronald W. Leigh

Library of Congress Cataloging-in-Publication Data

Leigh, Ronald W. (Ronald Wilson)
    AutoCAD : a concise guide to commands and features.

Includes index.
    1. AutoCAD (Computer program) I. Title.
T385.L42 1989          620'.00425'02855369          89-5766
ISBN 0-940087-31-6

Book design: Karen Wysocki, Ventana Press
Cover design: Dancing Bear Graphics, Raleigh, NC
Typesetting: Pixel Plus Desktop Publishing, Chapel Hill, NC
Editorial Staff: Elizabeth Shoemaker, Marion Laird, Terry Patrickis

First Edition, First Printing
Printed in the United States of America

Ventana Press, Inc.
P.O. Box 2468
Chapel Hill, NC 27515
919/942-0220
FAX 919/942-1140

## Limits of Liability and Disclaimer of Warranty

# TRADEMARK ACKNOWLEDGMENTS

# ABOUT THE AUTHOR

Ronald W. Leigh is chairman of the Computer Aided Design and Drafting Department, an authorized AutoCAD training center, at Indiana Vocational Technical College in Fort Wayne, Indiana.

He is also an AutoCAD and AutoLISP consultant.

Ronald W. Leigh
616 Pinetree Drive
Fort Wayne, IN 46819

# TABLE OF CONTENTS

# INTRODUCTION

## WHY ANOTHER BEGINNING AUTOCAD BOOK?

When AutoCAD was first unleashed on the world back in 1983, most of its users were accustomed to working with intricate reference manuals and had a good deal of previous CAD experience on minis and mainframes. As a result, many books on AutoCAD were—and still are—beyond the scope of today's beginner, who may have far less computer knowledge and programming experience.

In this book, I've deliberately tried to keep the content as straightforward as possible, so that new AutoCAD users can begin to draw without having to wade through complex material on database extraction, AutoLISP programming and other powerful features that should probably be reserved for more advanced treatments.

Those who have mastered the basics may wish to explore AutoCAD's more advanced capabilities; several excellent references are available, including complementary books published by Ventana Press: *The AutoCAD Productivity Book*, *The AutoCAD Database Book*, *The AutoCAD 3D Book* and *AutoLISP in Plain English*.

## WHAT'S INSIDE

*AutoCAD: A Concise Guide to Commands and Features* is a complete introduction to the terms, concepts, commands, skills and procedures required to use AutoCAD effectively. This book is arranged so that the new user can advance from the easiest to the more difficult skills in a logical progression.

Forty chapters take you from the preliminaries (working with DOS, managing your directories) to basic drawing and editing commands, then follow a logical sequence through dimensioning, polylines, attributes and some of AutoCAD's more complex features you'll want to master.

Several appendices provide invaluable exercises to help you get up and running, and information on tablet menus and overlays, working with attributes and creating batch files. Finally, a thorough index will help you find your way around this book.

## HOW TO USE THIS BOOK

*AutoCAD: A Concise Guide* is organized to serve two different purposes. First, it functions as a learning guide to help you progressively master AutoCAD's drawing and editing. Second, after you've learned to use AutoCAD, it serves as a reference book for looking up those details you don't use often enough to remember.

Consider the *AutoCAD Reference Manual,* supplied with AutoCAD. It's an excellent source of information—comprehensive and well organized. However, because the main body of the manual is divided according to major subjects into only 13 chapters, some advanced and difficult commands often were grouped with simple commands. Thus, advanced topics—such as meshes and 3D polylines—appear early in the manual, while basic topics—such as snap and zoom—appear much later.

While this sort of organization works well for a reference manual, it can make learning difficult. In contrast, *AutoCAD: A Concise Guide* organizes all the commands and topics into much smaller groupings and lists them under 40 chapter headings. Difficult, advanced commands are separated from basic, simple commands. By looking at the table of contents, you'll see that the easier and more basic sections appear at the beginning of the book and each subsequent section builds on the earlier sections.

If you start at the beginning and carefully work through each section in turn, you'll build a solid understanding of AutoCAD. And the exercises in Appendix A will help get you actually drawing and designing with this powerful program.

A reference book is useful only if you can find what you're looking for. There are two ways to find material in *AutoCAD: A Concise Guide.*

First, all commands and subjects are listed in the table of contents, and related commands and subjects are grouped together under appropriate headings. The easier and more basic commands and topics appear first.

Second, the index in the back of the book is thorough enough to let you find most any topic that comes to mind.

## HARDWARE/SOFTWARE REQUIREMENTS

*AutoCAD: A Concise Guide* was written for AutoCAD's Release 10, although most of the features and commands also apply to previous versions of

AutoCAD. This book was written for users of any PC-compatible hardware, including 8088, 286 and 386 model machines.

*AutoCAD: A Concise Guide* assumes that your equipment and software are fully installed, configured and ready to draw. For information on installing and configuring AutoCAD, see Chapters 2 and 3 of the *AutoCAD Release 10 Installation and Performance Guide*.

## A NOTE ON AUTOCAD'S TUTORIAL

AutoCAD comes with tutorial exercises that expose you to about one-third of the AutoCAD commands. If you have access to that tutorial, it can introduce you to the general flavor of AutoCAD and explain some of the basic concepts upon which AutoCAD is built.

Although the exercises in AutoCAD's tutorial are organized in different order from the material in this book, they can be used quite effectively with the exercises in Appendix A of *AutoCAD: A Concise Guide*. The table of contents in Appendix A places the AutoCAD tutorial exercises in their most appropriate locations for the best overall sequence of exercises.

## YOU'RE ON YOUR WAY...

...to learning how to use one of the most powerful, exciting computer applications ever written. Every step you master using AutoCAD will save you hours and hours of drawing time down the road. You'll draw faster, design more efficiently and explore a new way of problem solving that will change forever the way you think about your craft. Let's get started.

*Ronald Leigh*
*Fort Wayne, IN*

# 1 PRELIMINARIES

Welcome to computer-aided drafting and design. AutoCAD is a flexible computer drafting program that lets you create two-dimensional drawings and three-dimensional surface models for a wide variety of applications.

This book starts with the most basic concepts and procedures, leads you through all of AutoCAD's drawing and editing commands, and shows you how to customize AutoCAD to produce your particular kind of drawing.

## SUBDIRECTORIES

As you draw on the screen, AutoCAD compiles a body of information in the computer's memory that's continually updated during the drawing/editing process. This information can be filed on the computer's hard disk and/or floppy diskette.

A hard disk holds many more files than a floppy diskette. To manage all those files, the hard disk is divided into various branches or directories. One way of organizing a hard disk is illustrated in the diagram below. Files in each branch are located by a pathname. For example, the pathname C:\ACAD\ACAD3.OVL identifies drive C:, then subdirectory ACAD, then file ACAD3.OVL (one of the AutoCAD program files).

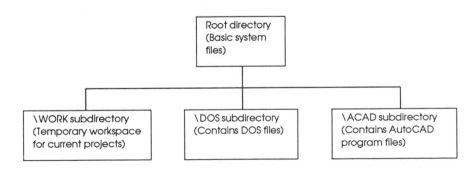

Placing your files on a separate directory (the \WORK directory), rather than mixing them with the AutoCAD program files, lets you manage your files more easily. (See Appendix D for more ideas on hard-disk organization, along with a simple system menu operated by batch files.)

In industry, drawings for each different project might be temporarily filed on a different directory of the hard disk. Drawing files from a particular project could then be copied to floppy diskette when the project is completed. In an educational setting, a different approach may be taken. With many students using each system, the hard disk would quickly become cluttered and drawing security would be hard to maintain. Therefore, students could be required to keep all their files on their own diskettes, using the hard disk only for temporary storage of files.

## FILE NAMES

Here are some sample drawing file names using combinations of letters, numbers and a few other selected characters. Notice that there are no spaces within the file names.

```
BRACKET      PROJ_1      ASSEM1

K123-85      PROJ_2      DET-37

84302875     PROJ_3      LAYOUT3$
```

Each different drawing must have a unique name of eight characters or less. When AutoCAD saves its drawings on the hard disk or on diskette, it automatically adds the file name extension, .DWG. When you're using items 1 and 2 on AutoCAD's main menu, you don't need to enter the .DWG extension. However, when you're using DOS or AutoCAD's File Utility menu (items 2–5), you must enter the entire file name, including the extension.

## CORRECTING KEYBOARD ENTRIES

If you've mistyped information and want to correct it, use the backspace key to return to the mistaken character, then continue typing. This works in both DOS and AutoCAD.

To cancel all characters on a line, use **CTRL-C** or **ESC** (escape key) while in DOS, or **CTRL-X** while in AutoCAD. CTRL-C means hold down the CTRL key, then press the C key. Use the same procedure for CTRL-X.

The computer makes a distinction between number 0 and letter O, and between number 1 and letter l. Don't substitute one for the other.

Beware of "heavy fingers." Most keys repeat when you hold them down.

## DOS COMMANDS

DOS stands for Disk Operating System. DOS is originally contained in a set of program files on the DOS diskette that's supplied with your computer.

DOS is the set of programs (system software) that tells your computer system how to carry out certain behind-the-scenes operations. These operations include placing information on the hard disk, getting a listing of all the files on a floppy diskette, loading a program into memory so it can be run, etc. In short, DOS lets your computer interpret and execute the commands that you enter.

DOS will be loaded into your computer's memory when you turn it on. In fact, it must be present in memory before other programs (applications software) can be run. The process of loading DOS is called "booting DOS" or "booting the system."

The floppy drive is labeled A: (sometimes both A: and B:), and the hard disk is labeled C:.

This book assumes that your computer is already set up and running properly, that DOS is on a directory called \DOS, AutoCAD is on a directory called \ACAD, and you know how to start your computer. If you make sure that the floppy diskette drive (drive A:) is empty when you turn your computer on, DOS will boot from the hard disk (drive C:) rather than from drive A:.

C> is the DOS prompt. The letter "C" indicates that drive C: is the default (current) drive. Unless DOS is directed to do otherwise, it will interact with the default drive. If you or your AUTOEXEC.BAT file have used the PROMPT command to alter the prompt, it may include more information than just the default drive. (See PROMPT below.)

DOS commands can be entered in uppercase or lowercase.

When you're typing DOS commands, spacing is important. Some DOS commands can stand by themselves (such as CLS). Other DOS commands take arguments (such as ERASE BRACKET.DWG). And others can stand alone *or* take arguments (such as DIR or DIR A:). The only spaces should be between the command and the first argument, or between arguments.

The commands below may be entered when you're in DOS. (See Appendix D for a system menu that can simplify some of the operations described below.) After you've started AutoCAD, most DOS commands aren't available again until you exit AutoCAD and thus return to DOS. (However, you can shell out to DOS from the AutoCAD drawing editor. See SHELL in Chapter 9.)

To do a warm boot (system reset) use **CTRL-ALT-DEL** (hold down the CTRL key, hold down the ALT key, and press the DEL key).

Full explanations of these and many more DOS commands are found in the DOS manual:

A:   makes drive A: (the floppy diskette drive) the current drive. "A" will appear in the DOS prompt.

C:   makes drive C: (the hard disk) the current drive. "C" will appear in the DOS prompt.

DIR   displays a list of files in the current (default) directory on the current drive.

DIR A:   displays a list of files on the diskette in drive A:.

DIR /W   displays an abbreviated directory across the screen, so more files can be viewed on a single screenful (W stands for wide).

DIR /P   displays a directory one screenful at a time. Press any key to proceed to the next screenful (P stands for pause).

DIR|SORT   lists directory in alphabetical or numerical order.

DIR|SORT /R   lists directory in reverse alphabetical or numerical order.

DIR|SORT /+10   lists directory with extensions in alphabetical order (sorting starts in column 10).

DIR|SORT /+14   lists directory in order of file size (sorting starts in column 14).

DIR A:|SORT /+14   lists directory of diskette in drive A: in order of file size.

CTRL-S   stops the scrolling of a directory. Press any key to continue.

CTRL-C stops the scrolling of a directory and returns to the DOS prompt.

CD displays the name of the current directory or subdirectory.

CD \XXXXX makes XXXXX (on the current drive) the current directory. For example, CD \WORK makes the subdirectory named WORK the current directory.

CD \ makes the root directory (on the current drive) the current directory.

CLS clears the screen.

DATE displays the present machine date and lets you change it.

TIME displays the present machine time and lets you change it.

PROMPT $p $g causes the DOS prompt to include both the drive letter and the path to the current directory. There's a space after "g" for readability.

FORMAT A: formats the diskette in drive A:.

*Important:* New diskettes must be formatted in order to hold files. Formatting erases all files that were on an old diskette. Be sure to specify drive **A:** when you use the **FORMAT** command, or you may unintentionally erase all files from the hard disk.

COPY A:XXXXXXXX.DWG copies the drawing file XXXXXXXX.DWG from the diskette in drive A: onto the \WORK directory on drive C: (assuming the \WORK directory is the current directory). The file also remains on the diskette in drive A:. The COPY command expects two arguments—**from** and **to**. In the example above, the first argument identifies the drive and file to be copied **from.** Since there's no second argument, DOS copies the file **to** the default directory.

COPY XXXXXXXX.DWG A: copies the drawing file XXXXXXXX.DWG from the \WORK directory on drive C: onto the diskette in drive A: (assuming the \WORK directory is the current directory).

ERASE XXXXXXXX.XXX erases file XXXXXXXX.XXX from the current directory.

ERASE A:XXXXXXXX.XXX erases file XXXXXXXX.XXX from the diskette in drive A:.

DEL (Short for DELETE) works the same as ERASE.

RENAME XXXXXXXX.XXX XXXXXXXX.XXX changes the name of a file on the current directory from the first file name to the second file name. RENAME can be abbreviated REN.

PATH C:\;C:\DOS;C:\ACAD establishes three paths that DOS will follow in searching for certain kinds of files not found on the current directory. One or more paths can be established at once. Each path must be separated from the others by a semicolon (;).

Wild cards: * stands for all remaining characters (all characters remaining in either the primary part of the file name or the extension). You can't place any characters after the asterisk (see note on wild cards under the FILES command). ? stands for any single character.

DIR *.BAK lists all files with the extension .BAK.

DIR PART?21.DWG lists, for example, the following files: PARTA21.DWG, PARTB21.DWG, PARTC21.DWG, PARTD21.DWG

COPY CUSTOM1.MNU PRN prints the file CUSTOM1.MNU on the printer.

COPY CUSTOM1.MNU LPT1—same as above.

TYPE CUSTOM.MNU > PRN—same as above.

SHFT-PRTSC prints the current text screen.

CTRL-PRTSC (or CTRL-P) prints each new line as it scrolls onto the bottom of the screen. Use CTRL-PRTSC (or CTRL-P) again to halt printing of subsequent lines.

COPY FILE1.TXT+FILE2.TXT+FILE3.TXT BIGFILE.TXT combines three files into a new file called BIGFILE.TXT.

COPY FILE1.TXT+FILE2.TXT+FILE3.TXT appends the second and third files onto the end of FILE1.TXT.

MD \UTILITY makes a subdirectory called UTILITY immediately under the root directory on the hard disk (assuming drive C: is the default drive).

RD \UTILITY removes a subdirectory called UTILITY immediately under the root directory on the hard disk (assuming drive C: is the default drive). A subdirectory can be removed only after all its files have been erased. Don't try to erase the "." and ".." files with the erase command. Instead, use the RD command.

TREE displays the structure of directories and subdirectories.

CHKDSK checks a disk (floppy diskette or hard disk) and displays error messages, status report, etc.

TYPE BSETUP.SCR displays the contents of the file BSETUP.SCR.

SET   displays the environment, including PATH, PROMPT and environmental variable settings.

SET ACADCFG=\TMO  sets the variable ACADCFG to the subdirectory \TMO (see "Using Two Menu Configurations" in Chapter 37).

## Using DOS Commands in AutoCAD

As a general rule, you use DOS commands when you're "in DOS" (at the DOS prompt) and you use AutoCAD commands when you're in AutoCAD (in AutoCAD's drawing editor). However, this general rule doesn't tell the whole story, because there are four ways to carry out DOS operations while you are in AutoCAD.

1. You can use AutoCAD's File Utility menu. This menu, which is accessed from the main menu, lets you list, copy, rename and erase files. See "Main Menu Organization" in Chapter 2.

2. You can use the FILES command. This command gives you access to the same File Utility menu that is accessed from the main menu. See FILES in Chapter 9.

3. You can use the SHELL command to gain access to all DOS commands. See SHELL in Chapter 9.

4. You can alter the ACAD.PGP file so that certain DOS commands and other programs can be called directly from the **Command:** prompt in the drawing editor. See "Changing the ACAD.PGP File" in Chapter 37.

## Using BASIC Commands

Several simple BASIC language commands are listed below. The first three commands, BASIC, BASICA and BASIC PRESSURE, are used while you're in DOS (or have shelled out to DOS; see SHELL in Chapter 9). The remaining commands are used while you are in BASIC or BASICA. The BASIC prompt is OK. See the BASIC manual for more details.

BASIC  loads the BASIC language.

BASICA  loads the Advanced BASIC language.

BASIC PRESSURE  loads the BASIC language and runs the program PRESSURE.BAS.

LOAD "XXXXXX" loads the BASIC program XXXXXX.

LIST lists the BASIC program that's currently loaded.

CTRL–NUMLOCK stops the scrolling of a BASIC program listing. Press any key to continue.

CTRL–BREAK stops the scrolling of a BASIC program listing and returns to the BASIC prompt.

RUN runs the BASIC program that's currently loaded.

SYSTEM exits BASIC and returns to DOS.

# ENTERING/EXITING AUTOCAD

## AUTOCAD STARTUP

1. Boot DOS and, if needed, enter the date and time. Make sure the floppy diskette drive is empty before turning the system on, so it will boot from the hard disk.

2. Enter **PROMPT $p $g**. For readability, include a space after the "g." This command makes the DOS promptly display the current directory as well as the current drive.

3. Enter **CD/WORK**. This makes \WORK the current directory.

4. Enter **PATH C:\;C:\DOS;C:\ACAD**. This establishes a path to the root, \DOS and \ACAD directories for DOS to use in later file searches.

5. If you plan to use a custom tablet menu overlay and have created a separate configuration directory called \TMO under the \ACAD directory, then type **SET ACADCFG=\ACAD\TMO** (see "Using Two Menu Configurations" in Chapter 37).

6. Enter **DIR**. The directory listing that appears on the screen should contain only two files—the file that identifies this as a subdirectory (.) and the file that identifies the parent directory (..).

7. If you find leftover files that you want to erase, use **ERASE \*.\*** (The asterisks are wild cards standing for any file name, any extension.) Be sure you're in the \WORK subdirectory before you erase all the files. You can tell which directory is current by looking either at the DOS prompt or at the top of a DIRectory listing.

8. If you'll be editing a drawing on floppy diskette, place that diskette in drive A: and enter **COPY A:XXXXXXXX.DWG**. (This copies file XXXXXXXX.DWG from drive A: onto the \WORK directory on drive C:.) You can copy several files at once by using wild cards. For example, entering **COPY A:\*.DWG** copies all drawings from the diskette in drive A: onto the \WORK directory on the hard disk.

9. Enter **ACAD**. This starts AutoCAD. If an opening message appears, press <RETURN> to proceed to the main menu.

The above start-up procedure reflects only one of many ways to run AutoCAD. It assumes that the DOS files are in the \DOS directory of the hard disk (as shown earlier under "Subdirectories") and that the AutoCAD program files are in the \ACAD directory. It also assumes that you're using AutoCAD in an educational setting, and will be copying your drawing files into the \WORK directory for use during the work session, then copying the new and edited files back onto floppy diskettes at the end of the session and clearing the \WORK subdirectory.

Steps 2 through 6 in the above procedure can be replaced with a batch file. See "Batch Files" in Chapter 26 for instructions on creating batch files and autoexec batch files. Also see Appendix D for two sample batch files you can use to start AutoCAD—18.BAT and 19.BAT. You can use these files as part of a system menu, or rename them and use them independently.

## CTRL-C (Control-C)

**Escapes from any procedure**

CTRL-C means hold down the CTRL key and press C.

If you use CTRL-C after selecting a menu item, you'll be returned to that menu for another selection.

If you're in the drawing editor and use CTRL-C after entering a command, you'll be returned to command mode. CTRL-C can also be used to exit a dialogue box or to halt a REGEN (regeneration) in order to save time.

## EXITING AUTOCAD

To exit AutoCAD, select **0** on the main menu.

If you're in the drawing editor and want to exit AutoCAD, you must enter **END** or **QUIT** to be returned to the main menu (see END and QUIT in Chapter 9).

When you exit AutoCAD, you're returned to DOS and the DOS prompt will appear at the bottom of the screen.

## MAIN MENU ORGANIZATION

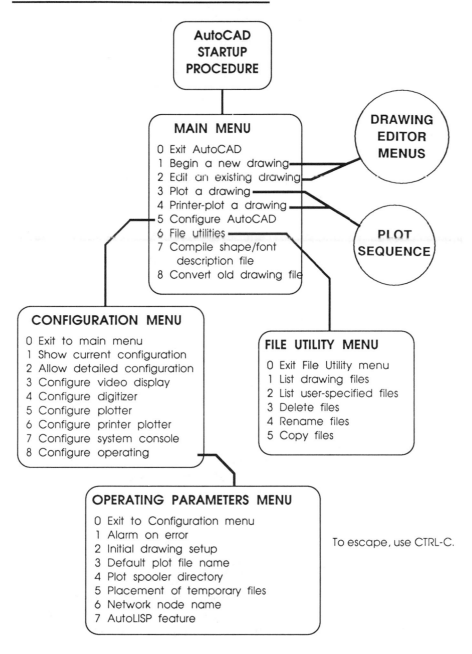

AutoCAD
STARTUP
PROCEDURE

MAIN MENU

0 Exit AutoCAD
1 Begin a new drawing
2 Edit an existing drawing
3 Plot a drawing
4 Printer-plot a drawing
5 Configure AutoCAD
6 File utilities
7 Compile shape/font
  description file
8 Convert old drawing file

DRAWING
EDITOR
MENUS

PLOT
SEQUENCE

CONFIGURATION MENU

0 Exit to main menu
1 Show current configuration
2 Allow detailed configuration
3 Configure video display
4 Configure digitizer
5 Configure plotter
6 Configure printer plotter
7 Configure system console
8 Configure operating

FILE UTILITY MENU

0 Exit File Utility menu
1 List drawing files
2 List user-specified files
3 Delete files
4 Rename files
5 Copy files

OPERATING PARAMETERS MENU

0 Exit to Configuration menu
1 Alarm on error
2 Initial drawing setup
3 Default plot file name
4 Plot spooler directory
5 Placement of temporary files
6 Network node name
7 AutoLISP feature

To escape, use CTRL-C.

## STARTING A NEW DRAWING

Select **1** on the main menu.

When prompted, enter the name of the new drawing (up to eight characters). Don't enter the .DWG extension. AutoCAD then loads its drawing editor and menu and places you in command mode.

If you enter only the name of the new drawing, AutoCAD will establish the limits, grid, snap, layers, etc. for the new drawing according to its default prototype. However, if you want to start a new drawing using a different prototype, type an equals sign and the name of that other prototype drawing immediately after the name of the new drawing. Or, you can tell AutoCAD to use no prototype drawing at all by typing just an equals sign right after the name of the new drawing.

Suppose you have a drawing called SHEET1 that includes border, title block, limits set at 18 x 12, grid set at 1, and several layers. Suppose also that you're starting a new drawing called PART15. When you're prompted for the name of the new drawing, you can enter any one of the following three options:

PART15   AutoCAD will use the default prototype drawing.

PART15=   AutoCAD won't use any prototype drawing; it will use system defaults.

PART15=SHEET1   AutoCAD will use SHEET1 as the prototype drawing.

When you call for a prototype drawing, as in the third option above, the name of the new drawing always comes first. Don't put any spaces before or after the equals sign.

Any drawing can serve as a prototype drawing. It can reside in the \ACAD or the \WORK directory, or you can include a path name to any other drive or directory. You can edit prototype drawings in the same way as any other drawing. See "Creating Prototype Drawings" in Chapter 17.

## DURING A DRAWING SESSION

Every 30 to 60 minutes, you should save the latest version of your drawing on the hard disk. To do so, enter **SAVE**, then press <**RETURN**> if you want to accept the default drawing name (the name you gave the drawing when you started it).

To save the latest version of your drawing on floppy diskette, place the diskette in drive A: and enter **SAVE**, then enter **A:XXXXXXXX**. Or, you can transfer the drawing from the hard disk to your floppy diskette after you exit AutoCAD's drawing editor, as explained in Step 3 below.

## ENDING A DRAWING SESSION

When you're drawing with AutoCAD, you're in the drawing editor. To end a drawing session completely (to exit both the drawing editor and AutoCAD), follow these steps:

1. Enter **END** (Saves the latest version of the drawing on hard disk and returns to the main menu.)

2. At the main menu, enter **0** (Exits AutoCAD and returns to DOS.)

3. Make sure that your diskette is in drive A:, then enter **COPY XXXXXXXX.DWG A:**.

> If you have edited several drawings and want to copy all of them onto the floppy diskette, enter **COPY \*.DWG A:**.

> Skip this step if you've saved your drawings on floppy diskette immediately before exiting the drawing editor, as explained above under "During a Drawing Session."

> *Suggestion:* Copy your drawing(s) onto two diskettes. After you place the second diskette in drive A:, you don't need to retype the same COPY . . . command. You can repeat any DOS command simply by pressing **F3**, then <RETURN>.

4. Enter **DIR**. Check this directory listing to make sure you've copied all the drawing files you should.

5. Enter **ERASE \*.\*** *Important:* Make sure you're in the \WORK directory before you erase all the files.

## EDITING AN EXISTING DRAWING

Select **2** on the main menu. When prompted, enter the exact name of the existing drawing. Don't enter the .DWG extension.

AutoCAD then loads its drawing editor and menu and places you in command mode. The units, limits, snap, grid, layer, text style and other settings will be exactly as they were when you last saved this drawing.

## SCREEN ORGANIZATION

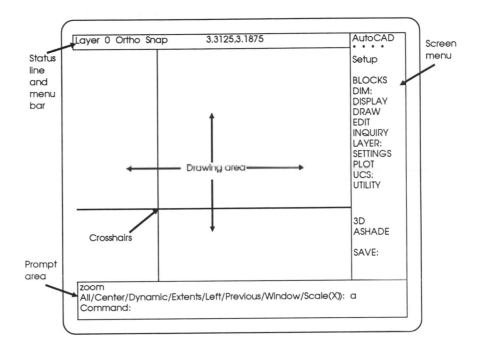

The User Coordinate System icon may appear in the lower left corner of the drawing area. To remove it, enter **UCSICON**, then **OFF** (see UCSICON in Chapter 31).

A box (aperture) appears on the crosshairs when OSNAP is activated (see OSNAP in Chapter 12). Also, the crosshairs change to a pick box when you're prompted to select objects (see PICKBOX in Chapter 6).

## CARTESIAN COORDINATES AND ANGLES

The basic 2D X-Y construction plane is described in this section. A more advanced coordinate system, which lets you place an X-Y construction plane anywhere in space, is described in "User Coordinate Systems" in Chapter 31.

Notice that when coordinates (pairs of X and Y distances) are given, the X coordinate is always given first and they are separated by a comma (no spaces).

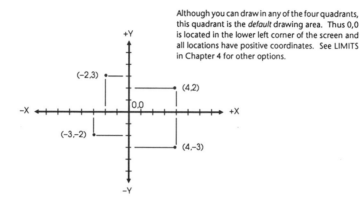

Although you can draw in any of the four quadrants, this quadrant is the *default* drawing area. Thus 0,0 is located in the lower left corner of the screen and all locations have positive coordinates. See LIMITS in Chapter 4 for other options.

The standard conventions for angles are as follows:

Angles are normally measured from the positive X direction. Positive angles normally revolve counterclockwise, while negative angles revolve clockwise.

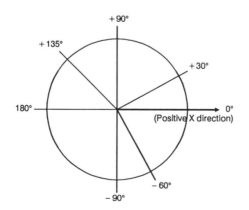

However, you can select any angle as the zero-angle, and you can select either counterclockwise or clockwise as positive rotation (see UNITS in Chapter 4).

## ENTERING AUTOCAD COMMANDS

You can enter AutoCAD commands in several different ways:

1. Keyboard: Type the command at the keyboard (in upper- or lower-case), then press <RETURN>. Be sure you're in command mode before you enter the command. You're in command mode whenever you're in the drawing editor and the **Command:** prompt is displayed. No matter what page of the screen menu is currently showing, you can enter any command from the keyboard as long as you're in command mode. You can return to command mode at any time by using **CTRL-C**.

There's an important difference between AutoCAD commands and DOS commands. Many DOS commands will accept a space, then one or two arguments. However, when you're in AutoCAD, the space bar usually works like another <RETURN> key. Each AutoCAD command that you type in at the keyboard must be entered first (using either the <RETURN> key or the space bar), then you'll be prompted for the remaining input.

You'll notice that screen menu items may be highlighted as you begin typing a command. Once the appropriate command is highlighted, you can enter it with the INS (Insert) key without having to type the full name of the command.

2. Screen menu: Use the pointer to enter the command from the menu that appears on the right side of the screen. See "Pointer Buttons" and "The Standard Screen Menu," below.

The screen menu contains two kinds of items. Items followed by a colon enter a command and call up a different page of the menu. Items that aren't followed by a colon merely call up a different page of the menu. Some submenus occupy two pages. Notice that most screen menu items are in alphabetical order.

You can also use the up- and down-arrow keys on the keyboard to highlight commands on the screen menu, then press the INS (Insert) key to enter the highlighted command.

3. Tablet overlay: Use the pick button on the pointer to enter the command from a tablet menu overlay. Before you can use AutoCAD's standard tablet template, you must configure the digitizing tablet using the **TABLET** command. See Step 3 in "Tablet Menu Overlay," in Chapter 37.

4. Pull-down menus: To display the menu bar, move the crosshairs into the status line at the top of the screen. Use the pointer's pick button to pull

down a menu, then select the command from that menu. Pull-down menus are explained in a separate section below.

5. Dialogue boxes: These boxes appear on the screen when you select certain options from AutoCAD's standard pull-down menu, when you enter special DD . . . commands at the keyboard, or when you're inserting blocks with attributes or editing attributes. They are explained in a separate section below.

The rest of this section explains aspects of command entry that are common to most of the entry methods mentioned above.

After you enter a command, AutoCAD prompts you for more information needed to complete the command. *Read these prompts carefully.* The most recent prompt always appears on the bottom line of the prompt area, and the previous prompts scroll upward until they disappear. By reading this bottom line carefully, you'll know what AutoCAD expects you to do. In many cases, you can enter options from the keyboard, the screen menu, the tablet overlay or a dialogue box.

Default responses appear in corner brackets <like this>. When these brackets contain numbers, the numbers can be entered simply by pressing <RETURN>. When the brackets surround one of several options, AutoCAD expects you to enter information in response to that option, or to enter one of the other options (usually by entering its first letter).

A prompt will often ask you to locate a point. You can do so either by entering the point's coordinates at the keyboard, or by moving the pointer to the desired position and pressing the pick button. Whenever you enter points from the keyboard, you must type in both the X and Y coordinates (X first) and separate the coordinates with a comma (no spaces) like this: 3.75,2.125

The space bar usually works just like the <RETURN> key. Thus, there are three different ways to press <RETURN>:

Press the actual <RETURN> key.

Press the space bar.

Press button 2 on the pointer.

Naturally, when you enter text (within the TEXT, DIM, ATTDEF commands, etc.) the space bar works in the usual way.

You can repeat any command simply by pressing <RETURN> (or the space bar or pointer button 2) when you're in command mode. Also, you can type **MULTIPLE** before entering a command (for example, **MULTIPLE ARC**). This will repeat that command automatically, until you use **CTRL-C** to stop the repetition or select another command from one of the menus.

**CTRL-Q** will turn the printer echo on/off, providing a record of all the AutoCAD prompts and your keyboard entries.

The descriptions of AutoCAD commands on the following pages are relatively brief. In many cases, a more detailed explanation of the same command can be found in the *AutoCAD Reference Manual*.

In this guide, commands are always printed in CAPITALS. Each section that describes a command begins with a capsule of the command immediately following the command name. Then we list the options you may enter after you've entered the command. In most cases, these options are described as they would be entered from the keyboard. Your responses, selected from the menus or dialogue boxes, will be obvious.

The options are not in any particular order. They aren't steps you should follow one after the other, but merely possible individual responses. When there's a definite set of steps to follow in a certain order, they'll be spelled out.

Finally, when we want you to enter a command or option, or when a command or option name requires special emphasis in text, we print it in **boldface** type.

## POINTER BUTTONS

When you use the pointer to enter commands from the screen menu, a tablet menu overlay, a pull-down menu, or a dialogue box, merely place the pointer at the appropriate location and press the pick button. On three- and four-button pointers, the buttons are assigned as follows:

Button 1— Pick button
Button 2— <RETURN> button
Button 3— Displays Tools pull-down menu
Button 4— Cancel (same as CTRL-C)

When you use the pointer to enter a 3D point (three coordinates), the X and Y coordinates are taken from the position of the pointer and the Z coordinate is taken from the current elevation (see ELEV in Chapter 32).

## FUNCTION KEYS

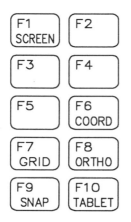

Six of the ten function keys have special uses in AutoCAD.

F1 Displays full screen of text or normal graphics screen simulating a two-monitor configuration

F6 (or CTRL-D) Makes the coordinate display in the status line active or inactive, or switches display from polar to rectangular coordinates, etc.

F7 (or CTRL-G) Turns GRID on or off

F8 (or CTRL-O) Turns ORTHO on or off

F9 (or CTRL-B) Turns SNAP on or off

F10 (or CTRL-T) Turns Tablet mode on or off after calibration

# THE STANDARD SCREEN MENU

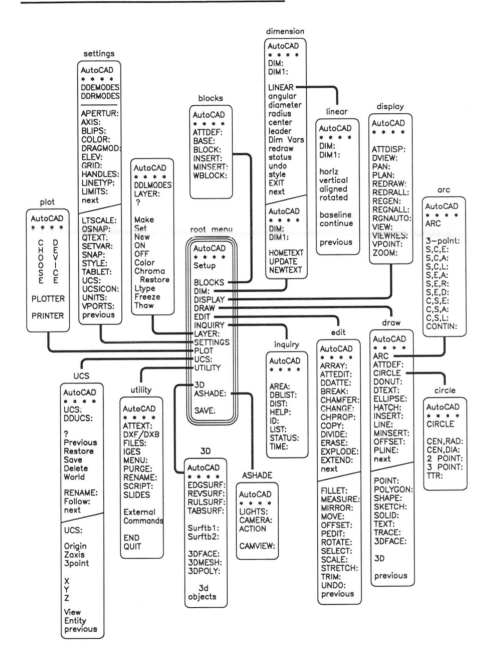

## PULL-DOWN MENUS

The pull-down menus supplied with AutoCAD include:

(1) Regular commands—approximately half of AutoCAD's commands

(2) Dialogue boxes

(3) Icon menus to help use certain commands

(4) Access to specialized AutoLISP routines

See Appendix B for a sample customized menu that contains pull-down menus listing all of AutoCAD's commands.

| Tools | Draw | Modify | Display | Settings | Options | File | Help |
|---|---|---|---|---|---|---|---|
| OSNAP | Line | Erase | Redraw | UCS Dialogue... | Ashade... | Save | Help |
| CENter | Arc | Move | ———— | UCS Options... | Fonts... | End | |
| ENDpoint | Circle | Copy | Zoom Window | UCS Previous | | Quit | |
| INSert | Polyline | Properties | Zoom Previous | | | ——— | |
| INTersection | 3D Polyline | Break | Zoom All | Drawing Aids... | | Plot | |
| MIDpoint | Insert | Fillet | Zoom Dynamic | Entity Creation... | | Print | |
| NEArest | Dtext | Mirror | ———— | Modify Layer... | | | |
| NODe | Hatch... | Trim | Pan | | | | |
| PERpendicular | 3D Construction... | Extend | Dview Options... | | | | |
| QUAdrant | | Stretch | Vpoint 3D... | | | | |
| QUICK, | | Edit Polylines | ———— | | | | |
| TANgent | | | Plan view (UCS) | | | | |
| NONE | | | Plan view (World) | | | | |
| ——— | | | ———— | | | | |
| FILTERS... | | | Set Viewports... | | | | |
| Cancel | | | | | | | |
| U | | | | | | | |
| Redo | | | | | | | |
| List | | | | | | | |

To pull down a menu, move the pointer into the status line, then pick the desired menu with the pick button. When the pull-down menu appears, use the pointer again to pick the desired item.

The Tools pull-down menu can be displayed with the third button on the pointer. You can use this menu to select immediate osnap modes, or select OSNAP, then select a running osnap mode (see OSNAP in Chapter 12).

When you select a menu item that's followed by an ellipsis (...), either a dialogue box or an icon menu will be displayed. See "Dialogue Boxes" below.

The Draw–3D Construction item on the pull-down menu (or the 3D–3D Objects item on the standard screen menu) uses AutoLISP programs that are supplied with AutoCAD. The Options-Ashade item on the pull-down menu also uses AutoLISP programs.

The first time you select one of these items, the AutoLISP programs are loaded automatically. (See the AutoSHADE manual for information on installing AutoSHADE.)

Many of the items in the pull-down menus are preset to operate in certain ways. For example, some of the drawing and editing commands repeat automatically, and some of the editing commands use a single, automatic selection mode (see SELECT in Chapter 6). For this reason you shouldn't become overly dependent on the pull-down menus. Instead, learn commands by entering them from the keyboard, from the standard screen menu and/or from the tablet overlay where all commands and options are available.

## DIALOGUE BOXES

Dialogue boxes appear when you select certain items from the pull-down menu. They can be summoned in other ways as well, as explained below. Some dialogue boxes can be used transparently (while you're in the middle of another command). A sample dialogue box is shown below.

Settings/Drawing Aids Dialogue Box

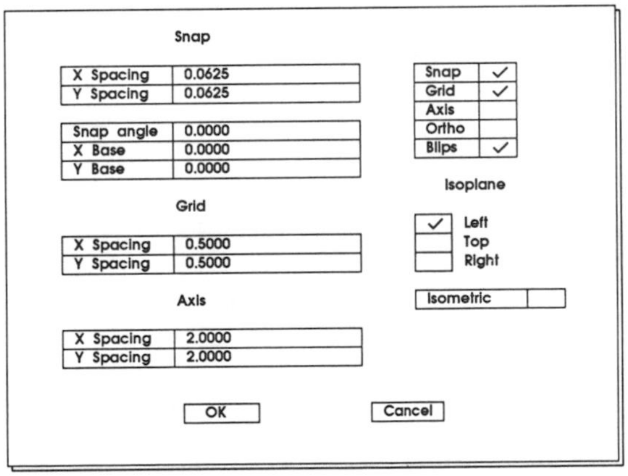

| | | |
|---|---|---|
| **Snap** | | |
| X Spacing | 0.0625 | Snap ✓ |
| Y Spacing | 0.0625 | Grid ✓ |
| | | Axis |
| Snap angle | 0.0000 | Ortho |
| X Base | 0.0000 | Blips ✓ |
| Y Base | 0.0000 | |

Isoplane

✓ Left  
Top  
Right

**Grid**

| X Spacing | 0.5000 |
| Y Spacing | 0.5000 |

Isometric

**Axis**

| X Spacing | 2.0000 |
| Y Spacing | 2.0000 |

OK       Cancel

When the dialogue box appears, the cursor changes to an arrow, which highlights the various options so you can select them with the pick button on the pointer.

When a dialogue box is on the screen, AutoCAD responds only to the pick button on the pointer and to the keyboard. To remove the dialogue box, pick either the **OK** button or **CANCEL** button on the screen, or use **CTRL-C** or **ESC** on the keyboard.

Dialogue boxes have several types of buttons:

The OK button causes the displayed values to be adopted as the current values, and removes the box.

The CANCEL button removes the box. If any values in the box were changed, they are discarded and the previous values are kept.

Check buttons, such as the Snap and Grid buttons on the right side of the box, indicate whether the item is on or off. You can toggle them on or off by highlighting them with the arrow, then by pressing the pick button on the pointer.

Input buttons, such as the X Spacing buttons in the illustration above, let you enter values from the keyboard. You must accept the value by pressing <RETURN> or picking that item's OK button. Neither the space bar nor the second button on the pointer will substitute for the <RETURN> key at this point. Some input buttons cause another dialogue box to appear in front of the main dialogue box. You must interact with this box before AutoCAD will return to the main box.

The main dialogue boxes are listed below:

| Dialogue Box | Related Commands | To select, pick this pull-down item |
| --- | --- | --- |
| Drawing aids | SNAP, GRID, AXIS, ORTHO, ISOPLANE, BLIPMODE | Settings/Drawing aids (or enter 'DDRMODES) |
| Entity creation | COLOR, LINETYPE Set, LAYER Set, ELEVATION and THICKNESS | Settings/Entity creation (or enter 'DDEMODES) |
| Modify layer | LAYER | Settings/Modify layer (or enter 'DDLMODES) |
| Entering attributes | INSERT | Draw/INSERT (or use SETVAR to set system variable ATTDIA to non-zero, then use INSERT command) |
| Editing attributes (single blocks) | ATTEDIT | Must enter DDATTE |
| Modify UCS | UCS, UCSICON | Settings/UCS Settings (or enter DDUCS) |

Some changes made in dialogue boxes will not take effect until the next command (if the dialogue box is used transparently) or until the next REGENeration.

## HELP

**Displays a list of commands, methods of point entry and specific information on each command**

When prompted for the command name, press <**RETURN**> for a list of all commands and methods of point entry, or enter the name of a command for specific information on that command.

You can get immediate help on any command while you're in that command (after you've entered the command and are being prompted for input). To do so, enter '**HELP** (notice the apostrophe). This same 'HELP command can be entered from the screen menu (pick the four asterisks near the top of the screen menu, then pick HELP) or from the pull-down menus (HELP is on the right end of the menu bar).

## TIME

**Displays time-related statistics**

When prompted, enter:

**D** to update the display.

**ON** to turn the elapsed timer on.

**OFF** to turn the elapsed timer off.

**R** to reset the elapsed timer to 0.

Press <**RETURN**> to return to command mode.

# SETUP

For more information on setup, see Chapter 17. Also see the setup exercise in Appendix A.

## UNITS

**Sets the format and precision for the display of coordinates and angles**

There are five possible formats for linear measure:

1. Scientific units—The base is always between 1 and 10, and the exponent following the E indicates how many places to move the decimal point to the right (positive) or left (negative).

Example: 1.8603E+03

2. Decimal

Example: 14.375

3. Engineering—Feet and inches with decimal fractions

Example:    4'–2.75'' (readout format)

4' 2.75'' (entry format, no spaces, inch designator optional)

Numbers entered without a unit designator are assumed to be inches.

4. Architectural—Feet and inches with regular fractions

Example:    2'–7 3/8'' (readout format)

2'7–3/8'' (entry format, no spaces, inch designator optional)

Numbers entered without a unit designator are assumed to be inches.

5. Fractional

Example:    27 3/8 (readout format)

27 –3/8 (entry format, no spaces)

Notice that only the Engineering and Architectural formats are locked into particular units of measure. The other three formats can be used with any unit of measure, such as microns, millimeters, inches, yards, miles, or even light years. A metric engineering drawing would typically use the decimal format.

There are also five possible formats for angular measure:

    1. Decimal degrees (360 degrees in a full circle)

       Example:    15.230

    2. Degrees-minutes-seconds (360 degrees in a full circle)

       Example:    15d13'48"

    3. Grads (400 grads in a full circle)

       Example:    16.922g (readout format only, don't use "g" when entering)

       1 grad = .9 degrees (exactly)

       1 degree = 1.111111 grads

    4. Radians (2-times-pi radians in a full circle)

       Example:    .2658r (readout format only, don't use "r" when entering)

       1 degree = .01745329 radians

       1 radian = 57.29578 degrees

    5. Surveyor's units

       Example:    N 74d46'12" E (readout format only, no spaces when entering)

The zero-angle direction is normally to the right (or 3 o'clock), but you can set it to any other direction. Positive angles are normally measured counterclockwise, but you can set them to be measured clockwise.

You can switch back and forth between the available linear formats, levels of precision, and angular formats at any stage during the drawing process. When you save a drawing, the options you selected are saved with the drawing, so they'll be the same the next time you edit the drawing.

If you're a new user, select an easy format for learning. Enter in the following order:

**2** to select decimal format

**4** to select four-decimal-place precision for linear measure

**1** to select decimal fraction format for angles

**4** to select four-decimal-place precision for angles

**0** to orient the zero-angle in the positive X direction (the standard 3 o'clock orientation)

**N** so positive angles will rotate counterclockwise

Naturally, anyone who customarily uses a format different from the one suggested above will want to set up that format from the start.

## USING METRIC UNITS

Suppose you want to draw in millimeters rather than inches. Drawing in units other than inches is just as easy as drawing in inches—you don't need to convert every dimension. However, there are several things you should do.

Remember that AutoCAD doesn't use specific units such as inches, feet, miles or meters. It works only in pure units, which may represent any form of linear measure from inches to miles or from microns to light years.

If you're going to draw in millimeters,

1) Reset the drawing aid values. For example,

SNAP 1 or .5          GRID 10          AXIS 50

2) Reset the dimensioning variables governing visual size to their metric equivalents (or set **DIMSCALE** to **25.4**).

3) Set **LTSCALE** to approximately **25**, then adjust as needed.

4) If you've been using text styles with fixed heights, you'll need to change their heights to the metric equivalents.

You can make these changes part of your metric prototype drawings.

When you plot, select **M** (millimeters), then set the size of the plotting and the pen width to their appropriate values.

Blocks that were created in inches and then written to disk can easily be reused in a metric drawing. Simply insert them at a scale factor of **25.4**.

## LIMITS

**Sets the rectangular drawing area or enables and disables the limits check**

When prompted, enter the coordinates of the lower left corner of the desired drawing area (this will often be 0,0), then enter the coordinates of the upper right corner. Remember that you can enter default values displayed in corner brackets simply by pressing <**RETURN**>.

To enable or disable the limits check, enter **ON** or **OFF**. When the limits check is on, AutoCAD won't let you enter points outside the limits.

If you have changed the limits and want to have the entire drawing area displayed on the screen, enter **ZOOM**, then enter **A** (for All). (See ZOOM in Chapter 11.)

You can reset the limits any time while you're working on a drawing, without affecting any of the entities you've already drawn.

## STATUS

**Displays a drawing's name, limits, extents, parameters and other statistics**

The screen will switch to text mode and display, among other things, these coordinates:

Drawing limits—define the rectangular drawing area.

Drawing extents—define the portion of the drawing limits that actually contains the drawing entities (can extend outside the limits).

Display extents—define the portion of the drawing currently displayed on the screen.

To return to graphics mode after viewing the status display, press **F1**.

## GRID

**Adjusts the spacing of the visible
grid (rectangular patterns of dots)
and turns the grid on/off**

When prompted, enter the following:

A number to set the spacing.

**ON** to turn the grid on.

**OFF** to turn the grid off.

**S** (for SNAP) to set the grid spacing equal to the snap spacing.

**A** (for Aspect). Then enter the X (horizontal) spacing of the desired grid, then enter the Y (vertical) spacing. The only time you need to use this response is when you want the X and Y spacings to differ from each other.

You can turn the grid on and off more conveniently with function key **F7**. The grid is initially off when a new drawing is started.

The grid, when on, fills up the drawing limits. The rotation and style of this visible grid always match the rotation and style of the invisible snap grid. If the grid spacing is set at 0, it automatically adopts the snap spacing (see SNAP in Chapter 5).

All the options available with the GRID command are also available in the Drawing Aids dialogue box. See "Dialogue Boxes" above.

## AXIS

**Adjusts the spacing of the hatch
marks along the edge of the
drawing display**

When prompted, enter the following:

A number to set the spacing. You'll usually want to use an even multiple of the grid spacing.

**ON** to turn the axis on.

**OFF** to turn the axis off.

A (for Aspect). Then enter the X spacing of the axis, then enter the Y spacing. The only time you need to use this response is when you want the X spacing to differ from the Y spacing.

The axis is initially off when a new drawing is started.

The axis can also be set and toggled on/off with the Drawing Aids dialogue box. See "Dialogue Boxes" above.

# 5 POINTS

## POINT

### Places points in the drawing

When prompted for the point, enter the X,Y coordinates separated by a comma (no spaces), or move the pointer to the desired location and press the pick button. A point can be entered with all three coordinates: X,Y,Z. (See Chapter 32.)

Don't confuse these points (which are separate drawing entities) with the points you must locate in order to define a line, circle, etc. The way points appear on the screen is controlled by the PDMODE and PDSIZE variables (see SETVAR, PDMODE and PDSIZE below).

## ENTERING POINTS

Whenever you place points, lines, circles, etc., in a drawing, you'll need to enter the points that define their location/direction/size. There are several ways to do this. Each method described below applies both to separate points (when using the POINT command) and to endpoints of lines, centerpoints of circles, etc. (when using the LINE, CIRCLE, etc., commands). See also "Using Point Filters" in Chapter 32.

| Kind of point entry: | |
|---|---|
| Keyboard—absolute | Enter absolute coordinates (X,Y distances from 0,0). For example, 8.25,6.8 (rectangular coordinates). |
| Keyboard—relative<br><br>Must precede coordinates with @ | Enter relative coordinates (X,Y distances from the last point entered): for example, @4.25,3.88 (rectangular coordinates). Or, enter distance and angle from the last point entered: for example, @1.5<30 (angular or polar coordinates). *Note:* The angle symbol in polar coordinates replaces the comma in rectangular coordinates. Entering @ (same as @0,0) identifies the same location as the last point entered. |
| Pointer (puck) | Move pointer to desired location and press the pick button. |
| Pointer and keyboard arrows | Move pointer to the general location, then refine it using the arrow keys on the numeric keypad. Then press <RETURN>. You can restore crosshair control to the pointer by pressing the backspace key. If SNAP is on, the cursor will move one snap distance at a time. |

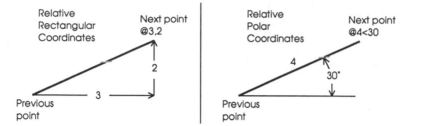

You can use relative coordinates to locate a point a certain distance from a reference point. See the REF.LSP file description in Chapter 39.

# SNAP

**Adjusts snap spacing and angle, and turns snap on and off**

The snap grid is an invisible grid (see GRID in Chapter 4). When you're locating a point with the pointer, the location is rounded to the nearest snap point if SNAP is on.

When prompted, enter the following:

A number to set the spacing.

**ON** to turn SNAP on.

**OFF** to turn SNAP off.

**A** (for Aspect) then enter X and Y spacings that differ from each other.

**R** (for Rotate) then locate the pivot point of the snap grid and enter the angle to rotate the grid (between +90 and 90 degrees).

**S** (for Style) then enter **S** for the standard rectangular snap grid or enter **I** for an isometric snap grid, then enter the desired spacing. (See "Isometric Drawings" in Chapter 30.)

SNAP is initially off when a new drawing is started. You can turn it on and off more conveniently with function key **F9**.

All of the options available within the SNAP command are also available in the Drawing Aids dialogue box. See "Dialogue Boxes," above.

## SETVAR

**Sets the values of AutoCAD's system variables**

AutoCAD remembers various parameters (such as the coordinates of the lower left and upper right corners of the drawing area, the grid status and spacing, etc.) by storing certain values in over 100 system variables.

The values in these variables are changed in the normal course of drawing and editing when you use such commands as LIMITS and GRID. For example, the LIMITS command changes the values in the LIMMIN and LIMMAX variables. And the GRID command changes the value in either the GRIDMODE or GRIDUNIT variable.

The values in these variables can also be changed directly by using the SET-VAR command.

When prompted for a variable name, enter the following:

> **?** to get a list of all system variables and their current values.

> The variable name, then enter the new value.

You can set a variable transparently (from inside any command) while being prompted for anything but a text string. To do so, enter **'SETVAR** (notice the apostrophe).

## PDMODE SYSTEM VARIABLE

**Selects the symbol used to display points**

Remember, system variables are set with the SETVAR command. If you're in the middle of another command and want to set a system variable, enter **'SETVAR**. Enter **SETVAR** (or **'SETVAR**) first, then enter **PMODE**, then its new value.

When prompted for the point display mode number, enter any of the following numbers (0 is the default):

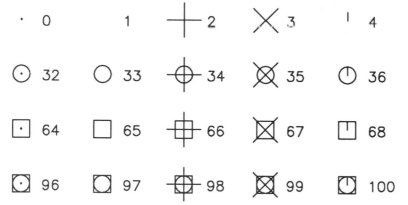

Using a **PDMODE** of **1** makes points inaccessible to other commands, such as LIST and OSNAP.

You can call up examples of these various point display modes by using the screen menu to select the **POINT** command, then select Examples.

## PDSIZE SYSTEM VARIABLE

**Sets the size of the point display symbol (if PDMODE is other than 0 or 1)**

Remember, system variables are set using the **SETVAR** command.

When prompted for the size of the point display, enter the following:

A positive number to set an absolute size (absolute in relation to the drawing units, but varies as you zoom in and out). For example, setting PDSIZE at .25 will make all points display at .25 high.

A negative number to set the size as a percentage of the screen height (appears same size on screen, regardless of zoom factor). For example, setting PDSIZE at -4 will make all points display at 4 percent of the current screen height, no matter how far you zoom in or out (assuming the screen regenerates when you zoom).

Both PDMODE and PDSIZE are global. After a REGENeration of the screen, all points that had been created under a different PDMODE or PDSIZE setting will now be displayed according to the current settings.

# ERASING

## ERASE

**Erases entities from a drawing**

The interactive selection options described below are also used in several other commands including MOVE, COPY, MIRROR, CHANGE, ARRAY and LIST.

When prompted to select objects, enter the following:

**P** to adopt the previous selection set (can be refined further).

Select one entity with the pointer (can be done repeatedly).

**M**, then select two or more entities with the pointer, then press **<RETURN>**. Do this when you're working with a very large drawing and want to speed up the process of selecting many entities.

**L** to select the most recent entity placed in the drawing.

**W** to select several items enclosed in a window, then locate two opposite corners of the window.

**C** to select items in or crossing a window, then locate two opposite corners of the window. The window is shown dashed or highlighted to distinguish it from a noncrossing (enclosing) window.

**BOX** to use either an enclosing or a crossing window. If the second corner of the window is to the right of the first, the window is an enclosing window. If it's to the left, the window is a crossing window. (This option has its greatest advantage when used in custom menus.)

**AU** (for automatic) to select one entity or to use an enclosing or a crossing window. If the pick box locates an entity, that entity is selected. If not, that pick location becomes the left corner for an enclosing window or the right corner for a crossing window.

**R** to remove an item from those already selected (can be followed with other responses, such as **W** to remove several items in a window).

**A** to add an item to those already selected (necessary only after using remove mode).

**U** to undo your last selection.

**SI** (for single) to cancel the interactive refinement of the selection set. This forces AutoCAD to accept the first object or group of objects you select. (This option has its greatest advantage when used in custom menus.)

After each of the above options, you're prompted to continue refining your selection, unless you're in single-selection mode. When you have completed the selection process, press <RETURN>.

## OOPS

**Restores the last item or group of items that was erased**

## SELECT

**Builds a selection set of drawing entities for later use in other commands**

You use this command to build a set of selected entities that you want to edit later as a group. The options are the same as those explained under the ERASE command above.

See the description of the SSX.LSP file under "AutoLISP Programs" in Chapter 39.

## PICKBOX SYSTEM VARIABLE

**Sets the size of the pick box—the square cursor that appears when you use SELECT, ERASE, LIST, etc.**

Remember, system variables are set with the **SETVAR** command.

When prompted, enter the size of the pick box in pixels. The default size is 3.

## LINES

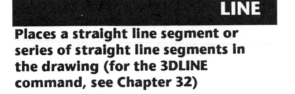

## LINE

**Places a straight line segment or series of straight line segments in the drawing (for the 3DLINE command, see Chapter 32)**

When prompted **From point:**

Locate the starting point of the line by entering coordinates at the keyboard or by moving the pointer to the desired location and pressing the pick button.

Press **<RETURN>** to begin the line at the end of the most recent line or arc. (If you're starting from the end of an arc, the direction is already set and you need to enter only the length of the line.)

When prompted **To point:**

Locate the end of the line or the next point in the series of lines, using keyboard or pointer.

Enter **U** to undo the last line segment drawn in this series of lines.

Enter **C** to close a polygon and return to command mode.

To end a series of lines and return to command mode, press <RETURN>.

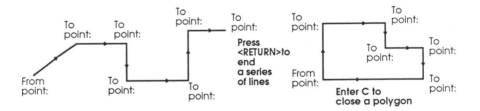

Although you'll often use the LINE command to produce regular 2D lines, the LINE command will also accept the Z coordinate just as the 3DLINE command will. If only X and Y are entered, or if the location is selected with the pointer, the Z location is adopted from the current elevation (see ELEV in Chapter 32).

You can use relative rectangular coordinates that include all three coordinates, such as @2,3,4. However, relative polar coordinates specifying distance and angle, such as @3.25 < 45, operate only in the X-Y plane. For other considerations, such as OSNAP and editing, see the 3DLINE command and "Using Point Filters," both in Chapter 32.

The line can be extruded in the **Z** direction with the **ELEV** and **CHANGE** commands.

See Appendix A for three exercises involving 2D lines.

## ORTHO

**Forces lines and traces to be horizontal or vertical when entered with the pointer**

When prompted, enter **ON** to enable ORTHO (make all subsequent lines orthogonal) or enter **OFF** to disable ORTHO (see the illustration below).

You can turn ORTHO on and off more conveniently with function key **F8**. You can do this several times during a series of lines.

When the endpoint of a line is entered from the keyboard, it's not affected by ORTHO.

If the snap grid has been rotated, newly created orthogonal lines will also be rotated. If the snap style is isometric, orthogonal lines are always parallel to one of the three isometric axes.

ORTHO also affects the displacement in the **MOVE** and **COPY** commands.

ORTHO may also be toggled on/off with the Drawing Aids dialogue box. See "Dialogue Boxes" in Chapter 3.

# 8 | REFRESHING THE SCREEN

## REDRAW

**Redraws the display**

This command removes unwanted point markers and restores apparently missing parts of the display resulting from the drawing/editing process. Turning the grid off or changing visible layers also automatically redraws the display.

Unless one of your pointer buttons is specifically assigned to the REDRAW command, the easiest way to redraw the screen is to press **F7** twice.

You can redraw the display from inside other commands while being prompted for anything but a text string. To do so, enter **'REDRAW** (notice the apostrophe).

## REGEN

**Regenerates the display**

The REGEN command forces a regeneration. An automatic regeneration also usually occurs when you zoom in a great distance, pan a great distance, or restore a previously named view. A regeneration of the drawing, since it goes all the way back to the drawing's database, can produce a more thorough update of the screen than a redraw, but it also takes more time.

## REGENAUTO

**Enables or disables the automatic regeneration performed by certain other commands**

The commands governed by REGENAUTO are: ATTEDIT (global editing), BLOCK (redefinition), INSERT (when you use *blockname=filename* to redefine a block), LAYER (changed linetype or freeze/thaw state) and LTSCALE.

When several of the above changes are made back to back, AutoCAD would normally regenerate the display after each change. On a complex drawing this would take considerable time. To save time, turn REGENAUTO off, make the series of changes, then turn REGENAUTO back on (will perform one regeneration).

ZOOM, PAN, VIEW Restore and REGEN aren't affected by REGENAUTO.

REGENAUTO is initially on when you begin a new drawing, unless the new drawing uses a prototype drawing in which REGENAUTO is off.

## BLIPMODE

**Enables or disables placement of marker blips**

When prompted, enter **ON** or **OFF** to enable or disable the placement of marker blips whenever you locate points (ends of lines, centers of circles, etc.).

BLIPMODE may also be toggled on/off with the Drawing Aids dialogue box (see "Dialogue Boxes" in Chapter 3).

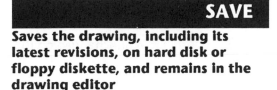

**FILES**

## SAVE

**Saves the drawing, including its
latest revisions, on hard disk or
floppy diskette, and remains in the
drawing editor**

When prompted for a file name,

> Press **<RETURN>** to accept the default name and thus update the drawing file. The updated version replaces the previous version on file. The previous version becomes the backup file (extension .BAK). To save the update on floppy diskette instead of the hard disk, enter **A:** immediately in front of the drawing name.

> Enter a new file name (different from the default) to save the updated drawing under that new name and retain the previous version under its original name.

Suggestion: Save your drawing every 30 to 60 minutes. If there's a power outage or other computer failure, you'll be glad you did.

Suggestion: At the end of a work session, save or copy your drawing onto two floppy diskettes.

## END

**Saves the drawing, including its
latest revisions on the hard disk,
exits the drawing editor and returns
to the main menu**

The drawing is saved under the exact file name you used when you began this drawing/editing session, and replaces the previous version of the drawing. The previous version becomes the backup file (extension .BAK).

If you're at the end of a drawing/editing session and want the backup file to be identical to the file of the latest version, enter **SAVE** and accept the default name, then enter **END**.

## QUIT

**Exits the drawing editor and returns
to the main menu, without saving
the latest revisions, if any**

The previously saved version of this drawing, if any, is left unchanged on the hard disk.

A prompt will ask you if you really want to discard all changes to the drawing. Enter **Y** to proceed, or **N** to cancel the command.

## FILES

**Lets you use the File Utility menu to
list, delete, rename or copy files
without leaving the drawing editor**

This command uses the same File Utility menu that's accessible from the main menu.

When the File Utility menu appears, enter the following:

**0** to return to either the main menu or the drawing editor (wherever you were before entering the File Utility menu).

**1** to list drawing files. Then press <RETURN> to list all the drawing files on the default (\WORK) subdirectory. Or, just enter **A:** to list all the drawing files on floppy diskette.

**2** to list other specified files. Then enter the **A:** drive specifier, if needed, and file name (with extension) and/or wild cards. For example,

*.* lists all files on the hard disk.

A:*.* lists all files on floppy diskette.

*.BAK lists all backup files on the hard disk.

GR*.DWG lists all drawing files on the hard disk whose names begin with GR.

*Note:* Although you can use * to stand for all characters in a file name or extension, or all remaining characters in a file name or extension (as in the example above), don't try to put characters after * (DOS won't see them). You can also use the wild card ? to stand for any single character.

**3** to delete a file. Then enter the drive specifier, if needed, and file name (with extension). If wild cards are used, each eligible file is displayed so you can decide whether to delete it.

**4** to rename a file. Then enter the drive specifier, if needed, and current file name (with extension). Then enter the new file name (with extension).

**5** to copy a file from one disk or diskette or directory to another. Then enter the drive specifier, if needed, and source file name (with extension). Then enter the drive specifier, if needed, and destination file name (with extension).

Use full path names when you're indicating a file that isn't in the current directory.

The following list gives various extensions with their corresponding file types.

ASC     ASCII text file

BAK     Backup of a drawing file

BAS     BASIC language program file

BAT     Batch file

COM     Compiled program file

DOC     Documentation file

DWG     Drawing file

DXB     Binary drawing interchange file

DXF     Drawing interchange file

DXX     Attribute extract file in DXF format (see TXT below)

EXE     Compiled executable program file

FLM     Filmroll file for use in AutoSHADE

IGS     IGES interchange file

LIN    File of line types

LSP    File of AutoLISP functions/commands

LST    Printer-plotter output file

MNU    Menu source file

MNX    Menu compiled file

MSG    Message file

OLD    Original version of converted drawing file

PAT    File of crosshatch patterns

PLT    Plotter output file

RND    Rendering file created by AutoSHADE

SCR    Command script file

SHP    Shape/font definition source file

SHX    Shape/font definition compiled file

SLB    Slide library file

SLD    Slide (single display) file

TXT    Attribute extract file in CDF or SDF format, or template file for making attribute extract files (compare DXX above)

$    Files whose extensions begin with $—usually temporary files that AutoCAD creates and then erases when you END or QUIT AutoCAD in the usual way.

Occasionally a drawing file won't load properly, and you must rely on a back-up file. The backup file must first be renamed, using either the File Utility menu or **RENAME** (DOS command), so its extension is changed from .BAK to .DWG.

For example, suppose you have a file called THING.DWG that won't load properly. If you have the backup file, THING.BAK, you can rename it so it has the .DWG extension. However, you can't have two files in the same subdirectory with the same name. So, you can temporarily move THING.DWG to another subdirectory while you rename THING.BAK to THING.DWG and try loading it. Or you can rename the backup file with a new and unique primary name as well as the .DWG extension. Once the old backup file has the .DWG extension, it can be used just as any other drawing file.

## SHELL AND SH

### Allow access to DOS commands

The File Utility menu, which is available from either the main menu or the drawing editor (using the **FILES** command), provides some options that are similar to certain DOS commands—listing, deleting, renaming and copying files. However, you may need to make more extensive use of DOS without leaving the drawing editor.

The SHELL and SH commands let you temporarily return to DOS and perform one or several DOS operations, as well as run other programs and utilities.

When prompted for **DOS command**:

> Reply with any valid DOS command. When the DOS command finishes, you'll be returned to command mode inside the drawing editor.

> Press <**RETURN**> if you want to use more than one DOS command. The usual DOS prompt is displayed with an extra > to remind you that you've "shelled out" of AutoCAD's drawing editor. To return to command mode inside the drawing editor, enter **EXIT**.

Each time you shell out, AutoCAD gives up a certain amount of memory so that the DOS command interpreter (COMMAND.COM) and possibly other programs can be loaded. Assuming you haven't altered the ACAD.PGP file supplied with AutoCAD,

> The SHELL command requests 127KB of RAM—sufficient for all DOS commands and certain other programs, such as the BASIC language.

> The SH command requests only 30KB of RAM, which is still sufficient for many DOS operations.

Because of the ACAD.PGP file, you also have direct access to several DOS commands and programs from within the drawing editor without having to enter either SHELL or SH. You can enter **CATALOG** to get a wide listing of files, **DIR** to get the usual directory listing, **DEL** to erase files, **TYPE** to type (list) text files and **EDIT** to use EDLIN.

See "Changing the ACAD.PGP File" in Chapter 37.

# 10    2D FIGURES

## CIRCLE

**Places a circle in a drawing**

When prompted,

> Locate the center, then the radius of the circle, using keyboard or pointer. When prompted for the radius, enter **D**, then enter the diameter.

> Enter **2P**, then locate the endpoints of any diameter of the circle.

> Enter **3P**, then locate three points on the circumference of the circle. You can use the tan (tangent) OSNAP mode to draw a circle tangent to three lines, three circles, two lines and an arc, etc. See OSNAP in Chapter 12.

> Enter **TTR** (for tangent-tangent-radius), then select the two lines/arcs/circles that the new circle will be tangent to, then enter the radius.

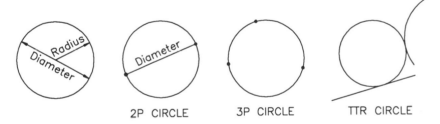

2P CIRCLE     3P CIRCLE     TTR CIRCLE

To drag the circle when DRAGMODE is on, you must enter **DRAG** when prompted for the final parameter and then use the pointer to place the circle. When you're dragging an entity, a location entered from the keyboard will override the location currently displayed.

See "Using Point Filters" in Chapter 32.

## DRAGMODE

**Enables or disables the use of DRAG**

Circles, arcs, blocks and shapes can be dragged dynamically if DRAGMODE is set to **ON** or **AUTO**.

When prompted, enter:

**A** (for Auto) to enable automatic dragging. Automatic dragging means that you don't have to enter DRAG to activate dragging.

**ON** to enable non-automatic dragging. To activate dragging when you're in a drawing or editing command, enter **DRAG** when prompted for the final parameter.

**OFF** to disable dragging.

DRAGMODE's initial setting is determined by the prototype drawing used, if any. When you save your drawing, the current DRAGMODE setting is saved with it.

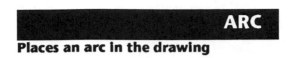

**ARC**

## Places an arc in the drawing

There are 12 ways to enter the data necessary to define an arc.

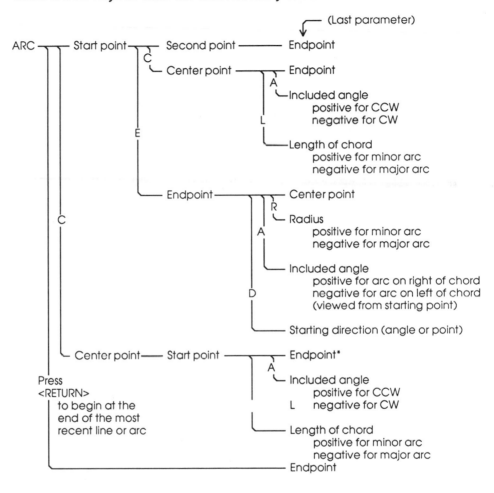

*\*Note: When relative coordinates (rectangular or polar) are
used, they are located relative to the center.*

When DRAGMODE is on, you can drag the arc by entering **DRAG** before entering the last parameter, then use the pointer to place the arc. See Appendix A
for an arc exercise.

# ARC TERMINOLOGY

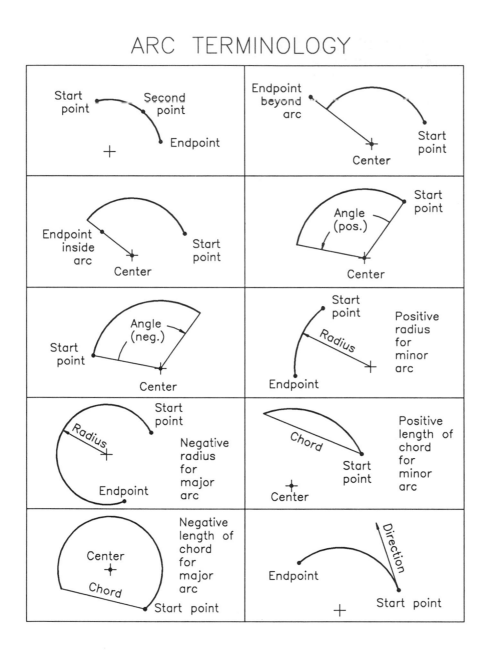

# POLYGON

**Draws a regular polygon**

When prompted, enter the number of sides. Then locate the center, then enter **I** for a polygon inscribed in a circle or **C** for a polygon circumscribed about a circle. Then enter the radius of the circle.

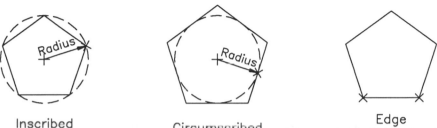

Inscribed          Circumscribed          Edge

Another way to define the polygon is to define one of its edges. After entering the number of sides, enter **E** (for Edge), then locate the endpoints of one side. The polygon will be drawn counterclockwise from that starting edge.

# ELLIPSE

**Draws an ellipse with specified axes**

Enter three points. The first two points are endpoints of one axis of the ellipse (major or minor axis). The third point is the endpoint of the other axis.

Or, you can begin at the center of the ellipse rather than the endpoint of one of the axes. To do so, enter **C**, then the center, then the endpoint of one axis, then the endpoint of the other axis.

Or, you can define the ellipse as though it were created by viewing a circle at a certain angle. To do so, enter the first two points to define the major axis (by either method above). Then enter **R**, then the number of degrees that you want the circle rotated around that axis. A rotation angle of 0 produces a circle, while a rotation angle of near 90 degrees produces an ellipse that's almost flat (nearly an edge view of a circle). *Note:* The system won't accept an entry of 90 degrees.

If you're drawing in isometric mode (SNAP style has been set to isometric), one more option appears in the prompt. You can enter **I** for an isometric circle, then locate the center, then the radius (or **D** and the diameter). AutoCAD will place the ellipse at the proper viewing angle and rotation for whichever isometric plane you are currently on (Left, Top or Right). See SNAP in Chapter 5 and "Isometric Drawings" in Chapter 30.

AutoCAD draws ellipses with polylines, so you can edit them with **BREAK** and **PEDIT**.

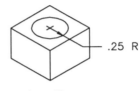

Rotated 60°
around
major axis

Begun with
center point

.25 R

Iso-ellipse

# 11 LOOKING AROUND

## ZOOM

**Displays a larger or smaller portion of the drawing**

When prompted, enter the following:

A scale factor. Enter a number greater than **1** to zoom in and magnify part of the drawing, or smaller than **1** to zoom out (demagnify) and show more of the drawing.

> The number by itself serves as the magnification factor by which the full drawing (limits) will be multiplied. Entering a magnification factor of **1** will display the drawing at full drawing scale, but centered at the center of the previous display. The number, followed by an **X**, serves as the magnification factor by which the current display will be multiplied.

**A** to display the full drawing (limits or extents, whichever is greater).

**E** to display the drawing extents. This fills the screen with all the drawing entities and thus produces the largest possible magnification of all the entities at once.

**C**, then enter the center point and height of the area you want displayed.

**L**, then enter the lower left corner and height of the area you want displayed.

**P** to return to the previous display. The 10 previous displays (whether zooms or pans) are saved for this purpose.

**W**, then locate opposite corners of the rectangular window you want displayed.

**D** to zoom and pan dynamically. A special display will appear that indicates:

> the current screen as a highlighted (dotted) rectangle,

> the drawing limits or extents, whichever is larger, as a white rectangle,

> the high-speed zooming area as four red corners, and

> the selection box.

To locate the selection box anywhere on the screen, move the pointer. To adjust the size of the selection box, press the pick button and then move the right edge of the box with the pointer. You can press the pick button as many times as you want to toggle back and forth and refine the location and size of the selection box. After the selection box has been adjusted to the desired location and size, press <RETURN>.

You can zoom while you're in other commands (while you're being prompted for anything but a text string). To do so, enter **'ZOOM** (notice the apostrophe). This transparent use of **'ZOOM** works only when **VIEWRES** is set for fast zooms (see VIEWRES below) and no regeneration is required. **ZOOM All** and **ZOOM Extents** always force a regeneration. But you can give a name to a view that's the equivalent of a ZOOM All, then use **'VIEW** transparently to restore that view, assuming a regeneration is not required (see VIEW below).

## PAN

**Shifts the displayed part of the drawing without changing the magnification**

When prompted for the displacement, enter:

The coordinates that define the direction (from 0,0) you want the picture moved. Then press <RETURN> when prompted for the second point.

Two points (using keyboard or pointer) that show where you want a point in the picture shifted from and to.

You can also pan by doing a dynamic zoom (**ZOOM D**) and retaining the same size for the selection box.

You can pan while you're in other commands (while you're being prompted for anything but a text string). To do so, enter **'PAN** (notice the apostrophe). This transparent use of **'PAN** works only when **VIEWRES** is set for fast zooms (see VIEWRES below), and no regeneration is required.

## VIEW

### Names a particular display so you can recall it easily

When prompted, enter the following:

**?** to get a list of the view names currently existing in the drawing.

**S** to save the current display as a view, then enter the name of the view. The name can have up to 31 characters, but short names are easier to use.

**W** to save a specified window area as a view, then enter the name of the view, then enter opposite corners of the window.

**R** to restore a view to the screen, then enter the name of the view.

**D** to delete a view, then enter the name of the view. The view itself isn't deleted, only its name.

You can use VIEW to restore a named view while you're in other commands (while you're being prompted for anything but a text string). To do so, enter **'VIEW** (notice the apostrophe). This transparent use of 'VIEW works only when **VIEWRES** is set for fast zooms (see VIEWRES below), and no regeneration is required.

## RENAME

### Changes the name assigned to an object

When prompted, enter the following:

**B** to rename a block.

**LA** to rename a layer.

**LT** to rename a linetype.

**S** to rename a text style.

**U** to rename a UCS.

**VI** to rename a view.

**VP** to rename a viewport.

Then enter the old name, then the new name.

Layer 0 and line type "continuous" can't be renamed.

## VIEWRES

**Controls the speed of zooms and
pans and the resolution of circles
and arcs in magnified views**

Enter **Y** if you want faster zooms and pans. If you enter **N**, all zooms and pans will cause a regeneration, which is slower than a redraw.

Then enter the number that defines the view resolution. The higher the number the rounder the circles and arcs, but the slower the regeneration. The default is 100.

If you have zoomed in and circles and arcs are too crude, do a **REGEN** to fix the current display, or reset VIEWRES either with **N** or a higher number.

## OSNAP

**Snaps new points to points already
in the drawing**

OSNAP, short for object snap, operates in two different ways—immediate osnap and running osnap.

Immediate—Enter one of the modes listed below each time you're about to enter a point. The osnap mode that you choose works only for that point; then you must reselect it or another osnap mode for the next point if desired.

Running—Enter the OSNAP command and then enter one or more modes that will apply to all subsequent points. When entering two or more modes, separate them with commas. To cancel running osnap, enter **OSNAP** and then enter **NON** or press <RETURN>.

You can enter any of the following modes from the keyboard or select them from the OSNAP submenu on the screen. To get the osnap page of the screen menu to appear, pick the asterisks (* * * *) at the top of any menu page, or press pointer button 3. The osnap target window or aperture appears on the crosshairs whenever an osnap mode is active. Enter the following:

    **NEA** (for Nearest) to snap to the point on a line, circle, arc, or point that's nearest to the crosshairs.

    **END** (for Endpoint) to snap to the closest endpoint of a line or arc.

    **MID** (for Midpoint) to snap to the midpoint of a line or arc.

    **CEN** (for Center) to snap to the center of a circle or arc.

    **NOD** (for Node) to snap to a point.

    **QUA** (for Quadrant) to snap to a point on a circle or arc that's located at 0, 90, 180 or 270 degrees.

    **INT** (for Intersection) to snap to the intersection of lines/arcs/circles.

    **INS** (for Insert) to snap to the insertion point of text, a block or a shape.

    **PER** (for Perpendicular) to snap to the point on a line that forms a perpendicular line with the last point entered, or the point on an arc or circle that's nearest the last point entered. You can apply PER to both the **from** and **to** endpoints of the line.

**TAN** (for Tangent) to snap to the point on a circle or arc that forms a tangent with the last point entered. You can also apply TAN to both the **from** and **to** endpoints of a line and thus draw a line tangent to two circles/arcs. And you can apply TAN to the three points of a three-point circle.

**NON** (for None) or **OFF** to turn running modes off for the next point.

## OSNAP Modes

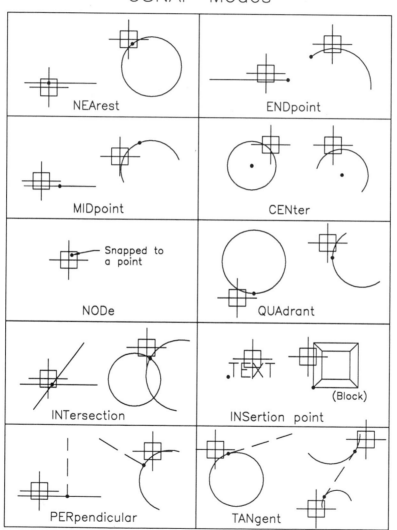

| NEArest | ENDpoint |
| MIDpoint | CENter |
| NODe | QUAdrant |
| INTersection | INSertion point |
| PERpendicular | TANgent |

When several points are found, AutoCAD selects the point closest to the cross-hairs. When quick mode is used with one or more of the above modes, AutoCAD selects the first point it finds that suits the requirements instead of the closest point.

No running osnap modes are present when a new drawing is started.

OSNAP overrides ORTHO, finds points only on visible layers, and won't snap to endpoints of spaces in hidden lines, center lines, and some parts of blocks. OSNAP sometimes overrides points entered from the keyboard. As a general rule, cancel running osnap modes as soon as you finish using them.

See Appendix A for an osnap exercise.

## APERTURE

**Adjusts the size of the osnap target box**

When prompted, enter desired height by entering the number of pixels (2 through 50).

You can also use **'SETVAR** to enter the desired number of pixels in the system variable APERTURE.

# INQUIRY

## ID

**Shows the coordinates or visual location of a point**

When prompted for the point,

Use the pointer to select the desired point, and its coordinates will be displayed.

Enter the coordinates of a point, and its location in the drawing will be displayed with a blip marker. ID will accept 3D locations (X,Y,Z).

It's often best to use **OSNAP** with the ID command (see OSNAP above).

## DIST

**Displays the diagonal and rectangular distances and the angle between two points**

When prompted, enter the two points using keyboard or pointer. The order in which you locate the points affects the sign of the rectangular distances and the size of the angle. DIST will accept 3D locations (X,Y,Z).

It's often best to use **OSNAP** with the DIST command (see OSNAP above).

## AREA

**Calculates areas of various shapes**

When prompted,

Locate the series of points (corners) defining a polygon. The prompt for the next point reappears until you press <RETURN>. If you have previously initiated the add/subtract mode, you'll then be prompted for further options for adjusting the running total. It's often best to use **OSNAP** when locating a series of points (see OSNAP above).

Enter **E**, then select an entity (circle or polyline). A polyline's width is ignored; its area is based on the centerline of the polyline. The prompt for the next circle/polyline reappears until you press **<RETURN>**. If you have previously initiated the add/subtract mode, you'll then be prompted for further options for adjusting the running total.

Enter **A** to initiate add mode—the next area(s) will be added into a running total.

Enter **S** to initiate subtract mode—the next area(s) will be subtracted from a running total.

The running total is reset to 0 each time the AREA command is entered.

## LIST

**Lists internal database information
and statistics on one or more entities**

When prompted, select the items you want listed. Handles are listed if they have been turned on with the **HANDLES** command. To return to your drawing, press **F1**.

## DBLIST

**Lists internal database information
and statistics on all entities in a
drawing**

When a drawing is complex, the database list is quite long and will scroll up the screen for several seconds or even minutes. To stop and restart the scrolling, use **CTRL-S**. To abort the listing, use **CTRL-C**.

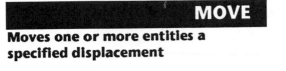

## MOVE

**Moves one or more entities a
specified displacement**

When prompted, select the entities you want to move.

When prompted for the displacement, enter:

The **Base point:** and **Second point:** of the displacement vector, using
the keyboard or pointer. You can fine-tune your placement of the entities by using the arrow keys on the numeric keypad, whether you're
using drag or not (Method 1).

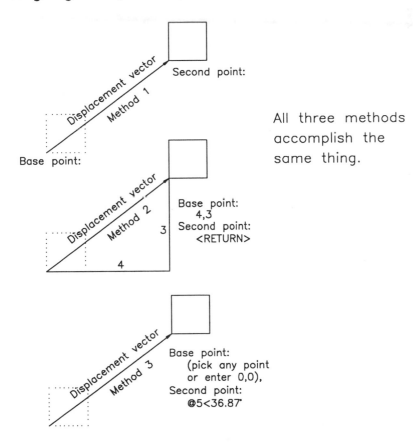

All three methods
accomplish the
same thing.

The relative X,Y displacement when prompted for **Base point:**. Press <RETURN> when prompted for **Second point:** (Method 2).

Any point (0,0 will do) when prompted for **Base point:**, then enter relative polar coordinates when prompted for **Second point:** (Method 3).

To drag the items when DRAGMODE is on, you must enter **DRAG** when prompted for the **to** point.

## COPY

**Places one or more copies of one or more entities a specified displacement from the original entities**

This command works like the MOVE command, but the original entities remain where they were.

Enter **M** to make multiple copies, then locate the base point and several points of displacement. Press <RETURN> to quit making copies.

## MIRROR

**Flips one or more entities around a specified axis**

When prompted, select the item(s) to be flipped. Then locate the endpoints of the flip axis. (You'll usually want to toggle ortho on when locating the second endpoint.) Then enter **Y** or **N** to delete or retain the original item(s).

You can drag the second point of the mirror line.

To keep text from being mirrored, use the **SETVAR** command to set **MIRR-TEXT** to **0**.

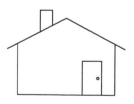 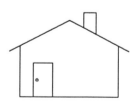

Mirror line
(flip axis)

*Special note on the next three commands:* When you use editing commands that change the actual geometry of the items you're editing, you'll have the most accurate visual control if you make sure that you're in a plan view (viewpoint 0,0,1) of the current UCS.

## OFFSET

**Draws parallel lines/arcs/polylines at a specified distance from the originals**

When prompted, enter:

> The distance for the offset, then select the object and indicate on which side of the original the new line is to be placed.

> **T,** then select the object and locate a point through which the new line is to run.

AutoCAD offsets connected lines/arcs differently from polylines, especially at the sharp corners.

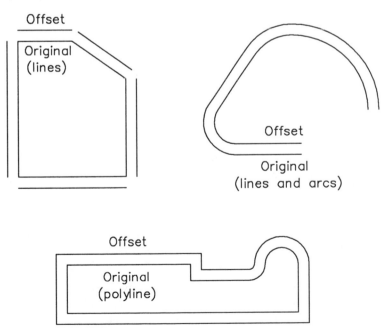

## FILLET

### Fillets lines, circles and arcs with a specified radius

When prompted, enter **R**, then enter the desired radius. Then re-enter the **FILLET** command if necessary and select the two lines/circles/arcs to be filleted.

The radius is stored in a system variable and, unless you change it, will be the same the next time you use the FILLET command. This means that you can simply enter the command and then select the two lines/circles/arcs.

The radius can be set to **0** to connect two lines/arcs forming a sharp corner.

When you're filleting a 2D polyline, all corners will fillet at once (see PLINE in Chapter 29). 3D polylines cannot be filleted.

You can select two lines, two arcs, a line and an arc, etc. Where you select the entity is important in determining where the fillet is placed.

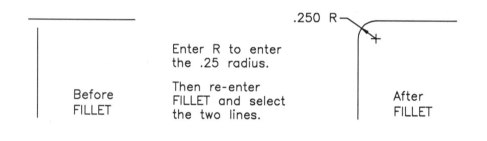

Before FILLET

Enter R to enter the .25 radius.

Then re-enter FILLET and select the two lines.

.250 R

After FILLET

## CHAMFER

### Chamfers (bevels) a corner with one or more specified distances

When prompted, enter **D**, then enter the first, then the second chamfer distance. (The default for the second distance is the first distance.) Then re-enter the **CHAMFER** command if necessary and select the first, then the second line.

The chamfer distances are stored in system variables and, unless you change them, will be the same the next time you use the CHAMFER command. This means that you can simply enter the command and then select the two lines.

When you're using CHAMFER on a 2D polyline, all corners will chamfer at once (see PLINE in Chapter 29). 3D polylines cannot be chamfered.

If the corner that you want to chamfer is a right angle (90 degrees) and you know the distance and the angle of the chamfer, you can find the second distance by multiplying the first distance by the tangent of the angle.

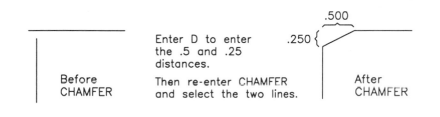

Before
CHAMFER

Enter D to enter
the .5 and .25
distances.

Then re-enter CHAMFER
and select the two lines.

.500

.250 {

After
CHAMFER

## ROTATE

**Rotates one or more entities in the X-Y plane around a specified point**

When prompted, select the object(s). Then enter the base point around which you want it rotated. Then enter the rotation angle, using keyboard or pointer.

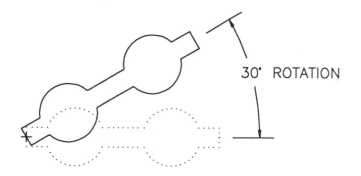

30° ROTATION

In place of the rotation angle, you can enter **R**, then indicate the reference angle by selecting two features of the objects (such as the endpoints of a line), then enter a new absolute angle for those two features. All the other selected objects will be rotated by the same amount. You can rotate an entire drawing.

The AXROT.LSP program (supplied on the release disks) lets you rotate entities around any point with the axis of rotation parallel to either the X, Y or Z axis.

## SCALE

**Scales the size of one or more entities in relation to a specified point**

When prompted, select the object(s). Then enter the base point and the scaling factor, using keyboard or pointer.

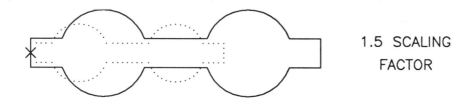

1.5 SCALING
FACTOR

In place of the scaling factor, you can enter **R**, then select a reference distance (such as the endpoints of a line), then enter a new absolute value for that distance. All the other objects will be scaled by the same amount. You can scale an entire drawing.

## U

**Undoes the previous command**

## REDO

**Redoes a command that was just undone**

## UNDO

**Lets you step back to an earlier stage in the drawing, or set up parameters for the U and UNDO commands**

Enter the following:

A number to undo several commands.

**A** to turn auto-undo on or off. Select this response only when you're using a menu that has macros (groups of commands triggered by one item on the menu). When Auto is on, these macros are treated as one command.

**M** to mark a place in the drawing process.

**B** to undo back to the last marked place in the drawing process. *Note:* If there are no previously marked places, entering **B** may undo the entire drawing.

**G** to group the next several commands (mainly for use with custom menus).

**E** to end the grouping begun with G. Subsequent UNDOs will treat this group of commands as one (mainly for use with custom menus).

**C** to control the range of the UNDO and U commands. Then enter **A** to let UNDO work with all commands, or enter **O** to limit UNDO to one command (same as the U command), or enter **N** (for None) to disable U and UNDO.

Selecting O or N clears the memory space that was holding UNDO information when it was fully active. Thus, after limiting UNDO, you can't return to a full-functioning UNDO for previous parts of the drawing.

# TEXT

## TEXT

**Places text in a drawing**

When prompted, locate the starting point or enter the following:

**R** to right-justify the text. Then locate the right-end point.

**C** to center the text horizontally. Then locate the center point.

**M** (for middle) to center the text horizontally and vertically. Then enter the middle point.

**A** to align the text between two points, then locate the two points. AutoCAD calculates the appropriate height.

**F** to fit the text between two points, then locate the two points and enter the height. AutoCAD adjusts the width of the text.

**S** to select a text style. Then enter the name of the desired style. One text style, called STANDARD, is created automatically when you start a new drawing. You must use the **STYLE** command to create other styles you want to use (see STYLE below).

```
ₓThis text is LEFT JUSTIFIED          This text is RIGHT JUSTIFIED
ₓThe default is left justified text   This line is also right justified


         CENTERED TEXT                 MIDDLE TEXT


⌐ₓThis text is ALIGNED⌐              ⌐ₓThis  text  is  FIT⌐
                                    
    (Height calculated                 (Height specified
    by AutoCAD so that                 by user, resulting in
    letter widths remain               letter widths that are
     proportional)                     not proportional)
```

When prompted for height, enter the height of capital letters, using the keyboard or pointer.

When prompted for rotation angle, enter the degrees from horizontal for the baseline of the text, using the keyboard or pointer.

When prompted for text, enter one line of text as you want it to appear in the drawing.

Each time you enter the TEXT command, the most recently entered text will be highlighted. If you want to place the new text immediately below this highlighted text with the same justification, height, etc., simply press <RETURN>. If you want the new text located someplace else, locate the starting point or select one of the options listed above.

| Special character | Produces |
|---|---|
| %%o | Overscore on/off |
| %%u | Underscore on/off |
| %%d | °(Degree symbol—same as %%127) |
| %%p | ± (Plus-or-minus symbol) |
| %%c | Ø (Circle diameter symbol) |
| %%nnn | ASCII character *nnn* or user-created character |

There are several AutoLISP enhancements to the TEXT command. See the CHGTEXT.LSP and ASCTEXT.LSP files under "AutoLISP Programs" in Chapter 39.

## DTEXT

**Places text in a drawing
dynamically, as it's being typed**

This command, while similar to the TEXT command, does some things differently. It places a square cursor on the screen where your text will start, then lets you see the text as it will appear in the drawing as you type it.

The DTEXT command assumes that you'll want to place subsequent lines of text below the present line, so it places the cursor at the beginning of the new line each time you press <RETURN>. You can backspace through one or more lines of text.

To quit entering text, press **<RETURN>** at the beginning of a line. The temporary text display is always left-justified, even though you may have selected right-justified, centered, etc.

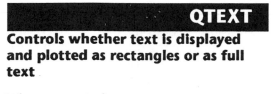

**Controls whether text is displayed and plotted as rectangles or as full text**

When prompted,

Enter **ON** to display text as rectangles, allowing faster redrawing and regenerating of the drawing.

Existing text is displayed as rectangles after QTEXT is turned on and after a regeneration (see REGEN below). However, new text is still displayed fully. Rectangles may not be exactly the same length as the actual text.

Enter **OFF** to display full text (displays only after a regeneration).

## STYLE

**Adjusts a text font according to your style specifications**

When prompted for text style name, enter:

**?** to get a list of styles already created.

The name of the new style you want to create, or the name of the style you have already created but want to alter. The name can be up to 31 characters long.

Then enter the information necessary to determine:

font to be styled—one of 22, shown below

height (use 0 if you want the height to remain variable)

width factor

slant degrees (positive slants to right, negative slants to left)

backwards

upside down

vertical

This newly created style automatically becomes the current style that the TEXT command will use.

You can redefine an existing text style. Most changes you make to an existing style will be reflected only in new text added to the drawing using the new style. However, if you redefine a style's text font or vertical/horizontal orientation, all lines of text that are already in the drawing and which use the redefined style will be affected.

## TEXT FONTS

Twenty-two text fonts are illustrated on the following pages. Most of these fonts are also pictured in an icon menu available from the Options/Fonts pulldown menu.

Some of the fonts are described as serif, some as sans-serif. A serif is an ending stroke on the arm or tail of a letter. "Sans-serif" means "without serif."

All 22 fonts can have either horizontal or vertical orientation.

The last five fonts are symbol fonts. You can tell which key on the keyboard produces any particular symbol by comparing that symbol's location with the same location in one of the non-symbol fonts.

| NAME & Description | Sample | NAME & Description | Sample |
|---|---|---|---|
| TXT — simplified letters for faster regeneration | ABC. DEF. GHIJ KLMN: OPQR° STUV WXYZ abc\ def/ ghi j1 klmn? opqr' stuv~ wxyz 1234567890 !@#$%^&*() _+-=:[](} | SCRIPTC — Script Complex | *ABC. DEF. GHIJ: KLMN: OPQR° STUV° WXYZ abc\ def/ ghij klmn? opqr' stuv~ wxyz ·1234567890 !@#$%~&*() _+-=<>[]{}* |
| MONOTXT — same as TXT but all characters have equal spacing | ABC. DEF. GHIJ KLMN: OPQR: STUV° WXYZ abc\ def/ ghi j1 klmn? opqr' stuv~ wxyz 1234567890 !@#$%^&*() _+-=:[]() | GREEKC — Greek Complex | ABX. ΔΕΦ. ΓΗΙϑ: ΚΛΜΝ: ΟΠϴΡ° ΣΤΥ° ΩΞΨΖ αβχ\ δεφ/ γηιϑ klmn? οπϑρ' στυϖ~ ωξψζ 1234567890 !@#$%~&*() _+-=<>[]{} |
| ROMANS — Roman Simplex sans serif single stroke | ABC. DEF. GHIJ: KLMN: OPQR° STUV° WXYZ abc\ def/ ghij klmn? opqr' stuv~ wxyz 1234567890 !@#$%~&*() _+-=<>[](} | CYRILLIC — Cyrillic - alphabetical | АВВ. ГДЕ. ЖЗИЙ: КЛМН: ОПРС° ТУФХ° ЦЧШЩ абвы\ где/ гхишщ клмн? опрсЯ стувэ цчшщ 1234567890 !@#$%~&*() Ю+-=юявбъ |
| SCRIPTS — Script Simplex | *ABC. DEF. GHIJ: KLMN: OPQR° STUV° WXYZ abc\ def/ ghij klmn? opqr' stuv~ wxyz 1234567890 !@#$%~&*() _+-=<>[]{}* | CYRILTLC — Cyrillic - transliteration | АВЧ. ДЕФ. ГХИЦ: КЛМН: ОПЏР° СТУВ° ШЖЙЗ абчы\ деф/ гхишща клмн? оппрЯ стувэ шжйз 1234567890 !@#$%^&*() 3+-=юявббъ |
| GREEKS — Greek Simplex | ABX. ΔΕΦ. ΓΗΙϑ: ΚΛΜΝ: ΟΠϑΡ° ΣΤΥϖ° ΩΞΨΖ αβχ\ δεφ/ γηιϑ klmn? οπϑρ' στυϖ~ ωξψζ 1234567890 !@#$%~&*() _+-=<>[]{} | ROMANT — Roman Triplex serif triple stroke | **ABC. DEF. GHIJ: KLMN: OPQR° STUV° WXYZ** abc\ def/ ghij klmn? opqr' stuv~ wxyz 1234567890 !@#$%~&*() _+-=<>[]{} |
| ROMAND — Roman Duplex sans serif double stroke | **ABC. DEF. GHIJ: KLMN: OPQR° STUV° WXYZ** abc\ def/ ghij klmn? opqr' stuv~ wxyz **1234567890** !@#$%~&*() _+-=<>[]{} | ITALICT — Italic Triplex | *ABC. DEF. GHIJ: KLMN: OPQR° STUV° WXYZ abc\ def/ ghij klmn? opqr' stuv~ wxyz 1234567890 !@#$%~&*() _+-=<>[]{}* |
| ROMANC — Roman Complex serif double stroke | ABC. DEF. GHIJ: KLMN: OPQR° STUV° WXYZ abc\ def/ ghij klmn? opqr' stuv~ wxyz 1234567890 !@#$%~&*() _+-=<>[]{} | GOTHICE — Gothic English | 𝔄𝔅𝔒. 𝔇𝔈𝔉. 𝔊𝔥𝔦𝔧: 𝔎𝔏𝔐𝔑: 𝔒𝔓𝔔𝔯° 𝔖𝔗𝔘𝔳° 𝔚𝔛𝔜𝔷 abc\ bef/ ghij| klmn? opqr' stuv~ wxyz 1234567890 !@#$%~&*() _+-=<>[]{} |
| ITALICC — Italic Complex | *ABC. DEF. GHIJ: KLMN: OPQR° STUV° WXYZ abc\ def/ ghij klmn? opqr' stuv~ wxyz 1234567890 !@#$%~&*() _+-=<>[]{}* | GOTHICG — Gothic German | 𝔘𝔅𝔒. 𝔇𝔈𝔍. 𝔊𝔥𝔍𝔍: 𝔎𝔏𝔐𝔑: 𝔒𝔓𝔔𝔯° 𝔖𝔗𝔘𝔳° 𝔚𝔛𝔜𝔷 abc\ bef/ ghij| klmn? opqr' stuv~ wxyz 1234567890 !@#$%~&*() _+-=<>[]{} |

# THESE CAPS .40"

## THESE CAPS .250 inch.

### THESE CAPITALS are .188 inch.

ALL FONTS CAN BE ORIENTED HORIZONTALLY OR VERTICALLY

THESE CAPITALS are .125 inch high.

THESE CAPITALS are .100 inch high.

THESE CAPITALS are .080 inch high.

THESE CAPITALS are .060 inch high.

This is a sample of the TXT font using a STANDARD style.

This is a sample of the TXT font using a COMPRESSED style. (.7 width factor)

This is a sample of the TXT font using an EXPANDED style. (1.4 width factor)

This is a sample of the TXT font using a SLANTED style.

| NAME & Description | Sample |
|---|---|
| GOTHICI Gothic Italian | (symbols) |
| SYASTRO Astronomical symbols | (symbols) |
| SYMAP Mapping symbols | (symbols) |
| SYMATH Mathematical symbols | (symbols) |
| SYMETEO Meteorological symbols | (symbols) |
| SYMUSIC Music Symbols | (symbols) |

# PROTOTYPE DRAWINGS

## CREATING PROTOTYPE DRAWINGS

Whenever you start a new drawing, AutoCAD normally uses a prototype draw-ing to set limits, snap spacing, grid spacing, layers, blocks, etc. A prototype drawing is simply any drawing—it can be blank (no drawing entities), or it can have a border and title block, predrawn blocks, etc. You can edit, then save prototype drawings just like any other drawing. Each time you start a new drawing, you have three prototype options (see "Starting a New Drawing" in Chapter 2).

You can configure AutoCAD to use a drawing that you've created as its default prototype drawing. At the main menu, select 5 to get the Configuration menu, then select 8 to get the Operating Parameters menu, then select 2 to get Ini-tial Drawing Setup. When prompted, enter the name of the drawing you want AutoCAD to use as its default prototype drawing. Or, enter . (period) if you want AutoCAD to have no default prototype drawing.

*Suggestion:* Create a set of drawings that you can use as prototypes, including the various size sheets/borders/formats you'll be using repeatedly. Create some for inches, some for millimeters, some with predefined blocks, etc.

## SETTING LIMITS

The following discussion of drawing limits applies both to prototype drawings and to any drawing you might create from scratch.

When you create prototype drawings, you must use the **LIMITS** command to set the limits. Don't use the sheet size for your limits. Rather, use the format (border) size—sheet size minus the margins.

If you're drawing at full scale (1=1), it's easy to set the limits for your prototype drawing. In many cases you'll want to set them at the maximum size your plotter will accept for each sheet size it handles. For example, suppose your plotter is a Houston Instruments DMP 42 that handles sheet sizes C (24 x 18) and D (36 x 24). The maximum plotting area for the C size sheet is 21.5 x 14.5 and for the D size it's 34 x 21.5. These maximum plotting sizes can be used as your limits.

If you want to end up with a plotted drawing at a scale other than 1=1, then you have to take the scaling process into account when you set your limits. Of course, you can select the "Fit" option every time you plot, but that can lead to very strange-looking drawings. The notes and dimension text will probably be too big or too small. And the plot probably won't be at one of the customary scales. It's much better to determine your limits precisely, so that after your drawing is scaled to its final proportions, (1) your drawing still fits within the maximum plotting area your plotter will accept, (2) the plot is at a customary scale and (3) your notes and dimension text are the desired size.

You can use the plotting scale chart below to help determine your drawing limits and final plotting scale. For example, suppose you want to draw a very small machine part (approx. .5" by .25") and then plot it on an A sheet that's 11 x 8.5 (10 x 7.5 border). If you need two views and also allow for extra space for dimensions and notes, you'll probably want a total drawing space of about 2.5" by 2."

Use the chart as follows: Look under the A size sheet (first column) and find the drawing limits that are 2.5 by 1.875 (closest to your desired total drawing space). Then look across to the plotting scale factor, which in this case is 4=1. Of course, you draw the part and dimension it at full scale. When you finally scale your drawing up by a factor of 4 (either in the drawing editor before you plot, or as you plot), your border will be exactly the size you need.

For another example, suppose you want to draw a floor plan of a 500' x 300' building and plot it on an E size sheet that's 48 x 36 (46 x 34 border). From the chart you can see that you need to use a final plotting scale of 1/16" = 1' (or smaller). Set your limits at 736' x 544', **DIMSCALE** at 192, then draw and dimension the part at full scale as usual. Then you can scale down the drawing by a factor of .00520833 (either in the drawing editor before you plot, or as you plot).

You can use this information to set up not only your limits, but also DIMSCALE, LTSCALE, etc. See "Drawing to Various Scales" in Chapter 23.

The sheet sizes given in the chart below are standard. However, the format sizes are merely generalized, since they were determined by subtracting nominal margins from the sheet sizes. Consult your plotter manual for the maximum plotting sizes available on your plotter for each size sheet. Once you adjust the format sizes according to the maximum plotting sizes, you can also adjust the drawing limits and thus create a chart that's suited to your particular plotter.

|  | A | A | B | B | C | C | D | D | E | E | Plotting Scale Factor |
|---|---|---|---|---|---|---|---|---|---|---|---|
| **Sheet size** | 11x8.5 | 12x9 | 17x11 | 18x12 | 22x17 | 24x18 | 34x22 | 36x24 | 44x34 | 48x36 | |
| **Margins** | .5 | .5 | .5 | .5 | .75 | .75 | 1.00 | 1.00 | 1.00 | 1.00 | |
| **Format (border) size** | 10x7.5 | 11x8 | 16x10 | 17x11 | 20.5x15.5 | 22.5x16.5 | 32x20 | 34x22 | 42x32 | 46x34 | |
| D | 1.00 x .75 | 1.10 x .8 | 1.60 x 1.00 | 1.70 x 1.10 | 2.05 x 1.55 | 2.25 x 1.65 | 3.20 x 2.00 | 3.40 x 2.20 | 4.20 x 3.20 | 4.60 x 3.40 | 10 = 1 or 10.00 |
| R | 2.5 x 1.875 | 2.75 x 2 | 4 x 2.5 | 4.25 x 2.75 | 5.125 x 3.875 | 5.625 x 4.125 | 8 x 5 | 8.5 x 5.5 | 10.5 x 8 | 11.5 x 8.5 | 4 = 1 or 4.00 |
| A | 5 x 3.75 | 5.5 x 4 | 8 x 5 | 8.5 x 5.5 | 10.25 x 7.75 | 11.25 x 8.25 | 16 x 10 | 17 x 11 | 21 x 16 | 23 x 17 | 2 = 1 or 2.00 |
| W | 10 x 7.5 | 11 x 8 | 16 x 10 | 17 x 11 | 20.5 x 15.5 | 22.5 x 16.5 | 32 x 20 | 34 x 22 | 42 x 32 | 46 x 34 | 1 = 1 or 1.00 |
| I | 20 x 15 | 22 x 16 | 32 x 20 | 34 x 22 | 41 x 31 | 45 x 33 | 64 x 40 | 68 x 44 | 84 x 64 | 92 x 68 | 1 = 2 or .50 |
| N | 40 x 30 | 44 x 32 | 64 x 40 | 68 x 44 | 82 x 62 | 90 x 66 | 128 x 80 | 136 x 88 | 168 x 128 | 184 x 136 | 1 = 4 or .25 |
| G | 80 x 60 | 88 x 64 | 128 x 80 | 136 x 88 | 164 x 124 | 180 x 132 | 256 x 160 | 272 x 176 | 336 x 256 | 368 x 272 | 1 = 8 or .125 |
| L | 10' x 7'6" | 11' x 8' | 16' x 10' | 17' x 11' | 20'6" x 15'6" | 22'6" x 16'6" | 32' x 20' | 34' x 22' | 42' x 32' | 46' x 34' | 1" = 1' or 1/12 or .08333333 |
| I | 20' x 15' | 22' x 16' | 32' x 20' | 34' x 22' | 41' x 31' | 45' x 33' | 64' x 40' | 68' x 44' | 84' x 64' | 92' x 68' | 1/2" = 1' or 1/24 or .04166667 |
| M | 40' x 30' | 44' x 32' | 64' x 40' | 68' x 44' | 82' x 62' | 90' x 66' | 128' x 80' | 136' x 88' | 168' x 128' | 184' x 136' | 1/4" = 1' or 1/48 or .02083333 |
| I | 80' x 60' | 88' x 64' | 128' x 80' | 136' x 88' | 164' x 124' | 180' x 132' | 256' x 160' | 272' x 176' | 336' x 256' | 368' x 272' | 1/8" = 1' or 1/96 or .01041667 |
| T | 160' x 120' | 176' x 128' | 256' x 160' | 272' x 176' | 328' x 248' | 360' x 264' | 512' x 320' | 544' x 352' | 672' x 512' | 736' x 544' | 1/16" = 1' or 1/192 or .00520833 |
| S | | | | | | | | | | | |

(Left-hand vertical label: DRAWING LIMITS)

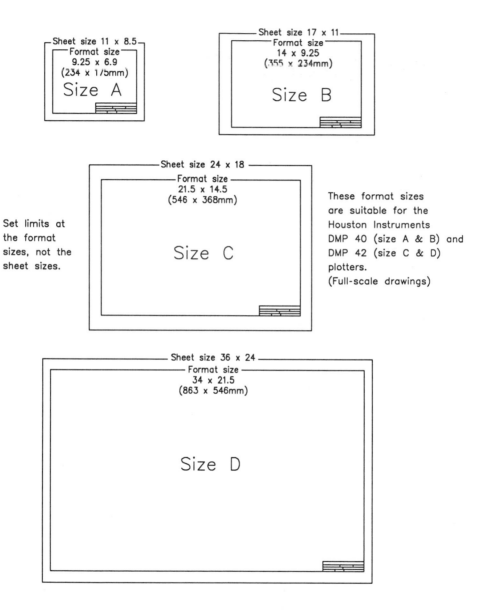

Sheet size 11 x 8.5
Format size
9.25 x 6.9
(234 x 175mm)
Size A

Sheet size 17 x 11
Format size
14 x 9.25
(355 x 234mm)
Size B

Sheet size 24 x 18
Format size
21.5 x 14.5
(546 x 368mm)
Size C

Sheet size 36 x 24
Format size
34 x 21.5
(863 x 546mm)
Size D

Set limits at
the format
sizes, not the
sheet sizes.

These format sizes
are suitable for the
Houston Instruments
DMP 40 (size A & B) and
DMP 42 (size C & D)
plotters.
(Full-scale drawings)

# 18 PLOTTING

## PLOT

**Plots a drawing**

Many variations are possible when you're plotting a drawing. This section describes only one way; see "Plotting Options" below for other possibilities.

The following setup will let you plot a small, full-scale drawing such as the fork profile in Appendix A.

## Preparing AutoCAD

First, select **3** on the main menu, then enter the name of the drawing you want to plot. Or, if you're currently working on a drawing and want to plot it without leaving the drawing editor, enter the **PLOT** command.

When prompted for **part of drawing**, enter **L** for Limits.

Certain plot specifications will be displayed, which you can change if needed. Check the plot specifications that are displayed. If you need to change any of them, enter **Y**. They should be as follows:

All plotting linetypes should be continuous **(0)**, even though some linetypes in your drawing are not continuous.

The plot is not sent to a file.

Size units can be **I** (inches) or **M** (millimeters), depending on the drawing units.

Plot origin should be **0,0**. If otherwise, both **X** and **Y** values must be positive.

Size should be a format size your plotter will handle.

The drawing should not be rotated.

Pen width should be **.010** (.25mm), which is suitable for a .35mm pen tip.

Area fill boundaries don't need to be adjusted for pen width.

Hidden lines don't need to be removed.

Plotting scale should be **1=1**.

## Preparing the Plotter

Each plotter model is different; see your plotter manual for information on plotter preparation. The items listed below are merely general procedures.

Make sure that the plotter is turned on and is on line.

Make sure the paper and pen(s) are in place.

You may need to set the baud rate, select large or small, etc., depending on the plotter you're using.

Then press <RETURN> to begin the plot. To abort a plot, use **CTRL-C**. The data that's already in the plotter's buffer will continue to plot.

When the plot is completed, press <RETURN> to return to either the main menu or the drawing editor.

Various sheet and format sizes suitable for the Houston Instruments DMP 40 and DMP 42 plotters and the JDL-850 EWS printer-plotter are listed in Appendix G.

## PRPLOT

**Plots a drawing on the printer**

Select **4** on the main menu, then enter the name of the drawing you want to plot. Or, if you're currently working on a drawing and want to plot it without leaving the drawing editor, enter **PRPLOT**.

The sequence of prompts is similar to the PLOT command.

Make sure the printer is turned on and is on line (selected) before you try to plot.

## PLOTTING OPTIONS

Basic plotting procedures are described under the PLOT command above.

## Picking the Part to Plot

Enter the following:

**D** to plot the current display as it appears on the screen. When you start from the main menu, the drawing isn't on the screen. In this case, the last part of the drawing that was displayed on the screen (just before the last time you saved the drawing) will be plotted.

**E** to plot the extents of the drawing (the rectangular area actually occupied by drawing entities).

**L** to plot the entire limits of the drawing (the area defined by the limits command).

**V** to plot a view you defined earlier with the VIEW command. Then enter the view name.

**W** to plot a window portion of the drawing that's smaller than the current display. If you began from the drawing editor so that the drawing is still displayed, you can locate a window with the pointer. If you began from the main menu, you'll have to use the keyboard to enter the coordinates of the window corners.

## Inches or Millimeters

All drawing is done in pure linear units, which can represent any measurement you have in mind. AutoCAD doesn't need to know how long these units are until you plot. Since inches and millimeters are the two most common units in engineering drawing, these are the only choices offered. If your units represent other distances, you'll need to select whichever unit (inches or millimeters) lets you calculate your plot-scaling ratio most easily.

## Plot Origin

The plot origin default of 0,0 is considered the plotter's home position. This home position is normally the lower left corner of the drawing sheet for the plotter, but the upper left corner for the printer-plotter.

You can enter the coordinates of a different plot origin (positive numbers only). These X-Y coordinates will move the origin over and up on the plotter, but over and down on the printer-plotter. The origin offset is full size, before any scaling factor is applied.

## Plotting Size

Enter plotting size either by entering the appropriate letter or mnemonic from the displayed options, or by entering the width and height, separated by a comma.

## Pen Width

If you set the pen width slightly smaller than the actual pen tip diameter, filled-in areas such as arrowheads, traces, solids, etc., won't contain gaps.

|  | Actual pen tip diameter | Suggested pen-width setting |
|---|---|---|
| If using inches: | .35mm (.014 inch) | .010 inch |
|  | .50mm (.020 inch) | .015 inch |
| If using millimeters: | .35mm | .25mm |
|  | .50mm | .40mm |

## Rotating a Drawing

Drawings can be rotated 90 degrees to the right as they are being plotted.

**Rotating a Drawing**

Drawings can be rotated 90 degrees to the right as they are being plotted.

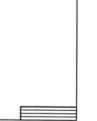

Not rotated
on screen

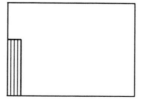

Rotated 90 degrees
as plotted

For example, the cylinder drawing in Appendix A is on a vertical, A-sized sheet. This drawing can be plotted (using Limits, and a scale of 1=1) and rotated while plotting if you enter a size of **9.25,6.9**, a plot origin of **0,0**, and enter **Y** when asked if you want a 2D plot rotated. Notice that the size of 9.25 wide by 6.9 high is the size after rotation. Also, if a plot is rotated 90 degrees, the plot origin offset is applied after rotation.

## Area Fill Adjustment

If you enter **Y** to adjust the area fill, the edges of solids, traces, etc. will be pulled back by one-half the indicated pen width so that the actual filled-in area represents its true dimensions. For most applications, this isn't needed.

## Scaling a Plot

When you want to plot a drawing so that one inch (or one millimeter) on the plot equals one drawing unit, enter **1=1** when prompted for the plotting scale. However, you may often need to plot at a scale other than 1:1.

There are two ways to end up with a scaled plot. One is to scale the drawing on the screen (see "Drawing to Various Scales" in Chapter 23). The other is to leave the drawing at full scale on the screen, but then scale it up/down on the plotter. Both examples below illustrate this second procedure.

Example 1—You have a drawing of a small machine part that's been drawn and dimensioned at full scale. You intend to plot it at 4:1 scale, so you've done the dimensioning with the **DIMSCALE** variable set at **.25** and have adjusted **LTSCALE** as needed. To plot the drawing at the intended scale, enter **4=1** when asked for the plotting scale.

Example 2—You have an architectural drawing that's been drawn and dimensioned at full scale. You intend to use a scale of 1/8 inch = 1 foot, so you've set **DIMSCALE** at **96** and have also adjusted **LTSCALE** as needed. To plot the drawing at the intended scale, enter **.125=12 (or 1/8''=1')** when asked for the plotting scale.

If you select **F** to fit the drawing to the plotting size you selected earlier, the drawing extents will be scaled up or down so that all drawing entities will fit on the sheet. However, the scale probably won't be any of the typical drawing scales.

## Changing Colors and/or Pen Widths

Different screen colors can be plotted with different pens. Thus, you can plot object lines in one color, hidden lines in another color, and center lines and dimension lines in still another color. Or, when you're plotting with black wet-ink, you can use different pen widths. For example, use a .50mm-tip pen for object lines (yellow on the screen), and a .35mm-tip pen for all other colors. See the notes at the end of the section on the LAYER command in Chapter 21.

To use different pens in a single-pen plotter, configure AutoCAD to pause for you to change pens. Use the configuration menu, select "configure plotter," and enter Y when asked if you want to change pens while plotting. At the start of the plotting procedure, enter Y when asked if you want to change anything, and enter the appropriate pen numbers when prompted. When AutoCAD pauses for you to change pens, remember that the colors mentioned in the prompts are screen colors, not necessarily the color pens to be used in the plotter.

## 3D Plotting

When you're plotting a drawing that has a viewpoint other than 0,0,1, a Limits plot becomes an Extents plot. For most options (Limits, Extents, Display and Window), the plotted viewpoint is the same as the most recent viewpoint shown on the display. However, the viewpoint for the View option is the same one that was in effect when that view was defined.

Hidden lines can be omitted from a plot by answering Y to the prompt **Remove hidden lines?** This accomplishes the same thing on the plotter that HIDE accomplishes on the screen.

## Plotting to File

In some cases, you may need to plot to a file. For example, suppose your computer isn't connected to a plotter. Suppose also that in the next room there's a computer connected to a Hewlett-Packard 7475A pen plotter, but that computer doesn't have AutoCAD. (The plotter is used to produce graphs and charts from a database program.) You can plot to a file on a floppy diskette at your computer, then use the other computer to send that file to the plotter. Here's how:

At your computer,

> Select **3** at the main menu (or enter **PLOT** in the drawing editor) to plot a drawing as usual.
>
> When prompted **Write the plot to a file?**, enter **Y**.
>
> When prompted for the file name, make sure you have a floppy diskette in drive A and then enter the name of the drawing, preceded by A:. For example, if the drawing name is P123, you'd enter **A:P123**. Since plot files have a .PLT extension, this will produce a file on the diskette in drive A: called P123.PLT.

At the other computer,

> Place your diskette in drive **A** and make sure you're at the DOS prompt.
>
> Since the Hewlett-Packard 7475A plotter receives data at 9600 baud, you need to use the **MODE** command to set up the serial port to send information at that same rate. Assuming the plotter is connected to the first serial port, known as COM1, you'd enter **MODE COM1:9600**.
>
> Enter **COPY A:P123.PLT COM1**.

Besides setting the baud rate, the MODE command can also set up the number of data bits, type of parity check and number of stop bits for the plotter you're using. Both commands, MODE and COPY, are explained in further detail in your DOS manual. Also see your DOS manual for an explanation of device names such as COM1.

If you want to printer-plot to a file (using **4** on the main menu or the **PRPLOT** command in the drawing editor), the procedure will be the same as above, except that AutoCAD gives the file name the extension .LST.

Printer-plotters are typically connected to a parallel port, so you don't need to set up a baud rate. Assuming your printer-plotter is connected to parallel port number 1, the COPY command line would be **COPY A:P123.LST LPT1**.

# chapter 19

# EDITING—Group Two

When you use editing commands that change the actual geometry of the items you're editing, you'll have the most accurate visual control of the editing process if you make sure that you're in a plan view (viewpoint 0,0,1) of the current UCS.

## BREAK

**Erases a part of a line, trace, circle or arc**

When prompted, select the item to be broken. If you select the item with the pointer, AutoCAD assumes that the point of selection is also the first breakpoint (an endpoint of the portion to be erased) and asks for the second breakpoint. If you want to pick a different first breakpoint, enter **F**.

The first breakpoint (assuming the item has already been selected) and the second breakpoint need not be on the item. They can be off to one side or off the end of the item. AutoCAD selects the nearest point on the item for the actual breakpoint. When you're breaking a circle, the erased portion runs counterclockwise from the first to the second breakpoint.

You can break an item into two portions without any gap by placing the second breakpoint at the exact same location as the first breakpoint. When prompted for the second breakpoint, enter **@**.

You can use the BREAK command to break 2D polylines.

See some examples of breaking procedures below.

## TRIM

**Trims off selected parts of an entity at the intersection of other selected entities**

When prompted, select one or more entities that will serve as cutting edges, individually or with a window. Then, with the pointer, select one or more items (lines, arcs, polylines) you want trimmed. Where you select the item determines which part of it is removed.

See some examples of trimming procedures below.

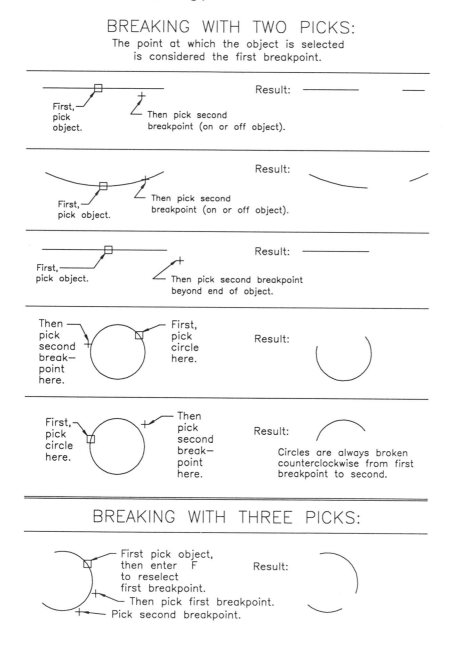

BREAKING WITH TWO PICKS:
The point at which the object is selected
is considered the first breakpoint.

First, pick object.
Then pick second breakpoint (on or off object).
Result:

First, pick object.
Then pick second breakpoint (on or off object).
Result:

First, pick object.
Then pick second breakpoint beyond end of object.
Result:

Then pick second breakpoint here.
First, pick circle here.
Result:

First, pick circle here.
Then pick second breakpoint here.
Result:
Circles are always broken counterclockwise from first breakpoint to second.

BREAKING WITH THREE PICKS:

First pick object, then enter F to reselect first breakpoint.
Then pick first breakpoint.
Pick second breakpoint.
Result:

# TRIM

Select the cutting edge(s) first, then select
the part of each entity you want to trim away.

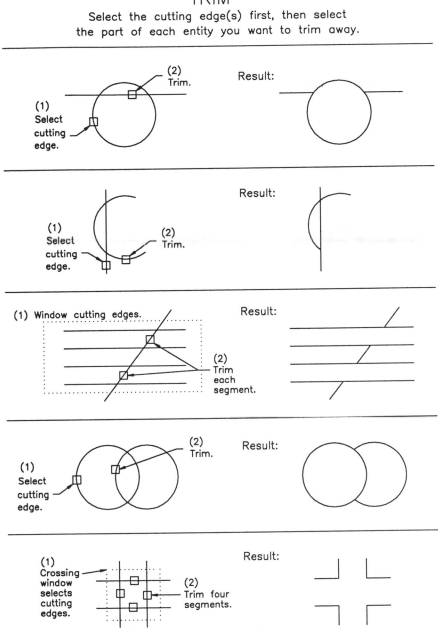

## EXTEND

**Extends selected lines, arcs and polylines to meet other selected items**

When prompted, select one or more entities that will serve as boundary edges, individually or with a window.

Then, with the pointer, select one or more items (lines, arcs or polylines) you want extended. Where you select the item determines which end will be extended.

You can reselect the same item several times to make it extend to subsequent boundary edges.

## CHANGE

**Modifies lines, circles, text, attributes and inserted blocks**

After selecting the items you want to change, you'll be prompted for **change point or properties**. If the viewing angle isn't perpendicular to the plane of the object being changed, a warning message appears.

Then enter the following:

**P** to change properties rather than the change point. Then:

**C** to change color.

**LA** to change layer.

**LT** to change line type.

**E** to change Z-axis elevation.

**T** to change Z-axis thickness.

If you want to change layers, there's a shortcut—when prompted for **change point**, enter **L** and you'll be prompted for the layer name.

If changing a line—The change point becomes the new endpoint of the line. The endpoint nearest the change point will shift to the change point. If ORTHO is on, the changed line will be orthogonal from its unchanged end. More than one line can be changed at a time, in which case the single change point will apply to all selected lines. You can change 3DLINEs in two ways: alter the X and Y coordinates with the pointer, or alter all three coordinates from the keyboard.

If changing a circle—The change point becomes the new radius of the circle.

If changing text—Enter the information for those aspects of the text you want changed: starting point/endpoint/center/middle, style, height, rotation angle of baseline or the text string (the alphanumeric content). For aspects you want to leave unchanged, simply press <**RETURN**>. See the CHGTEXT.LSP file under "AutoLISP Programs" in Chapter 39.

If changing an attribute definition that's not part of a block—Enter the new tag or text aspects, prompt or default value, etc.

If changing a block—Enter the change point (the new insertion point) and the rotation angle.

You can drag the change point for lines, circles and blocks; the rotation angle for blocks; and the starting point, height and rotation angle for text.

## CHPROP

**Modifies properties**

The CHPROP command works much like the CHANGE command, but doesn't change locations (of endpoints, etc.). Instead, it specializes in changing properties, including color, layer, linetype and thickness.

## STRETCH

**Moves parts of a drawing while retaining connections to parts not moved**

When prompted, select the objects that you want to move and/or stretch using a crossing window. (If you select this command from the screen menu, the crossing window option will be selected for you.) This selection set can be refined further if needed.

Then indicate the displacement, similar to the MOVE command. Items that are contained completely within the crossing window will be moved. Items that have one endpoint inside and one endpoint outside the window will be stretched.

BEFORE STRETCHING     Displacement vector     AFTER STRETCHING

.375

Crossing window

Dimensions can be stretched. If the dimension was created as an associative dimension (with variable DIMASO on), if the default dimension text was accepted, and if the dimension has not been exploded, the dimension text will be adjusted automatically when the geometry is stretched.

3DLINEs and 3DFACEs can be stretched in any of the three dimensions.

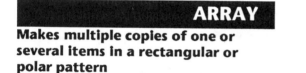

## ARRAY

**Makes multiple copies of one or several items in a rectangular or polar pattern**

When prompted, select item(s) to be copied to develop the array.

Then enter **R** for a rectangular array or **P** for a polar (circular) array.

For a rectangular array, enter the number of horizontal rows, then the number of vertical columns, then the distance between rows, then the distance between columns. Negative distances generate an array in the negative X and/or Y direction. Instead of entering distances from the keyboard, you can use the pointer to locate opposite corners of a box and thus indicate the spacing between rows and columns. The entire array can be rotated by setting the snap rotation before using the ARRAY command (see SNAP in Chapter 5).

There are three ways to define a polar/circular array. After selecting items, enter:

**P**, then center, then number of items, then angle to fill.

**P**, then center, then press **<RETURN>** when prompted for number of items, then enter angle to fill, then angle between items.

**C**, then center, then angle between items, then either number of items (positive) or number of degrees to fill (negative).

The last prompt to appear in the polar array sequence asks if you want the objects rotated as they are copied.

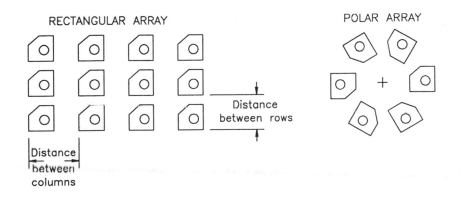

RECTANGULAR ARRAY

Distance between rows

Distance between columns

POLAR ARRAY

If you choose to make a polar array out of a group of entities and you don't rotate the group as it's copied, it may not array properly. (The system will select a reference point on one of the entities in the group.) This reference point will be arrayed properly, but the group of entities as a whole may not array as you intended, especially if the reference point isn't centrally located within the group.) To avoid this, create a block out of the group and select an insertion base point in the center of the group. Then make a polar array out of the block (see BLOCK in Chapter 22).

Objects are arrayed only in an X-Y plane by the ARRAY command. However, the AutoLISP program 3DARRAY (found on the release disks) will make polar arrays around any axis—X, Y, Z or oblique.

## DIVIDE

**Places points along a line, arc,
polyline or circle that divide it into a
specified number of segments**

When prompted, select the item to be divided. Then enter the desired number of segments. If you divide using points, you may want to change **PDMODE** to something other than 0 or 1 (see PDMODE in Chapter 5).

Before entering the number of segments, you can enter **B** to mark the divisions with a block rather than with points. Then enter the name of the block. Then enter **Y** to align each block with the item being divided, or **N** to leave all the blocks oriented as the block was oriented when it was defined.

## MEASURE

**Places points along a line, arc, polyline or circle that measure off a series of equal distances**

When prompted, select the item to be measured. Where you select the item will determine which end the measuring will start from. (Circles are always measured counterclockwise from the 0-angle point.) Then enter the length of the segments you want measured along the item. If you measure using points, you may want to change **PDMODE** to something other than 0 or 1 (see PDMODE in Chapter 5).

Before entering the segment length, you can enter **B** to mark the lengths with a block rather than with points. Then enter the name of the block. Then enter **Y** to align each block with the item being measured, or **N** to leave all the blocks oriented as the block was oriented when it was defined.

# 20 FILLED-IN ENTITIES

## TRACE

**Places a line of specified width in a drawing**

When prompted, enter the width of the trace using the keyboard or pointer. Then locate the centerline of the trace (the points at the centers of the ends of the trace or series of traces). To end a series of traces, press <RETURN>.

When **FILL** is off (and the drawing has been regenerated), only the outlines of the traces are displayed for faster picture regeneration (see FILL below).

## SOLID

**Places solid quadrilaterals or triangles in a drawing**

When prompted, enter the four points that define the first quadrilateral, or the three points plus <RETURN> that define the first triangle. (The third and fourth points must be oriented in the same basic direction as the first and second points or you'll get a "bowtie" instead of a quadrilateral.)

To continue the solid, consider the third and fourth points of the last quadrilateral as the first and second points of the next, then enter the new third and fourth points. To end the solid, press <RETURN> when prompted for the next third point.

When **FILL** is off (and the drawing has been regenerated), only the outlines of the solid are displayed for faster picture regeneration (see FILL below).

## DONUT (or DOUGHNUT)

**Draws wide rings or filled circles**

When prompted, enter the inside diameter, the outside diameter, then locate the center. To draw a filled circle, enter **0** for the inside diameter.

AutoCAD uses polyline arcs to make donuts, so they can be edited with PEDIT and BREAK.

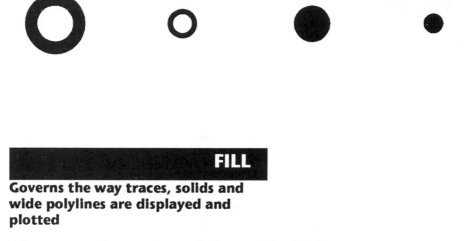

**FILL**

**Governs the way traces, solids and wide polylines are displayed and plotted**

When prompted, enter **ON** to display and plot filled-in traces, etc. Or enter **OFF** to display (and plot) their outlines only.

The display doesn't change until after the next regeneration.

FILL is initially on when a new drawing is started.

## LAYER

**Affects the creation and visibility of layers and their associated colors and line types**

When prompted, enter the following:

**?** then enter **\*** for a list of all layers and associated status, color and linetype.

**S** (for Set), then enter the name or number of the layer you want to draw on.

**N** (for New), then enter the name(s) or number(s) of the layers you want to create. If you enter more than one, separate them with commas. Creating a new layer doesn't change which layer is the current layer. Names that are 24 characters or less will fit on the list of layers in the SETTINGS—Modify Layers dialogue box, but only 17 characters will fit on the text screen listing (see **?** above), and only eight characters will be displayed in the status line. So try to keep your layer names to eight characters or fewer.

**M** (for Make) to create a new layer (similar to N above), and set it as the new current layer.

**ON**, then enter the name(s) or number(s) of the layers you want turned on; that is, visible on the display and plotted. Wild cards are accepted.

**OFF**, then enter the name(s) or number(s) of the layers you want turned off; that is, invisible on the display and not plotted. Wild cards are accepted.

**C** (for Color), then enter a color number or name (see list below) then enter the name/number of the layer(s) that you want that color assigned to.

**L** (for Line type), then enter a line type name (see list below), then enter the name/number of the layer(s) that you want that line type assigned to.

**F** (for Freeze), then enter the name/number of the layer(s) you want frozen. Freezing a layer turns that layer off (same as OFF above) and speeds up the commands that must regenerate the display, since the positions of entities on frozen layers are not calculated.

**T** (for Thaw), then enter the name/number of the layer(s) you want thawed.

Each time you enter the above information, you're returned to the LAYER command prompt. To exit the Layer command, press <**RETURN**>.

**Basic Colors**

1 Red

2 Yellow

3 Green

4 Cyan (light blue)

5 Blue

6 Magenta (hot pink)

7 White

You can look at the CHROMA.DWG drawing supplied with AutoCAD to see what additional colors your particular video card and monitor support.

**Line Types**

Continuous _____

Hidden __ __ __ __ __ __ __ __

Dashed ____ ____ ____ ____

Center _____ __ _____

Phantom _____ __ __ _____

Dot . . . . . . . . . . . . .

Dashdot ___ . ___ . ___

Border ___ ___ . ___ ___

Divide ___ .. ___ .. ___

Other custom line types can be created with the LINETYPE command.

Individual entities can be reassigned a color or line type regardless of the layer they were drawn on (see CHANGE in Chapter 19).

Also, you can use the COLOR and LINETYPE commands to establish a color or line type different from the current layer. This affects all subsequently drawn entities. (See COLOR and LINETYPE below.)

There are many ways to set up layers with their associated colors and line types, depending on the application. One possibility is given below. Colors in this setup work well when your system is configured for light vectors on a dark background. If you're using dark vectors on a light background, you'll want to alter some of the color settings suggested below for better contrast with the light background.

| Layer Name | Color | Line Type |
|---|---|---|
| 0 | 7 (white) | Continuous (established automatically by AutoCAD) |
| 1a | 1 (red) | Hidden (for short hidden lines) |
| 1b | 1 (red) | Dashed (for long hidden lines) |
| 2 | 2 (yellow) | Continuous (for object lines)* |
| 2h | 4 (cyan)** | Continuous (for cross-hatching) |
| 3 | 3 (green) | Center (for center lines) |
| 4 | 4 (cyan) | Continuous (for title block and border) |
| 5 | 5 (blue) | Phantom (for phantom lines) |
| 6 | 6 (magenta) | Continuous (for text and dimensions) |

*Note: For contrast when plotting with wet ink, use a .50mm-tip pen for yellow (layer 2-object lines) and a .35mm-tip pen for all other screen colors. See "Changing Color and/or Pen Widths" in Chapter 18. Also see the sample drawings in Appendix A.

**Note: When you're plotting with more than one pen, the pen is selected according to screen color rather than layer. Thus, when you're plotting with different color pens, you'd normally want cross-hatching to be plotted the same color as object lines; so you'd want layer 2h to be yellow (the same as layer 2). However, if you're plotting with different widths of wet-ink pens, you'd normally want cross-hatching lines to be plotted narrower than object lines, necessitating a different pen and thus a color for layer 2h different from screen yellow. The latter option is the one selected for the above chart.

All of the options available within the LAYER command are also available in the Entity Creation and Modify Layer dialogue boxes. See "Dialogue Boxes" in Chapter 3.

## COLOR

**Establishes a color for all entities
drawn subsequently**

Normally, a new entity's color is determined by the current layer. If you want subsequently drawn entities to have a different color, use this command to select it. When prompted, enter the name or number of the color (see list above).

If you want to revert to normal color assignment, enter **BYLAYER** when prompted for color.

Color may also be set using the Entity Creation dialogue box. See "Dialogue Boxes" in Chapter 3.

## LINETYPE (Set only)

**Establishes a line type for all entities
drawn subsequently**

Normally, a new entity's line type is determined by the current layer. If you want subsequently drawn entities to have a different line type, use this command to select it (see list above). When prompted, enter the name of the line type.

If you want to revert to normal line type assignment, enter **BYLAYER** when prompted for line type.

Line type may also be set by using the Entity Creation dialogue box. See "Dialogue Boxes" in Chapter 3.

You can also use the LINETYPE command to create and load your own custom line types, which are described later.

Centerlines can be clumsy to use. When you place them in a drawing, you control the locations of the endpoints but not the locations of the short segments which, in many cases, should fall at the centers of circles. AutoLISP helps solve this problem; see the CL.LSP file under "AutoLISP Programs" in Chapter 39.

## LTSCALE

**Adjusts the size of dashes and spaces
in hidden lines, center lines, etc.**

A scale factor of **1** is AutoCAD's default, but your prototype drawings can establish a different initial scale factor.

When prompted, enter a positive scale factor. A scale factor larger than 1 will lengthen dashes and spaces, whereas a scale factor smaller than 1 will shorten them.

If the final plot of your drawing will be at a scale other than **1:1**, keep the following things in mind in order to get your noncontinuous line types to plot as you desire. If you scale on the screen (using SCALE or inserting a block at a scale other than 1), the lengths of segments and gaps in noncontinuous line types remain constant while the number of segments and gaps changes. However, if you scale when you plot, the number of segments and gaps remains constant while the lengths change. See "Drawing to Various Scales" in Chapter 23.

LTSCALE is a global command that affects every noncontinuous line type in the entire drawing. This can create a problem when some parts of a drawing have fine details and need a relatively small LTSCALE setting, but at the same time have other parts that need a larger setting. The use of Layers 1a and 1b (see table of layers above) is a first step toward solving this problem. A more complete solution involves using the LINETYPE command (described later) to create additional line types. These new line types might include several new hidden and center lines, some with segments and spaces smaller than AutoCAD's standard hidden, dashed and center lines, and some with segments and spaces larger. Then you can establish additional layers that use these new line types.

## BLOCK

**Groups several entities for repeated
insertion anywhere in a drawing**

When prompted for the block name, enter a descriptive name up to 31 characters long.

When prompted for the insertion base point, find the point that will best serve as a reference point for future insertions of this block. This will often be the corner of a rectangle or the center of a circle.

When prompted, select the items that will make up the block. When these entities are formed into a block, they're erased. To restore them, enter **OOPS**.

A block is stored only in the current drawing. To store a block on hard disk or floppy diskette, use the **WBLOCK** command (see WBLOCK below).

Blocks may contain other blocks.

A block can be redefined. Enter **BLOCK**, then enter the name of the block you want to redefine. AutoCAD will remind you that a block by that name has already been defined, and will ask you if you want to redefine it. Then select the new or altered items that will make up the block. When a block is redefined, all prior insertions of that block will also change to the redefined configuration upon the next regeneration of the drawing (assuming the blocks were inserted as units; see INSERT below). You can also redefine a block by adopting a block definition from a file (see the end of the section on the INSERT command below).

## INSERT

**Places a previously defined block in
the drawing**

When prompted, enter **?** to list all the blocks present in the current drawing, or enter the name of the block. If the block is part of the current drawing, or is a drawing in the current directory, only the name is needed. If the block resides on a floppy diskette or in a directory other than the current directory, the pathname (drive and/or subdirectory) is also needed. See WBLOCK below.

Then locate the insertion point—the point at which the base point of the block will appear. You can enter a 3D location (X,Y,Z).

Then enter the **X** scaling factor, the **Y** scaling factor, and the rotation angle. Use the defaults for these three prompts to insert the block exactly as it was drawn. You can use negative scaling factors to flip the block. Blocks containing 3D elements (3DLINE, 3DFACE or a point with three coordinates) and 2D objects that have been assigned thickness are scaled in the Z direction the same as in the X direction.

Enter **DRAG** at the appropriate time to drag the insertion point, X and Y scaling factors or rotation angle (assuming DRAGMODE is on).

You can indicate the X and Y scaling factors with the pointer. To do so, pick a point when prompted for the X scaling factor. The X and Y distances between the block's insertion point and the point you pick become the X and Y scaling factors.

For dragging, AutoCAD normally assigns a scale factor of 1 and a rotation angle of 0. That is, even if you plan to insert a block at a scale factor of 2 and a rotation angle of −35 degrees, while you're dragging it its scale factor is still 1 and its rotation angle is still 0. However, when AutoCAD prompts you for the insertion point, you can enter one or more of the following:

      **S**  Overall scaling factor

      **X**  X-scale factor

      **Y**  Y-scale factor

      **Z**  Z-scale factor

      **R**  Rotation angle

Then AutoCAD resumes its request for the insertion point and the image that is dragged is scaled and/or rotated according to your instructions. The remaining prompts then skip requests for information you've already entered.

If you want to enter preliminary information for dragging purposes only, but want AutoCAD to prompt you for the final scaling factors and rotation angle, then instead of S, X, Y, Z or R, enter **PS, PX, PY, PZ** or **PR.**

By default, inserted blocks are treated as units by AutoCAD. That is, the individual entities in the block can't be edited in the usual manner. To overcome this, enter an asterisk (**\***) immediately in front of the block name (or immediately in front of the pathname if needed). Blocks that are inserted with the asterisk, called "star blocks," aren't treated as units and their individual entities can be edited. However, they cannot be scaled differently in the X direction than in the Y direction.

Entities in a block are inserted in a drawing on the same layers as when originally drawn. However, items that were originally drawn on layer 0 float to the current layer (unless the asterisk is used as explained above). Layer-0 elements in a block that is part of another block will float to the layer of that block.

Blocks can contain attribute information (see ATTDEF in Chapter 35 and related commands). When such a block is inserted, the attribute values may be entered in response to the prompts in the usual way, or with a dialogue box (see "Dialogue Boxes" in Chapter 3).

Even though a block might contain attributes, it can be inserted without entering any attribute values if you use **SETVAR** to set the system variable **ATTREQ** to **0**.

You can use a block on file to redefine a block in the current drawing by entering a block name in this form: blockname=filename. For example, suppose you have a block in your drawing called OLDPART, and a block on file called NEWPART(.DWG), and you want to replace OLDPART with NEWPART in your drawing. When you're prompted for the block name, enter **OLDPART= NEWPART**.

## MINSERT

### Places multiple insertions of a block in a rectangular array

After responding to the usual INSERT command prompts, enter the number of rows, number of columns, distance between rows and distance between columns.

The entire array is inserted as a unit. No star blocks (blocks inserted with the asterisk) are allowed.

## EXPLODE

### Breaks a block, polyline or associative dimension into its parts

When you're exploding a unit block, the block is redrawn as individual elements so they can be edited in the usual way (see INSERT above). This produces the same result as if the block had originally been inserted as a star block. Everything should remain the same visually, except that layer-0 (floating) elements may change color or line type.

A block that has been inserted with differing X and Y scaling factors cannot be exploded.

When a polyline is exploded, it's replaced with ordinary, zero-width lines and arcs.

When a mesh is exploded, each element becomes a separate 3DFACE.

When an associative dimension is exploded, it will no longer function associatively (see DIM and DIM1 below).

## WBLOCK

### Writes (files) a block on disk as a separate drawing

When prompted, enter the file name (with drive specifier and pathname if needed). Then enter the name of the block you want written onto disk (enter = if you want to use the block with the same name as the file name). If you haven't already defined the block, you'll be prompted for the base insertion point and the entities to include in the block.

If you want the entire current drawing written onto disk, enter * for the block name. This does the same as the SAVE command, but unreferenced blocks and layers are not written.

## BASE

### Specifies a base point for future insertion of one drawing into another

When you create a block using the BLOCK command, you're prompted for an insertion base point. However, when you want to insert an entire drawing into another drawing, the 0,0 point of that drawing is assumed as the insertion base point unless you use the BASE command to specify a different point while you're creating/editing that drawing.

BASE will accept 3D locations (X,Y,Z).

## PURGE

### Deletes named objects no longer referenced by a drawing

You must use this command early in an editing session, before the drawing database has been changed with one of the drawing or editing commands.

When prompted, enter:

**B** to purge unused blocks.

**LA** to purge unused layers.

**LT** to purge unused line types.

**SH** to purge unused shape files.

**ST** to purge unused text styles.

**A** to purge all unused named objects.

Each unused object will be listed for you to decide whether you want to delete it.

Layer 0, line type "continuous" and text style "standard" can't be purged.

## ORGANIZING A BLOCK LIBRARY

You can save a lot of drawing time by inserting predrawn blocks, especially if you have a well-organized library of blocks. Your block library is most useful when It's fully documented. That includes a sample printout of each block, with block name/number and insertion point shown.

You'll want to group similar blocks together. This can be done in several ways. One way is to store all related blocks as individual wblocks (drawings) in a separate subdirectory of the hard disk. Whenever a block (from a subdirectory other than the current subdirectory) is first inserted into the drawing, its path-name must be included as part of the block name.

Another way to group related blocks is to store all similar blocks in a certain drawing (called the *library drawing*). All of these block definitions can then be simultaneously called into a different drawing if you insert the library draw-ing. To do so, use the **INSERT** command and answer the prompt for the block name with the name of the library drawing. When prompted for the insertion point, use **CTRL-C**. Although CTRL-C prevents the insertion of the actual library drawing into your present drawing, the block definitions it contains have al-ready been loaded and are now available from within the present drawing.

## DIM and DIM1

### Give access to the dimensioning subcommands

A dimension is usually made up of two extension (witness) lines, a dimension line and the dimension text or notation. A leader (see the drawing below) is an arrow pointing from a notation to a feature on the object.

Once you enter the DIM or DIM1 command, you're in dimensioning mode and a new set of subcommands is available to you. These subcommands work only in dimensioning mode. Similarly, most of the regular commands will not work in dimensioning mode.

Use **DIM** when you want to add several dimensions to your drawing. To get out of dimensioning mode, enter **EXI** or **EXIT** or use **CTRL-C**. Use **DIM1** when you want to add only one dimension and then return immediately to the regular command mode.

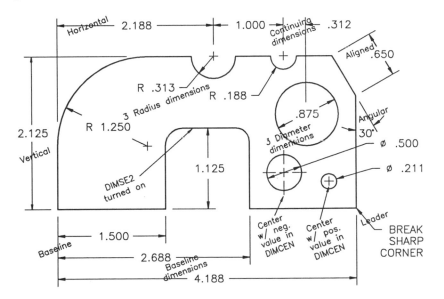

LINEAR dimensioning subcommands—when prompted for **Dim,** enter:

**HOR** for a dimension with a horizontal dimension line.

**VER** for a dimension with a vertical dimension line.

**ALI** for a dimension whose dimension line is aligned with an angular feature of the object.

**ROT** for a dimension with a dimension line rotated to a specified angle.

When prompted for first and second extension line origins, you may want to use **OSNAP** with the above four dimensioning subcommands. Or you can press <RETURN>, select the line, arc, or circle you want to dimension, and AutoCAD will find the extension line origins (doesn't work with unit blocks).

**BAS** to stack dimensions from the baseline (the first extension line) of the previous dimension.

**CON** to continue a dimension from the second extension line of the previous dimension.

When the dimension text and arrows don't fit inside the extension lines, they are placed outside according to the following rule: on the side of the second extension line origin selected, or furthest from the point at which the line, arc or circle was selected.

NONLINEAR dimensioning subcommands—when prompted for **Dim,** enter:

**ANG** to dimension an angle (doesn't work with unit blocks).

**DIA** to dimension a diameter (doesn't work with unit blocks).

**RAD** to dimension a radius (doesn't work with unit blocks). Automatically adds center mark or centerlines if DIMCEN is nonzero.

UTILITY dimensioning subcommands—when prompted for **Dim,** enter:

**CEN** to place a center mark (if DIMCEN is positive) or centerlines (if DIMCEN is negative.).

**LEA** to draw a leader and leader extension(s). Works like the LINE command.

**STA** to display the current status of the dimensioning variables.

**UND** to undo (erase) the most recently added dimension.

**UPD** to update selected dimensions (assuming they are associative dimensions) to reflect the current settings of the dimension variables, text style, and/or UNITS command. You can window an entire drawing to update all associative dimensions at once. (See "Associative Dimensions" below.)

**NEW** (for newtext) to replace text in one or more associative dimensions. When prompted for the text, press <RETURN> if you want the actual distance to be used as the text.

**HOM** (for hometext) to restore the text of an associative dimension to its default position (for example, after it's been stretched to a different position).

Let's assume that either you've been drawing at full scale, or you've set the dimensioning variable **DIMLFAC** to compensate for a scale other than 1:1. In this case, the correct distance will be displayed as the default dimension text in the prompt.

You can enter this text by pressing <RETURN>, or you can type in your own text. Or, you can add a prefix or suffix to the displayed text without having to type out the entire text. Add a prefix to the default text by typing the prefix, then <>. Or add a suffix to the default text by typing <>, then typing the suffix.

The text style that appears in the dimension will be the most recently created style or the style most recently used in the TEXT command. If that style has a fixed height, that height will override the value in DIMTXT (see DIMTXT below).

## DIMENSIONING VARIABLES

The dimensioning variables listed below hold the values that determine how any given dimension will be placed in a drawing. When you're in dimensioning mode, you can change a variable by entering its name, then entering the appropriate value. You can change these variables either while you're at the **Dim:** prompt, or while you're in the middle of a dimensioning sequence. However, you can't change them while you're being prompted for the dimension text. The variables can also be changed with SETVAR.

The suggested values given in the table below are somewhat different than AutoCAD's default values. The values in this table can be used in dimensioning drawings similar to those in Appendix A; use them for your first few attempts at dimensioning.

| Variable | Explanation | Suggested Value |
|----------|-------------|-----------------|
| **Default numbers and text** | | |
| DIMLFAC | The factor by which all lengths will be multiplied before being displayed as defaults. | 1.000 |
| DIMRND | Rounds all default dimensions to nearest value (although they're still displayed according to the precision set by the UNITS command). | .001 |
| DIMALT | If on, adds alternate dimension (such as metric), determined by factor in variable DIMALTF. | OFF |
| DIMALTF | Factor for calculating alternate dimensions. | 25.4 |
| DIMALTD | Number of decimal places in alternate dimension. | 2 |
| DIMZIN | (Applies to architectural and fractional units—0 is the default). If 0, omit zero feet, omit exactly zero inches If 1, include zero feet, include exactly zero inches If 2, include zero feet, omit exactly zero inches If 3, omit zero feet, include exactly zero inches | 3 |
| DIMPOST | Holds a text string added as a postscript (suffix) to all dimensions except angular. | "." (suffix disabled) |
| DIMAPOST | Same as DIMPOST, but for alternate dimensions. | "." (suffix disabled) |

**Visual size and appearance**

| | | |
|---|---|---|
| DIMSCALE | A scale factor applied to most other dimensioning variables in this group. | 1.000, if drawing at full scale (otherwise, use the inverse of the final drawing scale) |
| DIMTXT | Governs text size (only when the last text style used has a variable height). | .100 |
| DIMASZ | Arrowhead size. | .100 |
| DIMTSZ | Tick size (in place of arrowheads), overrides DIMBLK, DIMBLK1/2 and DIMSAH if nonzero. | 0 |
| DIMBLK | Name of block that replaces normal arrowheads or ticks. (The block should be created one unit long, pointing to the right, with the insertion base point at the tip of the arrowhead.) A DOT block is built in. | "." (none) |
| DIMBLK1/2 | Blocks for first and second ends of dimension line (see DIMSAH below). | "." (none) |
| DIMSAH | If on, allows different arrowheads at each end of dimension line (see DIMBLK1/2 above). | OFF |
| DIMEXO | Extension line offset (gap). | .100 |
| DIMEXE | Amount extension lines extend past arrowheads/ticks. | .100 |
| DIMDLE | Amount dimension lines extend past extension lines if using ticks. | 0 |
| DIMDLI | Spacing increment between dimension lines in successive dimensions from the same baseline. | .300 |
| DIMCEN | Center mark size (use negative value for centerlines instead of centermarks). | .080 |

| DIMSE1 | If on, suppresses first extension line. | OFF |
| DIMSE2 | If on, suppresses second extension line. | OFF |

**Tolerances**

| DIMTP | Tolerance (plus). | 0 |
| DIMTM | Tolerance (minus). | 0 |
| DIMTOL | If on, the tolerance from DIMTP and DIMTM is automatically added if default text is used. | OFF |
| DIMLIM | If on, default text is written in limits form. | OFF |

**Placement of text**

| DIMTIH | If on, text inside extension lines is always horizontal. | OFF |
| DIMTOH | If on, text outside extension lines is always horizontal. | OFF |
| DIMTOFL | If on, extra line is placed between arrowheads when text and arrowheads are placed outside extension lines. | OFF |
| DIMTIX | If on, text is forced inside extension lines (text may conflict with extension lines and arrowheads). | OFF |
| DIMSOXD | If on, suppresses dimension line; works only when DIMTIX is on. | OFF |
| DIMTAD | If on, text is placed above dimension line (distance between dimension line and text is one-half text height). See DIMTVP below. | OFF |

| DIMTVP | Governs distance text is placed above or below dimension line; the value is a factor multiplied by the value in DIMTXT to locate the center of the text; DIMTAD must be off. | 0.00 |

### Associative dimensions

| DIMASO | If on, dimensions are created as associative dimensions (applies to all linear dimensions, plus ANGular, DIAmeter and RADius). | ON |

| DIMSHO | If on, dimension shape and text is adjusted as it's dragged while using STRETCH. | OFF |

## ASSOCIATIVE DIMENSIONS

Any dimensions created while the dimension variable DIMASO is on will be associative (this is the default). Any dimensions created while DIMASO is off will be composed of independent lines, arcs, arrows and text. LEAder and CENter never produce associative dimensions.

Associative dimensions are created in the same way as regular dimensions, but they have several special properties. They can be stretched/scaled/rotated at the same time an object is being stretched/scaled/rotated, and the dimension will be realigned and its text will be corrected automatically.

Also, one, several or all associative dimensions can be updated using the UPDate command so they reflect the current settings of the dimension variables, text style and/or UNITS command.

And, although associative dimensions behave somewhat like blocks (they're listed, erased, moved, etc. as units), the text can be changed with the NEWtext command and repositioned to its default position with the HOMetext command.

The UPDate, NEWtext and HOMetext commands work only inside dimensioning mode.

STRETCHING OBJECT AND ASSOCIATED DIMENSIONS

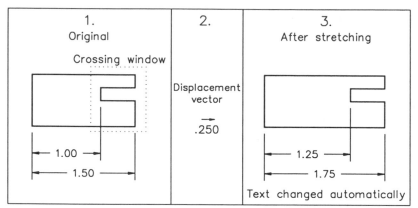

Associative dimensions are controlled by special definition points. For example, a HORizontal dimension would have definition points located at the origin points of the witness lines, at the first end of the dimension line and at the midpoint of the text. Two of these definition points lie under object lines, so they should be automatically included in the selection set when an object is STRETCHed with a crossing window.

However, if you scale or rotate some objects, and select them individually with the pick box, you won't include the definition points and the associated dimensions won't be adjusted automatically. As you edit a dimensioned object, notice whether the dimensions are highlighted, to see whether they've been selected.

When you want only one end of a dimension stretched, that end's dimension point must be included in the crossing window.

Definition points are placed on a layer called DEFPOINTS. AutoCAD automatically creates this layer and turns it off the first time you create an associative dimension. As you'd expect, while the DEFPOINTS layer is off, the definition points won't plot. However, the screen visibility of definition points is determined by the on/off status of the layer containing the actual dimensions, not by the DEFPOINTS layer.

Besides STRETCH, SCALE and ROTATE, other editing commands, including TRIM, EXTEND, MIRROR and ARRAY, can affect associative dimensions.

You can STRETCH a dimension's text to a different place along the dimension line, or even outside the dimension line, and the dimension line will adjust.

When you EXPLODE an associative dimension, its elements are placed on layer 0.

## DRAWING TO VARIOUS SCALES

The following is only one way of drawing to a scale other than 1:1. This method lets you take full advantage of commands such as DIST, LIST and AREA.

1. Draw all objects at full scale. Adjust **LTSCALE** as needed.

2. Dimension with **DIMSCALE** set to the inverse of the intended final scale.

3. Shrink or enlarge all objects and dimensions to their final size by making the entire dimensioned object into a block and reinserting it as a star block with the appropriate scale factor. (Don't use SCALE, or all the dimensions' texts will also be scaled.)

4. Reset **DIMSCALE** to **1.** (If you were to stretch or update any dimensions after Step 3, your current dimension variables would cause the adjusted dimensions to appear a different size. Resetting DIMSCALE to 1 avoids this problem.) Also set **DIMLFAC** to the inverse of the final scale, for the same reason.

5. Reset **LTSCALE** (multiply the adjusted LTSCALE factor from Step 1 by the final scale).

For example, suppose you want to draw a small machine part at a scale of 4:1.

1. Draw the part at full scale. As you draw, you may need to adjust **LTSCALE** somewhat.

2. Dimension the part with **DIMSCALE** set to .25.

3. Make the dimensioned part into a block and reinsert it as a star block, using a scaling factor of **4**.

4. Reset **DIMSCALE** to **1**. Set **DIMLFAC** to .25.

5. Reset **LTSCALE** to approximately four times the adjusted value used in Step 1.

After you shrink or enlarge your drawing, DIST, LIST and AREA won't give true readings. However, automatic dimensioning can be adjusted to give true readings if you set the dimensioning variable DIMLFAC to the inverse of the drawing scale.

A variation of the above procedure would be to follow Steps 1 and 2 as above, but then to keep the drawing at full scale and adjust its scale only on the plotter. See "Plotting Options—Scaling a Plot" in Chapter 18. This variation has the advantage of keeping the drawing at full scale for later editing. However, it also has some disadvantages, particularly when a large number of drawings are made at various scales. The appropriate scale must be entered each time a drawing is plotted. A different format (border and title block) is required for each different scaling as well as for each different sheet size. Notes and title block entries must be scaled with the final plotting size in mind.

# 24 TABLET AND SKETCHING

## TABLET

**Lets you use the digitizing tablet to copy a drawing into the computer or reset the tablet's menu areas**

Tape the drawing that you want to digitize onto the tablet. The drawing doesn't need to be aligned squarely. Make sure that **UCS=WCS** (if not, see the explanation in the *AutoCAD Reference Manual* ).

When prompted, enter the following:

**CAL** to calibrate the tablet with the paper drawing. Then enter **first known point** with the pointer, then enter its coordinates from the keyboard. Then do the same for the **second known point**.

**ON** to turn the tablet mode on (assuming the tablet has been calibrated). It's easier to use **F10** while you're digitizing.

**OFF** to turn the tablet mode off. This is also more easily done with **F10**.

**CFG** to configure the tablet with up to four menu areas. See "Tablet Menu Overlays" in Chapter 37.

When tablet mode is on, the location of the pointer on the tablet is what's important. In fact, the crosshairs don't need to be on the screen (although that is not recommended practice). When tablet mode is off, the location of the crosshairs on the screen and the corresponding coordinate readout are what matter. When you're digitizing a drawing on the tablet, tablet mode should be on while drawing, off while editing.

SNAP and ORTHO still work in tablet mode; use them whenever possible.

You can digitize a paper drawing that's larger than your tablet by doing one section at a time and recalibrating the tablet each time the paper is shifted. Use **ZOOM** and **PAN** to ensure that the area you're digitizing is displayed on the screen.

# SKETCH

**Places freehand or irregular curves
in a drawing**

Curves produced by SKETCH are made up of a series of short, straight line segments.

ORTHO and SNAP should be off. Your current layer should have a continuous line type.

When prompted, enter the record increment. This determines the length of the line segments that will make up the freehand curves, and thus determines the resolution of the sketch. The smaller the record increment, the finer the resolution and the smoother the curve. For experimentation, try a record increment of .1 inch.

While you're in sketch mode you can press the following:

**P** or the pick button to raise or lower the pen. When the pen is down, a temporary sketch will appear on the screen in a different color as the pointer is moved. The pen is initially up. (Don't confuse "pen" with "pointer.")

**R** to record lines already placed on the screen, and remain in sketch mode. Or press button **3** on the pointer to record lines. Recorded lines are displayed in the current color and they can be edited with the usual editing commands—MOVE, ERASE, etc.

**X** to record lines already placed on the screen, and exit to command mode. Or press <RETURN>.

**Q** to discard temporary lines and exit to command mode.

**E** to erase part of a temporary sketch (not yet recorded). The pen is raised automatically. Move the pointer to the point on the temporary sketch where you want the sketch to end, then press **P** (or the pick button). To abort the erase, press **E** again or any other sketch subcommand. (Don't confuse this erasing feature with the regular ERASE command.)

**C** to connect to the end of the most recent temporary sketch (the location of the most recent "pen up"). The pen is automatically lowered when the crosshairs come within one record increment. To abort, press **C** again or any other sketch subcommand.

. (period) after raising the pen in order to draw a straight line from the end of the most recent temporary sketch to the current pointer location. The pen remains raised. Or press button 2 or the space bar.

*Note:* Sketching produces a large number of lines, especially when the record increment is small. A little sketching uses relatively large amounts of memory and disk space. You should use a record increment only as small as required by the type of sketch you plan to make.

Moving the pointer too quickly can result in lost points.

Sketching can also be done in tablet mode (see TABLET).

You can sketch with polylines by setting the system variable **SKPOLY** to a number other than 0 (see PLINE in Chapter 29).

## HATCH

**Fills an area with a cross-hatch pattern**

The current layer should have a continuous line type.

When prompted, enter the following:

> **?** to get a list of available pattern names, or select **HATCH** from the DRAW pull-down menu to see the available patterns.
>
> The hatch pattern name, then the pattern scale, then the angle.
>
> **U** to define your own hatch pattern. Then enter angle, then line spacing, then **Y** or **N** to indicate whether you want the pattern doubled at 90 degrees.
>
> You can follow the pattern name (or U) with a comma and then one of the following letters to indicate hatching style:
>
> > **N** Normal hatching style—fills every other area when one closed area contains other closed areas (this is the default).
> >
> > **O** Outermost hatching style—fills outer area only.
> >
> > **I** Hatching style that ignores internal entities—fills entire area.
> >
> > Enter an asterisk (*) immediately in front of the pattern name if you want the hatch pattern to be drawn so that you can edit the lines individually (similar to a star block).

Then select items that form the perimeter of a closed area to be hatched. They can be selected individually or with a window, but they must form a closed area or the hatching may not work properly.

Some lines/arcs/circles may need to be broken into two or more segments so that the perimeter is one continuous closed boundary (see BREAK in Chapter 19). If the perimeter is complex, breaking many entities into smaller segments can be time-consuming, so it may be quicker to use OSNAP to reconstruct the perimeter on a different layer and then erase the perimeter after hatching it.

Normal

Outermost

Ignore

# 26 EDLIN AND BATCH FILES

Batch files, which are simply text files containing DOS commands, can make DOS much more efficient. Similarly, other text files can add efficiency and power to AutoCAD. AutoCAD uses many text files, particularly for customization: script files, template files, line-type files, shape and font files, menu files and AutoLISP programs.

It would be worth your while to learn EDLIN well. It's even more profitable to master a good word processing program; the full-screen editor makes it much easier to work with longer files. If you plan to advance to the point of customizing AutoCAD, take time to learn word processing. Nevertheless, since everyone has EDLIN (it's packaged with DOS), we discuss it below.

## STARTING EDLIN

EDLIN is a line editing program. While it's not a full word-processing program, it's handy for creating and editing batch files and many other types of files for use with AutoCAD. EDLIN is explained fully in the DOS manual (see the chapter in that manual on EDLIN and the section on DOS editing keys).

EDLIN is entirely separate from AutoCAD. It resides among the DOS files in the \DOS directory (assuming your subdirectories are set up as described under "Subdirectories" in Chapter 1 of this manual, and you've copied EDLIN into the \DOS directory from the IBM DOS master diskette).

You can use EDLIN from the \WORK directory, assuming your path includes the \DOS directory, such as the path illustrated under "AutoCAD Start-up," Step 4, in Chapter 1.

You can use EDLIN any time you're in DOS. Also, you can shell out of AutoCAD's drawing editor to use EDLIN (see SHELL in Chapter 9). Or you can enter the AutoCAD command EDIT, assuming you haven't altered the ACAD.PGP file.

This section assumes that you're getting into EDLIN from DOS rather than from AutoCAD's drawing editor.

To create a file with EDLIN, enter **EDLIN XXXXXXXX.XXX** (EDLIN, then a space, then the complete name of the file that you want to create, including the extension). You can use a drive specifier and/or path in the filename. Don't put any spaces in the filename. EDLIN will respond: **New file**.

To edit an existing file with EDLIN enter **EDLIN XXXXXXXX.XXX** (same format as when you're creating a new file). The file must already exist and you must enter its name accurately. EDLIN will respond **End of input file** when the entire file has been loaded.

*Beware:* EDLIN can erase or overwrite your drawing backup files. Both EDLIN and AutoCAD create backup files with a .BAK extension.

When you create a file with EDLIN and then use **E** to save and exit the file for the first time, EDLIN erases any backup (.BAK) file with the same primary name. Later, when you use EDLIN to edit the same file, any existing .BAK file with the same name will be overwritten with the EDLIN backup file.

If your EDLIN file has the same primary name as one of your drawings, that drawing backup file will be lost when you exit EDLIN. One solution is to avoid giving any EDLIN file the same name as a drawing file. Another is to create and edit your EDLIN files in a directory that contains no drawing backup files.

## EDLIN COMMANDS

EDLIN's prompt is the asterisk (*). When the asterisk is located at the left margin, you can enter one of the EDLIN commands listed below. When the asterisk follows an indented line number you can enter a line of text, up to 253 characters. The asterisk identifies the current line or the most recently edited line.

EDLIN generates the line numbers automatically, but they aren't saved with the file.

**I** Begins a new file at line 1 if no lines presently exist in the file, or inserts one or more lines of text immediately in front of the current line. To stop inserting lines, use **CTRL-C**.

**6I** Inserts a line of text immediately in front of line 6. Line 6 and following lines are renumbered. After the line is entered, EDLIN assumes that you want to insert another line. To stop inserting lines, use **CTRL-C**.

**#I** Inserts a line at the end of the file.

**L** Displays the lines in the file. If the file is longer than 23 lines, the 23 lines surrounding the current line are displayed.

**1L** Displays the first 23 lines of the file.

**14L** Displays 23 lines starting with line 14.

**14,18L** Displays lines 14 through 18.

To page through a file that's longer than 23 lines, enter **1P**. Then for each subsequent page of 23 lines, enter **P**.

**8D** Deletes line 8. Following lines are renumbered.

**8,11D** Deletes lines 8 through 11. Following lines are renumbered.

**D** Deletes the current line. Following lines are renumbered.

**3** Edits line 3. The existing line 3 is displayed and the line number is repeated. You can now enter a new line 3, or use the editing keys described below to make changes in the existing line. Press the following keys:

> The **right cursor key** (or **F1**) to retype one or more characters from the existing line.
>
> **DEL** to delete one or more characters after the cursor.
>
> **INS** to insert one or more characters, then press INS again (or one of the editing keys such as the right cursor key) to cancel insertion mode.
>
> **F3** to retype all characters after the cursor.

To discard the editing done to the current line and place the cursor back at the beginning of the line for a fresh start, press the **ESC** key. To exit from editing this line while the cursor is at the beginning of the line, use **CTRL-C** or press **<RETURN>**.

**7,9,12M** Moves lines 7 through 9 in front of line 12.

**7,7,12M** Moves line 7 in front of line 12.

**7,9,12C** Copies lines 7 through 9 in front of line 12.

**7,7,12C** Copies line 7 in front of line 12.

**1,50Sapple** Searches for the first occurrence of "apple" in lines 1 through 50. EDLIN will find "apple" even if it's embedded in another word. When it's found, the line containing "apple" will be displayed. To repeat the search for the same word beginning with the next line, enter **S**. The search is case-sensitive—capitalization must match exactly.

**6,20RchampoinF6champion** Replaces all occurrences of "champoin" with "champion" in lines 6 through 20 (F6 is function key F6 and displays as ^Z). The lines in which the replacement was done will be displayed. Case-sensitive.

**6,20?RchampoinF6champion** Same as above, except each occurrence of "champoin" will be displayed with the replacement string and you can enter Y or N to indicate whether you want to accept the replacement. Case-sensitive.

**19Tfile3.scr** Transfers the contents of the file FILE3.SCR into the present file immediately in front of line 19.

**E** Saves file and ends the editing session (exits EDLIN and returns to DOS).

**Q** Does not save file, but ends the editing session (exits EDLIN and returns to DOS).

You can put your own sign-on message in a file called ACAD.MSG. The contents of this file will be displayed each time AutoCAD is started.

# BATCH FILES

A batch file is a file made up of a series of DOS commands. It must have the extension .BAT in order to function as a batch file. The computer responds to the commands from a batch file just as though you had entered them from the keyboard. To run a batch file, simply enter its name (without the extension).

If the name of the batch file is AUTOEXEC.BAT, and if the file is located in the root directory of the hard disk, DOS will run this file automatically when you boot the system from the hard disk.

Two different ways to create batch files are explained below.

## Method 1

Suppose you want to create a file called FILE1.BAT, and place three DOS commands in it.

First, enter **COPY CON FILE1.BAT** (press <RETURN>).

Then enter the three DOS commands (one command per line), pressing <RETURN> after each line.

Then press **F6** (will display ^Z) , then press <RETURN>.

You can check to see if your new file is on the disk by entering **DIR**. And you can check to make sure your three commands are in the batch file by entering **TYPE FILE1.BAT**.

You can run this batch file by entering **FILE1**.


## Method 2

Batch files can also be created using the EDLIN program or a word processing program in programming or nondocument mode. Using a line editor such as EDLIN or a word processor lets you edit the file easily.

# SCRIPTS

## SCRIPT

**Uses a predetermined series of commands and responses from a script file**

The SCRIPT command "runs" the commands stored in a script file. The commands that are unique to script files are explained in separate sections below.

A script file is a file made up of a series of AutoCAD commands and responses to prompts. (A script file is to AutoCAD as a batch file is to DOS.) A script file must have the extension .SCR. Script files can be created using EDLIN or a word processor in programming (nondocument) mode.

When prompted, enter the name of the script file (with drive specifier and path if necessary). The commands and responses to prompts stored in the script file will be executed just as though they had been entered from the keyboard.

A script file can be useful for setting up such drawing configurations as UNITS, LIMITS, SNAP and GRID, and for establishing several layers with associated colors and line types. Prototype drawings will do the same thing, but you use those only when a new drawing is started. In contrast, scripts can be run at any time—at the beginning of a drawing or while the drawing is being completed.

You might also use script files to add a predetermined set of layers to a drawing; to change several dimensioning variables; to change DIMSCALE and LTSCALE and heights of text styles for drawings that are done at a scale other than 1:1; to create certain text styles; or to run a slide show.

To stop a running script, press the backspace key. To restart a script after it's been stopped (whether because of an error in the script file, or because you stopped it intentionally), enter **RESUME**.

Here's a sample script file. This script converts all dimensions in a drawing from decimals to fractions. In some situations, a designer might prefer to work with decimals while the people in the shop might prefer to work with fractions. The script illustrated below would let the designer do all of his dimensioning in decimals, then convert all the dimensions to fractions just before plotting.

When the plot is finished, you can convert the dimensions back to decimals again either by using the **U** command or by running a second script designed for the purpose. The file name for the following script could be something like DEC-FRAC.SCR.

```
units 5 32 (Four spaces at end of line)
```

dim upd w -9999,-9999 99999,99999 (One space at end of line)

```
exi
```

Remember that a space in AutoCAD works the same as **<RETURN>**. Thus, in the above script, the space after "units" enters the UNITS command, the space after "5" enters the 5, and the first space after "32" enters the 32. The remaining three spaces, along with the carriage return (which occurs automatically at the end of every line in the file when you enter the line) enters each of the defaults for the four remaining prompts in the UNITS command.

For the UPD command to work, the dimension must be associative, created by accepting the default distance (see "UTILITY dimensioning subcommands" under "DIM and DIM1" in Chapter 23).

The same script file could be formatted as shown below. Carriage returns are used in place of the extra spaces at the ends of the lines, which makes their presence more apparent when you look at the file.

```
units 5 32 (Four blank lines)
```

dim upd w -9999,-9999 99999,99999 (One blank line)

```
exi
```

Any time you find yourself repeating a sequence of several commands over and over, you might consider writing a script to accomplish the same thing. Once a script is written and saved on file, it can be used in any drawing.

The scripts described above are ones that are run while you're in the drawing editor, after entering the SCRIPT command. However, the name of a script can be included in the command line that starts AutoCAD. For example at the DOS command you could enter:

```
ACAD DRAWING1 SCRIPT1
```

This command line starts AutoCAD and establishes DRAWING1 as the default drawing name. AutoCAD proceeds to its main menu, skipping any opening message from the ACAD.MSG file. At the main menu, SCRIPT1 takes over. SCRIPT1 might begin like this:

```
2 (One space at end of line)
```

```
...remainder of script file...
```

The space after the "2" enters the 2 at the main menu. The carriage return at the end of that line "accepts" the default drawing name. The remaining lines in the script file are executed as soon as the command prompt appears in the drawing editor.

If the last line in the script file returns to the main menu, the entire script is automatically repeated (see RSCRIPT below).

The command line illustrated above, which would normally be entered at the DOS prompt, could be part of a batch file.

Scripts have one advantage over AutoLISP programming—they're easier to write, since you don't have to learn a programming language and you already know the AutoCAD commands. However, scripts also have a major drawback—they aren't interactive. You can't write a script that asks for information in the middle of the script. However, AutoLISP programs are interactive. They can also make complex calculations, work with files and access the drawing's database, which makes AutoLISP a far more powerful and flexible tool. Nevertheless, scripts are just right for the sorts of repetitive tasks mentioned earlier.

## RESUME
**Restarts a script that's been stopped**

Scripts will stop when they come to an invalid command or an invalid response to a prompt. You can also stop a running script by pressing the backspace key.

In either case, enter **RESUME** to restart the script at the next command in the script file.

## DELAY
**Delays execution of the next command in a script file**

In a script file, to delay the execution of the next command use the DELAY command, followed by a space, followed by a number to indicate the length of the delay. Different computer models will vary. You can experiment with **DELAY 1000,** or **DELAY 5000** to see how many seconds your computer delays. On some models, DELAY 1000 will take approximately one second.

## RSCRIPT

**Restarts the currently running script
from within a script**

Include RSCRIPT as the last command of a script to rerun that script (assuming the script was started from within the drawing editor).

## GRAPHSCR and TEXTSCR

**Display the graphics screen or the
text screen from within a script**

You can use these commands in single-screen systems to do what **F1** does. Like F1, you can use them in the middle of another command by placing an apostrophe in front of them.

# 28    SLIDES

## MSLIDE

**Makes a slide**

A slide is a file of a particular display. A slide can be viewed (see VSLIDE below) even when you're working with a different drawing. However, you can't edit a slide.

You can use slides for quickly referencing other drawings, charts or tables. Or you can produce a slide show that automatically displays any number of slides by means of a script. See SCRIPT above.

Before entering the MSLIDE command, set up the display exactly as you want it to appear in the slide (using ZOOM, PAN, LAYER, etc.).

When prompted, enter the name of the slide.

The slide is placed in a file with an .SLD extension.

## VSLIDE

**Displays a slide**

When prompted, enter the name of the slide without the .SLD extension.

If the slide is in a library (see "Slide Libraries" below), enter the library name, including path if needed, then (in parentheses) the name of the slide. For example: LIBRARY7(SLIDE36).

To return to your current drawing, enter **REDRAW** (or press **F7** twice).

Don't try to edit the slide.

VSLIDE can be used in a script to display a series of snapshots from different drawings.

## SLIDE LIBRARIES

You can place a group of individual slide files into a larger file, called a *slide library*. The program that constructs a slide library is called SLIDELIB.EXE and Is found on the support disk. It's assumed here that this program resides with your AutoCAD program files.

Before you can use the SLIDELIB program, you must create a text file containing the names of the slides (one per line, with or without the .SLD extension) that you want included in the larger file. This file containing the list of slides becomes the input for the SLIDELIB program. You must redirect the input for the SLIDELIB program using the DOS redirection symbol <.

For example, if your file of slide names is called SLIST1, and the name of your new library file is going to be LIBRARY1, you'd use this command line at the DOS prompt:

```
SLIDELIB LIBRARY1 <SLIST1
```

The SLIDELIB program produces a file with an extension .SLB.

When you want to add slides to your library file, or remove slides from it, you must revise the text file that contains the slide names, then rerun the SLIDELIB program, making sure that all the original slides are present.

Storing a large number of slides in slide libraries uses disk space more efficiently than storing each slide separately.

The icon selections that are available through the pull-down portion of AutoCAD's standard menu are in the slide library file called ACAD.SLB.

## PLINE

**Draws a polyline (a sequence of lines/arcs with special properties) on the current X-Y construction plane**

A polyline, in contrast to a series of regular lines and arcs, is treated as one entity by AutoCAD. Also, a polyline can have varying widths in its various segments.

When prompted, enter the endpoint of a line (this is the default response, and if you're starting a polyline this is your only choice). Or enter the following:

**W,** then enter the starting and ending widths for the next segment. The default width is **0**. The ending width is retained for the beginning and ending widths of subsequent segments unless you change them.

**H,** then enter the starting and ending half-widths. This choice is especially suitable if you use the pointer to indicate the half-width.

**L,** then enter the length to draw a line from the end of the most recent line or arc. The direction is already determined by the most recent line or arc.

**C** to close the polyline (draw a line back to its origin).

**U** to undo the most recent line or arc. You can use U repeatedly.

**A** to draw an arc. A new prompt will appear with several options unique to arcs. However, the Undo, Width and Half-width options operate just as they do when you're drawing straight segments. The options are:

> **L** to return to line mode.
>
> **CE,** then locate the center of the arc. The remaining prompts are self-explanatory.
>
> **R,** then enter the arc's radius. The remaining prompts are self-explanatory.
>
> **A,** then enter included angle (**positive** for CCW, **negative** for CW). The remaining prompts are self-explanatory.
>
> **S,** then enter the second point of the arc. The remaining prompts are self-explanatory.

**CL** to close a polyline with an arc.

**D** to set a starting direction other than the direction of the most recent line or arc.

If DRAGMODE is on, you must enter **DRAG** before entering the final parameter in order to dynamically drag the arc.

You can find the area inside a closed polyline by using the **LIST** command or the **AREA** command (select **Entity**).

See Appendix A for a polyline exercise.

## 3DPOLY

**Draws a polyline made up of straight line segments, anywhere in space**

Unlike the polyline created with the PLINE command, this polyline can have vertices anywhere in space. However, it's constructed with zero-width straight line segments only.

The 3DPOLY command operates much like the LINE command, but its result is more like the PLINE command. You can enter endpoints anywhere in space by entering the X-Y-Z coordinates from the keyboard or by using **OSNAP** and point filters. The result is considered by AutoCAD to be one entity and it can be edited with the **PEDIT** command.

Begin by entering the **from point**. Then, enter:

One or more vertex points (endpoints).

**C** to close the polyline and return to command mode.

**U** to undo the last segment.

Press <**RETURN**> to complete the series of segments and return to command mode.

3DPOLY lines can be extruded in the Z direction with the **ELEV** and **CHANGE** commands.

## PEDIT

**Edits a polyline**

PEDIT can be used to edit 2D polylines, 3D polylines and meshes, as well as other entities that are created out of polylines such as donuts, polygons and ellipses.

When prompted, select the polyline. If the line or arc you select isn't a polyline, AutoCAD will say so and give you the option of turning it into a one-segment polyline.

If the polyline is a regular 2D polyline created with the PLINE command, the prompt that appears will include all the options listed below. But if it's a 3D polyline created with the 3DPOLY command, the prompt will not include Join, Width or Fit curve. If the polyline is a mesh, the only way you can edit it with PEDIT is to open or close it, move one or more vertices or smooth its surface. See the discussion of mesh surfaces at the end of this section and under MESHES in Chapter 34.

Enter the following:

**X** to exit from PEDIT.

**C** to close an open polyline (adds a closing line if necessary).

**O** to open a closed polyline (removes the closing line or arc if it was created by entering C).

**J** to join a line/arc that already meets the end of an open polyline (2D polylines only). Several lines/arcs can be selected at once. If a spline has been fit to a polyline that is joined, it's automatically decurved.

**W** to specify a new uniform width for the entire polyline (2D polylines only).

**F** to fit a curve to a series of straight line segments (2D polylines only). This curve is made up of pairs of arcs and it passes through all vertices.

**S** to apply a B-spline to the polyline based on the frame that connects its present vertices. This spline passes through only the first and last vertices of an open polyline. The more vertices a polyline has, the more closely the spline will conform to the shape of the frame. Three system variables control the shape and appearance of the spline, as explained below.

> Set system variable **SPLINETYPE** to **5** for a quadratic B-spline, or to **6** for a cubic B-spline. The quadratic B-spline conforms more closely to the spline frame, while the cubic B-spline is more generalized or smoother.

To display the frame, set the system variable **SPLFRAME** to non-zero, then use **REGEN**.

The spline is composed of short straight line segments. The number of segments employed is governed by the variable **SPLINESEGS** (default – 8). If the polyline is a 2D polyline, a negative value for SPLINESEGS creates a spline that's both "splined" and then automatically fitted (see F above).

Changing SPLINESEGS affects only newly splined or resplined polylines.

**D** to de-curve a polyline (cancels the effect of F or S).

**U** to undo the effect of the most recent PEDIT operation. You can enter U more than once within a single PEDIT command to undo several operations.

**E** to edit a vertex or segment(s) between two vertices. If you're editing a regular 2D polyline, all of the options listed below will appear in the prompt. But if you're editing a 3D polyline, the prompt won't include Width or Tangent. AutoCAD will mark the vertex to be edited with an X, beginning with the first vertex. Enter the following:

**X** to exit vertex editing (return to PEDIT).

**N** to move the marker to the next vertex.

**P** to move the marker to the previous vertex.

**B** to break between the current vertex and another selected vertex.

Then enter **N** (Next) or **P** (Previous) to move the marker to another vertex. Then enter **G** (Go) to effect the break.

Or enter **X** to exit the break procedure.

If you enter **G** without moving the marker, the polyline will be broken into two segments with no visible gap.

Breaking a closed polyline converts it to an open polyline with the closing segment removed (if the closing segment was created with the C option).

**I** to insert a new vertex after the marker, then locate the new vertex.

**M** to move the marked vertex, then locate the new position.

**W** to change beginning and/or ending widths for the single segment following the marker (2D polylines only). New widths aren't displayed until the display is regenerated.

**R** to regenerate the display.

**S** to place a straight line segment between the current vertex and another selected vertex.

Then enter **N** (Next) or **P** (Previous) to move the marker to another vertex. Then enter **G** (Go) to effect the straight line.

Or enter **X** to exit the straightening procedure.

If you enter **G** without moving the marker, the next segment (assuming it is an arc) will be straightened.

**T** to indicate a tangent direction (using keyboard or pointer) for later curve fitting (2D polylines only). Does not affect a spline.

The **BREAK** command can be used on a 2D polyline.

The **EXPLODE** command, when applied to a polyline, converts the polyline into individual lines and arcs with a width of 0, and when applied to a mesh converts the mesh into individual 3DFACES.

When you're editing a mesh, most options are similar to those described above. The operations unique to editing meshes are as follows. Enter:

**M** to close/open the mesh in the M direction.

**N** to close/open the mesh in the N direction.

**E** to identify and move a vertex.

**S** to smooth the mesh surface.

Three types of surfaces are used to smooth a mesh. The type is determined by the value in system variable SURFTYPE. The degree to which the smoothed surface conforms to the original mesh is further governed by system variables SURFU and SURFV. (See "Smooth Surfaces" in Chapter 34.)

## ISOPLANE

**Selects the left, top or right
isometric plane**

Assuming you've already set snap style to isometric (see SNAP in Chapter 5), you can use this command to select the left, top or right isometric plane by entering **L**, **T**, or **R**, respectively.

It's much easier to use **CTRL-E** to switch from one isometric plane to the next (left, then top, then right, etc.). This can be done while you're in the middle of another command, without having to enter the ISOPLANE command.

Isoplane can also be set by using the Drawing Aids dialogue box (see "Dialogue Boxes" in Chapter 3).

## ISOMETRIC DRAWINGS

In isometric drawings, the two receding axes are at 30 degrees to horizontal. Distances are measured on the vertical and on the receding axes.

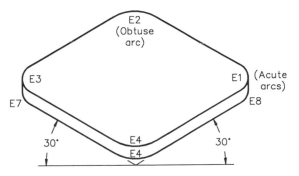

You get an isometric snap and grid by using the SNAP command. Enter **S** for Style and then enter **I** for Isometric. The vertical spacing that you enter will be applied both to the vertical direction and the directions of the two receding axes. However, the coordinate readout on the status line still operates in rectangular coordinates.

When circular objects are drawn in isometric, they're most accurately represented by ellipses. Three different ways to draw ellipses are explained below. (See the iso-ellipse comparison drawing in Appendix A.)

## Method 1—Using ELLIPSE

Use **CTRL-E** to place the crosshairs on the desired isometric plane, then enter the **ELLIPSE** command, select **I** for isometric circle, then locate the center, then enter the radius (or **D** and the diameter). A full ellipse will be placed on the current isometric plane. The ellipse will be constructed with a polyline, so you can edit it with the **BREAK** and **PEDIT** commands. (The ellipse is actually constructed from 16 polyarcs and is fairly accurate—within .5 percent of the radius for most of the ellipse.)

This is perhaps the quickest method when full ellipses are needed. When you need only a segment of an ellipse, or when you need a hidden ellipse (non-continuous line type), one of the other methods may be better.

## Method 2—Inserting Elliptical Blocks

Whole ellipses and elliptical segments can be created as blocks for insertion into a drawing.

Use these circular shapes to create these elliptical shapes:

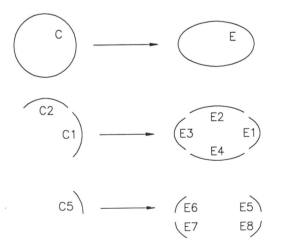

For example, to make E1, follow these steps:

Construct **C1** with a one-inch radius and known center coordinates, extending **45** degrees below horizontal and **45** degrees above horizontal.

Make it into a block (name=C1) using the known center coordinates as the insertion base point.

Insert this new block C1 at the same center coordinates with an **X** scale factor of **1.224745** and a **Y** scale factor of **.707107**.

Make this elliptical segment into another block (name=E1) using the known center coordinates as the insertion point.

E1 can now be inserted as an elliptical arc and scaled as needed.

These elliptical arcs are suitable for top isometric surfaces (horizontal planes). They can be rotated 120 degrees for use in left-side vertical planes, or −120 degrees for use in right-side vertical planes.

One advantage of these blocks is that they're accurate ellipses or elliptical segments. Also, since most of them are segments to begin with, they're already broken for use in a drawing similar to the square plate shown above. However, since they were created from blocks that were inserted with differing X and Y scaling factors, they cannot be broken further, so they're not suitable for more complex drawings such as the swivel bracket in Appendix A.

## Method 3—Using FILLET and Blocks

Approximations of isometric arcs (similar to those constructed with a compass) can be made by constructing the straight line portions of the isometric drawing first, then using **FILLET** to create the arcs. Set the fillet radius as follows:

For acute arcs—multiply the object radius by **.5773502**.

For obtuse arcs—multiply the object radius by **1.7320508**.

These arcs have the disadvantage of not being true isometric arcs (they're circular rather than elliptical). Their accuracy is off by about 7 percent of the object radius at the acute corner, but they're suitable for most visual representations (see the iso-ellipse comparison and swivel bracket drawings in Appendix A). They do have the advantage of being easily constructed and easily broken.

You can create these arcs ahead of time and save them as blocks. If they're created as illustrated below, the block will represent a one-inch object radius and can be scaled easily when inserted into a drawing. First construct the straight line segments, each exactly two units long. Then fillet the corners using the fillet radii given above. Then form the four arcs into one block, or create a series of blocks that contain various combinations of the arcs. When inserted as a star block, unnecessary portions can be erased or broken off.

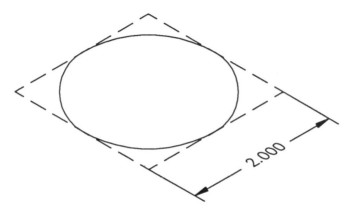

In some situations, such as when the center of the arc is hard to locate on the isometric grid, it's easier to make these constructions on the fly than it is to insert a block. Of course, it's rather clumsy to have to multiply the object radius by the appropriate factor and enter the adjusted radius each time. But this process can be made much easier with AutoLISP.

A routine can be written that automatically multiplies the object radius by the specified factor and enters that radius in the system variable used by the FILLET command.

# 31   COORDINATE SYSTEMS

## USER COORDINATE SYSTEMS

This section gives a general description of User Coordinate Systems (UCS) and X-Y construction planes. A UCS involves two commands (UCS and UCSICON) and several system variables (including UCSICON and UCSFOLLOW) that are described in further detail in separate sections below. There's a UCS exercise in Appendix A.

Don't confuse User Coordinate Systems and their construction planes with viewpoints.

### The World Coordinate System and User Coordinate Systems

The standard (default) coordinate system is called the World Coordinate System (WCS) to distinguish it from coordinate systems established by the user. The WCS is adopted at the beginning of a new drawing (assuming that it hasn't been replaced by a different UCS in your prototype drawing).

The WCS, with its X-Y construction plane, was described in Chapter 3 under "Cartesian Coordinates and Angles." That basic coordinate system is adequate for most 2D drawings. However, for many 3D drawings you'll want to establish one or more User Coordinate Systems with the 0,0,0 origin located in different places and/or the axes pointing in different directions. You can set up as many different UCS's as you need.

Complex 3D geometry would be difficult to construct if all entities had to be located from an X-Y construction plane in the WCS. AutoCAD lets you place an X-Y construction plane anywhere in space and orient it at any angle. This lets you place various entities in a complex configuration using simple X-Y distances in the new X-Y plane.

Once you've defined a new UCS, all coordinates that you enter and all coordinates that are displayed are based on this new UCS. However, coordinates preceded by an asterisk (such as *2,4,6 or @*5<30) are interpreted as WCS coordinates. You can easily switch between various coordinate systems at any time during the drawing process.

The UCS is independent of the current viewpoint (although the viewpoint can be automatically tied into the current UCS). Only one UCS will be active at any given time, even though you may have various viewports displayed. The view from 0,0,1 toward 0,0,0 is called the *plan view*.

Since the UCS and the viewpoint don't necessarily coincide, you'll want to pay close attention to the UCS icon to help you see the current orientation of the three axes. (See UCSICON below.)

When you save a drawing, the current UCS is saved with it and will automatically become the initial coordinate system when you begin to edit that drawing the next time.

## Right-Hand Rules

The X-Y-Z axes will always be oriented in relation to each other according to a right-hand rule. When your right hand is positioned as shown below, with the thumb representing the positive X axis and the first finger representing the positive Y axis, the positive Z axis will point in the direction of the second finger.

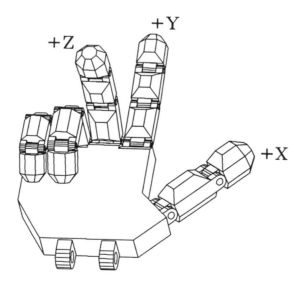

Also, rotation around any given axis will follow another right-hand rule. When the thumb of the right hand points along the positive direction of any given axis as shown below, then positive rotation around that axis follows the direction of the curled fingers.

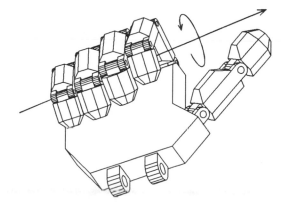

## Grid and Pointer

The grid always appears on the construction plane—the X-Y plane at the current elevation in the current UCS.

Remember that whenever you place entities in your drawing with the pointer, all locations will be on the X-Y construction plane (at the current elevation), even when your current viewpoint or your current UCS makes the crosshair appear to be somewhere above the construction plane.

### UCS

**Establishes, saves or recalls a User Coordinate System**

All of the UCS options described below are also available in the Modify UCS dialogue box, which can be brought up by entering **DDUCS** at the keyboard. The User Coordinate System Options dialogue box is also available from the menu bar (Settings—UCS Options).

Remember that when you're defining a new coordinate system, all input is interpreted according to the current coordinate system, not the World Coordinate System (unless, of course, the WCS is the current system).

You'll want to use immediate osnap modes to enter many of the points requested below.

When prompted, enter the following:

**W** to make the World Coordinate System the current coordinate system. W is always the default response in the UCS prompt.

**O**, then enter the coordinates of the origin of the new UCS. This new coordinate system will have an origin that's shifted from the current coordinate system, but its X, Y and Z axes will point in the same direction as the current system.

**ZA**, then enter the coordinates of the origin of the new UCS (if different from the origin of the current system), then a point through which the positive Z axis will pass. This option is handy if you merely want to designate a Z direction to extrude an object but don't care where the X and Y axes are pointing.

**3**, then enter three points to define the new UCS: (1) the origin, (2) a point on the positive X axis and (3) a point on the positive Y half of the X-Y plane. Once the X and Y axes are so determined, the Z axis is determined by the right-hand rule.

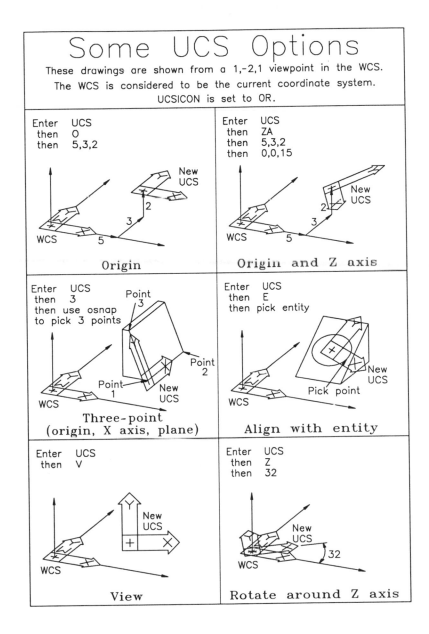

# Some UCS Options

These drawings are shown from a 1,-2,1 viewpoint in the WCS.
The WCS is considered to be the current coordinate system.
UCSICON is set to OR.

Enter  UCS
then  O
then  5,3,2

New UCS

WCS

Origin

Enter  UCS
then  ZA
then  5,3,2
then  0,0,15

New UCS

WCS

Origin and Z axis

Enter  UCS
then  3
then use osnap
to pick 3 points

Point 3

Point 1

Point 2

New UCS

WCS

Three-point
(origin, X axis, plane)

Enter  UCS
then  E
then pick entity

New UCS

Pick point

WCS

Align with entity

Enter  UCS
then  V

Y

New UCS

X

WCS

View

Enter  UCS
then  Z
then  32

New UCS

32

WCS

Rotate around Z axis

The defaults for these three points are as follows:

First point—the origin of the current system.

Second point—the direction of the positive X axis in the current system.

Third point—a direction parallel to the current X-Y plane.

This option is handy if you want to attach the new coordinate system to certain features of an object using various osnap modes.

**E** to define the new UCS by using an entity already in the drawing. Whenever you use this option, the positive Z axis will be oriented in the same direction as it was when the entity was created. This, in turn, forces the X-Y plane to be parallel to the X-Y plane that was current when the entity was created; however, the direction of the X and Y axes may differ.

Various entities determine the new coordinate system in various ways:

Circle—its center becomes the new origin and the X axis runs through the pick point.

Arc—its center becomes the new origin and the positive X axis runs through the end of the arc that's visually nearest the pick point.

Line—its end visually nearest the pick point becomes the new origin and the positive X axis usually runs through the other end of the line.

Point—its location becomes the new origin and AutoCAD determines the rest.

2D polyline—its start point becomes the new origin and the positive X axis runs through the next vertex.

Trace—its start point becomes the new origin and the positive X axis runs through its next endpoint.

Solid—its first point becomes the new origin and the positive X axis runs through its second point.

3D face—its first point becomes the new origin, the positive X axis runs through the second point and the fourth point lies on the positive half of the X-Y plane.

Dimension—the middle point of the text becomes the new origin and the positive X axis runs the same direction as the positive X axis in effect when the dimension was drawn.

Inserted item (shape, text, block, attribute tag or value)—its insertion point becomes the new origin and its rotation angle will be 0 in the new UCS.

**V** to adopt the current viewing direction as the direction of the negative Z axis (the origin remains unchanged). This option is handy when you want to plot a drawing from a particular viewpoint and still want to place text in the drawing so that it will appear straight on when plotted.

**X** (or **Y** or **Z**), then enter an angle (from the keyboard or by picking two points) to rotate the new coordinate system around the X (or Y or Z) axis. The origin will remain unchanged. The right-hand rule will determine the direction of rotation.

**P** to return to the previous coordinate system. AutoCAD remembers the 10 previous coordinate systems that you have used (named or unnamed).

**?** to get a listing of the names and orientations of all the saved coordinate systems. The World Coordinate System is listed first. The current coordinate system is also listed and called *NO NAME* unless you've given it a name.

Remember that each coordinate system is listed according to the current coordinate system. If you change coordinate systems and then look at the same listing, the numbers will be different. The prompt reappears after the listing. Since W is always the default in the prompt, be careful not to press <RETURN> to return to Command mode unless you intend to change to the WCS at the same time. Instead, use **CTRL-C** to exit the listing and return to Command mode.

**S** to save the current coordinate system, then enter its name (up to 31 characters). When you save a coordinate system, you do not save the current viewpoint.

**R**, then enter the name of the coordinate system you want to restore. The viewpoint will remain the same unless system variable **UCSFOLLOW** has been set to **1**.

**D** to delete the name of a saved coordinate system. You can list several names separated by commas, or use wildcards.

Whenever you create a new UCS you can establish a plan view by using the **VPOINT** command and entering **0,0,1**. Or you can use the **PLAN** command. Or you can set system variable **UCSFOLLOW** to **1** and AutoCAD will automatically establish the plan view each time you change to a new UCS.

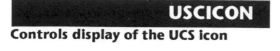

### Controls display of the UCS icon

The UCS icon is pictured below. It provides information about the current coordinate system. The settings for the UCSICON command affect only the current viewport unless you use the **A** option explained below.

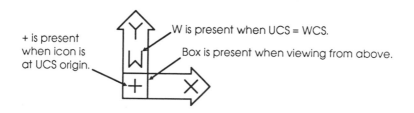

If the current coordinate system is the WCS, a W appears in the Y-arm of the icon. If the icon is positioned at the origin of the current coordinate system, the plus sign will be present in the icon. If the current viewpoint looks at the object from the underside (originates from a negative Z location), the box at the elbow of the icon will be missing.

When prompted, enter the following:

**A** to make all UCS icon settings (changed during this use of the UCSICON command) apply to all viewports.

**ON** to enable the UCS icon.

**OFF** to disable the UCS icon.

**OR** to place the icon at the origin of the current coordinate system. If this moves the icon off the current screen/viewport or too near the edge, it's displayed in the lower left corner of the screen.

**N** (for Not at origin) to place the icon at the lower left corner of the screen.

The UCS icon also appears in two other forms. When your viewing direction is parallel to the X-Y construction plane of the current UCS, the icon appears as a broken pencil in a box. When this icon occurs, you should change your viewing direction before trying to indicate any locations with the pointer. When you're using perspective (see DVIEW in Chapter 33), the icon appears as a cube.

## UCSICON SYSTEM VARIABLE

**Holds settings for the current coordinate system**

**0** = icon at lower left of screen/viewport, **1** = icon off, **2** = icon at origin if current display allows. **0** is the default.

## UCSFOLLOW SYSTEM VARIABLE

**Enables or disables automatic display of the plan view each time you change coordinate systems.**

Use **SETVAR** to set this variable to **1** if you want AutoCAD to make the plan view (0,0,1) the initial viewpoint each time you select a different coordinate system. Any viewpoint can be adopted thereafter, as usual. The default value for UCSFOLLOW is 0.

# 32  3D ENTITIES

## 3D DRAWING

AutoCAD uses several drawing commands to generate three-dimensional entities, including ELEV, LINE (described above), 3DLINE, 3DFACE, 3DPOLY (described above), 3DMESH, TABSURF, RULESURF, REVSURF and EDGESURF. AutoCAD also uses several display commands to help you see these entities from various angles and perspectives, including VPOINT, DVIEW, PLAN and HIDE. These commands are discussed separately below and in the following two sections.

This section provides a background for using 3D entities, discusses point filters, which are very handy in 3D drawing and describes three simple 3D commands—ELEV, 3DLINE and 3DFACE.

Certain 3D shapes can be constructed using built-in AutoLISP commands. These commands are available under "3D" on the screen menu.

3D drawing makes use of the X, Y and Z axes according to the right-hand rule (see "User Coordinate Systems" in Chapter 31). On the screen, when positive X extends to the right and when positive Y extends up, positive Z extends toward you.

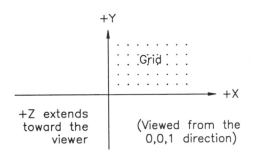

+Y

:Grid

+X

+Z extends toward the viewer

(Viewed from the 0,0,1 direction)

Here the X and Y axes are in their normal (default) 2D orientation, also called the plan view.

If a normal 2D drawing were placed flat on a table with positive X to the right of the table and positive Y to the far side of the table, positive Z would extend above the table. When such a drawing is viewed from a +X, −Y, +Z quadrant, it appears as illustrated below.

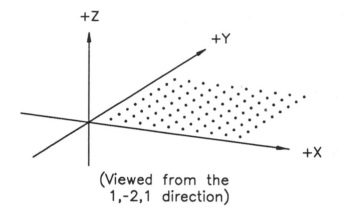

(Viewed from the
1,-2,1 direction)

A new drawing normally begins on the X-Y construction plane (at an elevation of 0) in the current UCS, unless your prototype drawing is set up differently. The drawing is viewed straight on from a positive Z direction. When you use regular 2D drawing commands such as CIRCLE, ARC, TRACE, SOLID and PLINE, all drawing is done on an X-Y plane at a certain Z elevation in the current UCS (Z locations will all be the same). To give these objects depth in the Z direction, use the **ELEV** command or the **CHANGE** command to assign a certain thickness that's figured from the elevation, as illustrated below.

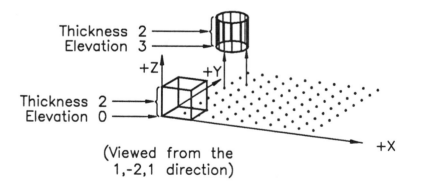

(Viewed from the
1,-2,1 direction)

To draw the above picture,

First use **ELEV** to set the elevation at **0** and the thickness at **2**, then draw a two-unit square with its lower left corner at **0,0**.

Then use **ELEV** to set the elevation at **3** and keep the thickness at **2**, then draw a two-unit-diameter circle centered at **1,7**.

Finally, use **VPOINT** to set the viewpoint at **1,-2,1**. The grid will appear at the current elevation of **3**. To move the grid back to its original location so the display looks like the picture above, use **ELEV** to set the elevation back to **0**.

These extruded 2D entities will give a visual appearance of surfaces, but they are different from the true surfaces created, for example, with the 3DFACE command.

In addition to the regular 2D drawing commands, a number of 3D commands —including LINE, 3DLINE, 3DFACE, 3DPOLY and the meshes—accept X,Y,Z coordinates. A command that expects a 3D point (three coordinates) will accept just the X and Y coordinates from the keyboard or pointer and adopt the current elevation as the Z coordinate.

When you use one of these 3D drawing commands, all drawing is done in relation to the current X-Y construction plane but various parts of a single entity can have Z locations that differ from each other. As illustrated below, these commands can produce lines/edges/surfaces that are slanted with respect to the X-Y construction plane (they intersect an X-Y plane instead of lying completely within it).

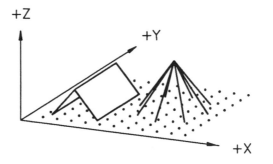

## USING POINT FILTERS

Partial coordinates can be extracted from various kinds of 3D locations. For example, you can extract one or two coordinates from the endpoint or mid-point of a LINE or 3DLINE or 3DPOLY, the corner of a 3DFACE or midpoint of the edge of a 3DFACE, etc. To do so, enter **.X, .Y, .Z, .XY, .XZ** or **.YZ** when prompted for a point.

Suppose you have a 3DLINE that ends at 4,5,8. To begin another 3DLINE at the same Y and Z coordinates, enter **.YZ** when prompted for the **From point** of the new 3DLINE. AutoCAD will respond with **of**. Then **OSNAP** to the end of the line. AutoCAD will prompt you for the missing X coordinate.

Point filters can also be used with 2D entities to extract one of the two needed coordinates.

## ELEV

**Sets Z elevation and thickness for subsequent entities**

When prompted, enter the new elevation and new extrusion thickness. The elevation can be positive, negative or 0. The thickness can also be positive, negative or 0.

You can **OSNAP** to the extruded portion of an object if your viewpoint is something other than 0,0,1 (plan view) in the current UCS and if your current command would accept a Z coordinate.

To change the elevation or thickness of an existing entity, use the **CHANGE** command.

You can use **STATUS** to check the current elevation and thickness.

The ELEV command will be dropped from the next major release of AutoCAD. You're advised to use the **UCS** command to control the placement of the X-Y construction plane, and use the system variable **THICKNESS** to control its thickness.

## 3DLINE

**Draws straight line segments
(similar to the LINE command)**

3DLINE works just like the regular LINE command. You'd normally enter all three coordinates (X,Y,Z). If only X and Y are entered, or if the location is selected with the pointer, the Z location is adopted from the current elevation.

3DLINE accepts relative rectangular coordinates in all three dimensions, such as @2,3,4. However, relative polar coordinates specifying distance and angle, such as @3.25<45, operate only in the X-Y plane.

Some of the OSNAP modes work with 3DLINEs in space. For example, if you snap to a 3DLINE while creating another 3D element (LINE, 3DLINE, 3DFACE, 3DPOLY, etc.), all three coordinates will be adopted. However, if you snap to a 3DLINE while creating a 2D element (CIRCLE, ARC, TRACE, PLINE, etc.), only the X and Y are adopted from the 3DLINE, while the Z location is adopted from the current elevation.

3DLINEs can be extruded in the Z direction with the **ELEV** and **CHANGE** commands. 3DLINEs can be edited in the Z direction with **MOVE**, **COPY**, **CHANGE**, **SCALE**, and **STRETCH**. But **MIRROR**, **ROTATE** and **ARRAY** operate only in the X-Y plane.

If you need a group of entities rotated in a plane other than the X-Y plane, remember that you can make the entities into a block, create a new UCS that's rotated as desired, and then simply insert the block in the new UCS.

3DLINE will be replaced by LINE in the next major release of AutoCAD.

## 3DFACE

**Creates a surface bounded by three
or four edges (corners can have
different Z locations)**

3DFACE works much like SOLID, except that the third and fourth points should continue around the perimeter (the third and fourth corner points should relate to each other in the opposite direction from the first and second corner points).

To create a 3D face that has only three edges instead of four, press <RETURN> when prompted for the fourth corner.

Only the edges of 3D faces are displayed. However, they will hide other entities if all four corners are in the same plane, or if the face has only three corners. 3D faces never have thickness.

To make an edge invisible, enter I before entering the coordinates of the corner preceding the edge (and before entering osnap modes or point filters), as illustrated below. This lets you combine several 3D faces into complex shapes with only the outer edges visible.

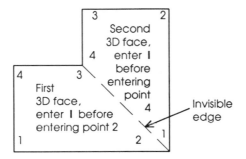

If you create a 3D face with all edges invisible, you won't be able to list or edit it while the edges remain invisible. However, you can set system variable **SPLFRAME** to 1 and then **REGEN** in order to display hidden edges. Also, an AutoLISP program called EDGE (found on the release disks) lets you turn selected visible edges into invisible ones, and vice versa. The program also lets you highlight invisible edges so they can be selected.

You can move the vertices of 3D faces with the CHFACE AutoLISP program supplied on the release disks.

Regarding relative coordinates, OSNAP, the construction of 3D and 2D elements and editing, the same limitations that apply to 3DLINE also apply to 3DFACE.

See "3DMESH" in Chapter 34. Also see the 3DLINE/3DFACE drawing exercises in Appendix A.

# CHAPTER 33

# 3D VIEWING

## HIDE

**Hides (or displays in different colors)
entities that are behind other
entities according to the current
viewpoint**

The HIDE command remains active only until the next time the display is regenerated (using ZOOM, PAN, VPOINT, etc.). Depending on the complexity of the drawing, hiding may take a lot of time.

To display hidden lines in different colors, use the **LAYER** command to create layers with the same names as the layers on which the entities are drawn, except with the prefix hidden immediately in front of the layer name. For example, if your object lines are on layer **2** in color **2** (yellow), create a layer called **hidden2** and assign it a different color, such as **5** (blue). Then use the **HIDE** command. Lines on the hidden layer will retain their linetype.

Solids, traces, circles and wide polyline segments have tops and bottoms when assigned a thickness, so the HIDE command treats them accordingly.

Entities on layers that have been turned off may still obscure entities on visible layers. Solution: Freeze the layers that were off.

There are many pitfalls when you're using HIDE with a complex drawing. See the *AutoCAD Reference Manual,* "Tips on Use of the HIDE Command."

Text and attribute definitions are always 0 thickness, but you can give them a thickness with the **CHANGE** command.

Axis lines are displayed only when the viewpoint is **0,0,1** (plan view).

The insertion point assigned to a block and the base assigned to a drawing adopt the current elevation for their Z coordinate, unless explicitly assigned a Z coordinate.

The thickness of sketched lines isn't displayed until the lines are recorded.

## VPOINT

**Sets the location in space from which the viewing line of sight originates**

You can set a viewpoint with: 1) **X,Y,Z** coordinates, (2) the compass and axis tripod or (3) two angles to rotate the viewpoint.

1) When prompted, enter the **X,Y** and **Z** coordinates, separated by commas. The line of sight is the vector from the selected coordinates to **0,0,0**. The distance from the coordinates to 0,0,0 isn't important, only the direction. Thus, a viewpoint location of 1,−2,2 is identical to 5,−10,10.

2) You can also set the viewpoint by using the compass and axis tripod pictured below. To get the compass and tripod, press <**RETURN**> when prompted for the viewpoint coordinates.

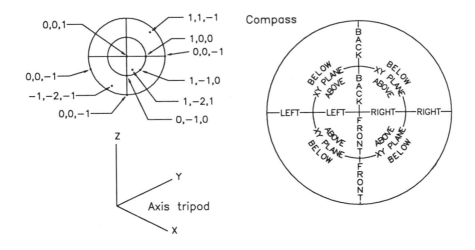

To use the compass, imagine yourself above the surface of a globe at the North Pole, looking toward the center of the globe. Think of the compass as a flattened globe with the center as the North Pole, the outer circle as the South Pole and the inner circle as the equator.

As you move the pointer around the compass, the tripod shows the relative positions of the positive X, Y and Z axes. Select your viewpoint by locating the appropriate point on the compass. The vector from that point to the center of the (round) globe defines the line of sight.

3) You can also set the viewpoint by using two angles (similar to spherical coordinates). When prompted, enter **R** (for Rotate), then enter the angle in the horizontal plane, then the angle in the vertical plane. Rotation of the line of sight begins from the positive X axis (1,0,0). The two angles that you enter rotate the viewpoint around 0,0,0 first in the X-Y plane, then toward the +Z or −Z axis.

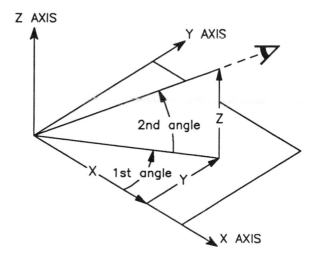

To get a view of an object that's similar to the normal isometric view (top, front and right sides), use a viewpoint of 1,−1,1.

The ZOOM and PAN commands work as usual, no matter what viewpoint you've selected.

# PLAN

**Displays the plan view of a selected UCS**

The plan view is the straight-on view of the X-Y construction plane in the current User Coordinate System. It's the same view you get when you use the VIEW command and enter coordinates 0,0,1.

When prompted, enter:

**C** for a plan view of the current UCS. C is the default.

**U** for a plan view of a previously saved UCS, then enter the name of the desired UCS.

**W** for a plan view of the World Coordinate System.

## USING VIEWPORTS

This section gives a general description of viewports. A viewport is a window on your drawing. When you begin a new drawing, you have only one viewport, which occupies the entire graphics screen (unless your prototype drawing is set up differently).

Viewports are controlled by the VPORTS command and the CVPORTS system variable, which are explained in greater detail in separate sections below.

By using the VPORTS command you can establish a pattern of two, three or four viewports (if you're using an MS-DOS/PC-DOS operating system), or more viewports if you're using certain other operating systems. Viewports are always rectangular.

A particular pattern of viewports is called a *viewport configuration*. Below is a sample viewport configuration involving one possible pattern of three viewports.

Each viewport can have its own unique settings for commands such as GRID, SNAP, AXIS, VIEWRES, UCSICON, VPOINT, ZOOM, PAN and DVIEW.

```
Layer 0 Ortho Snap          3.3125,3.1875              AutoCAD
                                                       • • • •

                    ┌─────────────────────────┐   BLOCKS
                    │                         │    DIM:
                    │                         │    DISPLAY
      Viewport      │                         │    DRAW
         1          │                         │    EDIT
                    │                         │    INQUIRY
                    │                         │    LAYER:
                    │        Viewport         │    SETTINGS
                    │           3             │    PLOT
                    │                         │    UCS:
                    │                         │    UTILITY
      Viewport      │                         │
         2          │                         │    3D
                    │                         │
                    │                         │

zoom
All/Center/Dynamic/Extents/Left/Previous/Window/Scale(X): a
Command:
```

However, only one UCS is active at any given time. Viewport 1 could have a VPOINT of 1,–2,1. At the same time Viewport 2 could show a plan view (VPOINT 0,0,1) and ZOOM All with GRID set to 1. And Viewport 3 could show one small area of the drawing, with GRID set to .25 and SNAP set to .0625.

Generally, drawing and editing commands affect all viewports, whereas display commands affect only the current viewport.

When a viewport configuration contains more than one viewport, each viewport in that configuration is considered to be active. However, only one is considered current; it's indicated by a wider border. All drawing and editing is done in the current viewport, but all other active viewports are updated automatically at the completion of each drawing or editing command.

When you move the crosshairs out of the current viewport into another viewport, the crosshairs change to an arrow. To select a different viewport as current, simply move the arrow into that viewport and press the pick button on the pointer.

You can create as many different viewport configurations (patterns of windows) as you like. Each different configuration can be named, saved and restored at any time.

Even though all drawing and editing is done in the current viewport, you can change current viewports in the middle of most drawing and editing commands. However, you can't select a new current viewport while you're in the middle of a display command such as SNAP, GRID, ZOOM, PAN, VPOINT, DVIEW or VPORTS.

You can build a selection set by selecting some entities from one viewport and other entities from a different viewport. Entities will be highlighted only in the viewport in which they were selected. When you drag entities, they'll all drag in the current viewport but only those selected in other viewports will drag in those viewports.

The **REDRAW** command affects only the current viewport. However, if you redraw the screen by pressing **F7** twice, all viewports are redrawn. Also, the **REDRAWALL** command redraws all viewports. Likewise, **REGEN** affects only the current viewport, but **REGENALL** regenerates all viewports.

## VPORTS (or VIEWPORTS)

**Establishes, modifies, saves or restores viewport configurations**

Enter the following:

**?** for a list of viewport configurations. The list indicates the location of each viewport in the configuration by giving the coordinates of that viewport's lower left and upper right corners.

The coordinates range between **0** and **1**, with **0,0** indicating the lower left corner of the screen and **1,1** indicating the upper right corner of the screen. The current configuration is listed first, with each viewport's ID number and coordinates. Then each saved viewport configuration is listed with its name and the coordinates of each of its viewports.

**S** to save the viewport configuration presently displayed, then enter the name of the configuration, up to 31 characters.

**R** to restore a viewport configuration you've already saved, then enter its name.

**D** to delete a viewport configuration already saved, then enter its name.

**SI** to select a screen containing a single viewport. The current viewport is enlarged to fill the screen and its settings are adopted. The other viewports are removed.

**J** to join two viewports into one larger viewport. The two viewports to be joined must be adjacent and must form a rectangle. When prompted, select the viewport you want to be dominant (its settings will apply to the new larger viewport). If you want the current viewport to be dominant, simply press **<RETURN>**. Then select the other viewport you want joined to the dominant viewport.

**2** to split the current viewport into two smaller viewports, then enter **V** to divide the current viewport vertically or **H** to divide it horizontally.

**3** to split the current viewport into three smaller viewports. Then enter:

>   **H** to establish three new viewports of equal size, oriented horizontally.

>   **V** to establish three new viewports of equal size, oriented vertically.

>   **A** to establish one larger viewport above two smaller viewports.

>   **B** to establish one larger viewport below two smaller viewports.

>   **L** to establish one larger viewport to the left of two smaller viewports.

>   **R** to establish one larger viewport to the right of two smaller viewports.

**4** to split the current viewport into four equal viewports.

When you're entering numbers to split the current viewport into a number of smaller viewports, AutoCAD will display an error message if you try to establish too many viewports.

The above options give you eight different configurations when you start from the default, single viewport. However, by joining and then redividing viewports, you can create many more viewport configurations.

There are also several preset viewport configurations in the DISPLAY—Set Viewports pull-down menu.

## REDRAWALL

**Redraws all viewports**

You can redraw all viewports either by entering **REDRAWALL** or by pressing F7 twice. REDRAWALL can be used transparently. The regular REDRAW command redraws only the current viewport.

## REGENALL

**Regenerates all viewports**

This command regenerates all viewports, whereas the regular REGEN command regenerates only the current viewport.

## CVPORT SYSTEM VARIABLE

**Establishes the current viewport**

Use **SETVAR** or the AutoLISP function **setvar** to establish a new current viewport by entering the ID number of the viewport. You can find a viewport's ID number by using **vports** and **?**.

## DYNAMIC VIEWING

Dynamic viewing includes a wide variety of viewing options especially designed for 3D drawing. The regular ZOOM and PAN commands are adequate for 2D drawing, but 3D drawing demands more.

### Advantages of dynamic viewing

When you're drawing a 3D item, it's helpful to be able to see:

The item from all sides and all angles.

The item being dragged; that is, changing dynamically on the screen as you select your desired view.

The item in either parallel projection or in perspective.

Inside the item by clipping entities near the observer.

The DVIEW command lets you do these, and more.

## Parallel projection and perspective

Every view you select can be seen in either parallel projection or in perspective.

Parallel projection is the standard projection used in engineering drawings. The theoretical viewpoint is an infinite distance from the item being viewed, so the projectors (projection rays) from the item to the projection plane (the sheet of paper or the display screen) are always parallel.

An item that's far away from the viewer will appear the same size on the projection plane as one that's closer to the viewer. A typical engineering drawing is made to show how to manufacture a certain item, so precise alignment and dimensioning are important features of engineering drawings. Parallel projection helps make alignment and dimensioning precise.

Perspective has been used since the 1400s, but it shows items differently. The projectors converge at the theoretical viewpoint, which is a certain distance from the item being viewed rather than at infinity. This makes the item appear differently on the projection plane than it does in parallel projection.

In perspective, an item that's far away from you will appear smaller on the projection plane than one that's closer. Also, edges that would be parallel on the actual item appear to meet at a distant vanishing point. This type of projection makes items look more like they do in the real world, especially if the real viewer's location is close to the theoretical viewpoint established when the projection was made.

If the real location and the theoretical location are very different, distortions can occur. One such distortion mentioned below (DVIEW command, Zoom option) occurs when the focal length of the camera is too short.

## Terms

Camera—the viewer or viewpoint.

Target—the point near or within the item at which the camera aims.

Line of sight—the line from the camera to the target.

Field of vision (or field of view)—the amount of the item that's visible when you're looking in any one direction.

Lens focal length—in photography, the distance between the lens and the focal point of the lens (the point where parallel rays of light converge after passing through the lens). A lens with a lot of curvature (small diameter and thick) will have a short focal length and a wide field of vision. One with less curvature will have a longer focal length and a narrower field of vision. In AutoCAD, changing the lens focal length changes the field of vision. A short focal length gives a wide field of vision and, if too short, produces a distorted image. A long focal length gives a narrow field of vision and, if too long, produces a perspective image that's difficult to distinguish from a parallel projection.

Clipping—Removing items or parts of an item from the display. Items closer to the camera than the front clipping plane won't be seen. Items farther from the camera than the back clipping plane won't be displayed. Clipping planes are always perpendicular to the line of sight.

## DVIEW
### Controls the display of 3D items

You'll be prompted to **Select objects**. These will be the preview objects that AutoCAD will drag dynamically if you select your desired view with the pointer.

You'll need to select the right number of objects—not too few and not too many. If you select too few, the preview may not provide enough information for you to select your view wisely. If you select too many objects, AutoCAD won't be able to generate all of the preview objects quickly enough and, to compensate, you'll have to move the pointer very slowly. After you select your desired view, all objects are redisplayed in the new view.

For several of the options described below, you can use slider bars that appear on the screen to dynamically indicate your choice of angle, magnification, etc. As you move the pointer, the preview objects change and a diamond moves in the slider bar indicating the amount of the change. A rubber band connects the diamond to the old value, which is also the default value. The default value can be accepted by pressing <RETURN>.

After selecting the preview objects, enter the following:

**CA** to rotate the camera (your viewpoint) around the target. Then enter the angle up or down from the current X-Y construction plane, using the keyboard or slider bar. Then enter the angle around the Z axis in the current construction plane, using the keyboard or slider bar.

**TA** to rotate the target (the point you're looking at) around the camera. This is like turning your head. Then enter the angle up or down, then the angle left or right, using the keyboard or slider bar.

**D** to change your distance from the objects. Since distance makes no sense in parallel projection (the theoretical viewpoint is always at infinity), this option automatically turns on perspective viewing and the usual UCS icon is replaced by a perspective icon. You can enter the distance with the keyboard or slider bar. If you want to view more, or less, of the object without turning perspective on, use the **Z** option instead of this option.

**PO** to enter point coordinates for the target, then the camera. Object snap and point filters apply. If you're in perspective when you select this option, you're temporarily returned to parallel projection until the points have been selected.

**PA** to pan the display in any direction. You can use the keyboard or the pointer if you're in parallel projection. If you're in perspective, you must use the pointer.

**Z** to zoom in/out or increase/decrease your field of vision. If you're in parallel projection, this works much like the regular ZOOM command. You simply enter the zoom scale factor to apply to the current display. However, if you're in perspective, this option lets you change the focal length of the camera lens.

The default focal length when you first enter perspective is **50mm**, which gives a view similar to that of a 35mm camera. If you use a very short focal length, you'll get a very wide view but you'll also get more distortion, like the distortion you get with a fish-eye lens on a regular camera. If you use a long focal length, you'll get a narrow view like the view you get with a telephoto lens on a regular camera.

When the focal length is very long, the image on the screen will appear almost identical to parallel projection (the projectors from object to camera are close to parallel).

**TW** to twist (rotate) the view around the line of sight from camera to target. The twist angle can be entered with keyboard or pointer.

**CL** to clip the drawing. Then enter **B** to set the distance of the back clipping plane, or turn it on or off. Or enter **F** to set the distance of the front clipping plane (**E** sets it at the camera "eye"), or turn it on or off. The default position for the front clipping plane is at the camera "eye." Distances for both the front and back clipping planes are measured along the line of sight with the zero distance located at the target. Positive distances are measured toward the camera, negative distances away from the camera. Distances can be entered with the keyboard or with the slider bar. Front clipping is always on when you're in perspective.

**H** to remove hidden lines in the preview objects.

**OFF** to turn perspective off. To turn it back on, use **D**.

**U** to undo the previous DVIEW operation. You can undo as often as necessary while you remain in the DVIEW command.

Each time one of the above options is performed, you're returned to the same DVIEW prompt. To exit the DVIEW command, enter **X** or simply press **<RETURN>**. When you exit the DVIEW command, the entire drawing will be regenerated, with the same options as in the last setting.

*Note:* After you use DVIEW Distance to turn perspective on, ZOOM, PAN and SKETCH won't work.

## USING MESHES

A mesh is a network of surface elements. Like a net, it can curve in any direction in space. AutoCAD uses meshes to approximate different kinds of 3D surface shapes; see the illustrations on the next several pages.

Each of a mesh's surface elements has four sides and four vertices (corners), and has up to four edges in common with adjoining surface elements. You can imagine a mesh as a rectangular matrix of surface elements with columns (running in the M direction) and rows (running in the N direction). Even though each individual surface element in a mesh acts somewhat like a small 3D face, the entire mesh is one entity. Meshes never have thickness.

AutoCAD uses five commands to create five different types of meshes. These commands are described in separate sections below. Four of them (TABSURF, RULESURF, REVSURF and EDGESURF) create a large number of surface elements automatically when you select certain entities that define the mesh. The fifth command (3DMESH) lets you define an irregular mesh by entering the location of every vertex, one by one. This command is designed mainly for use in AutoLISP programming.

Two system variables, SURFTAB1 and SURFTAB2, which are also described below, determine the density or resolution of meshes (number of surface elements in each direction).

A mesh is said to be open or closed in the M and/or N direction. It's open in a given direction if the last surface elements in that direction are separate from the first ones; it's closed if the last surface elements are joined to the first.

A mesh can be edited as a unit with the usual editing commands. Also, a mesh lists as a polyline and you can use the PEDIT command to move individual vertices and fit a smooth surface to the mesh.

When you explode a mesh, the elements become individual 3D faces.

When you use the HIDE command, the surface elements of the mesh will hide other entities and other mesh surfaces that are behind them.

A variety of standard shapes constructed from meshes are available in the DRAW–3D Construction icon menu.

## 3DMESH

**Creates a mesh, one vertex at a time**

When prompted, enter the number of vertices in the **M** direction, then the number in the **N** direction. The number in either direction can range from 2 through 256.

AutoCAD then prompts for the **X-Y-Z** coordinates of each vertex. The vertices are identified by their M and N positions, so you'll be prompted for vertex 0,0, then vertex 0,1, etc. You'll be asked for all the vertices in the N direction before proceeding in the M direction.

As with regular points, you can enter either 2D points or 3D points (the Z coordinate is optional). If the vertices are entered in the order illustrated below, the M and N directions will be as shown. After you've located all the vertices, AutoCAD draws the mesh. 3DMESH always produces an open mesh, but you can close it, in one or both directions, with the **PEDIT** command.

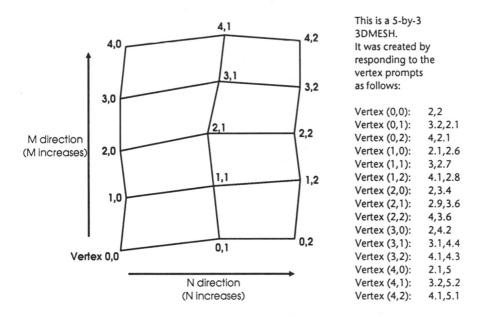

This is a 5-by-3 3DMESH. It was created by responding to the vertex prompts as follows:

|  |  |
|--------|-------------|
| Vertex (0,0): | 2,2 |
| Vertex (0,1): | 3.2,2.1 |
| Vertex (0,2): | 4,2.1 |
| Vertex (1,0): | 2.1,2.6 |
| Vertex (1,1): | 3,2.7 |
| Vertex (1,2): | 4.1,2.8 |
| Vertex (2,0): | 2,3.4 |
| Vertex (2,1): | 2.9,3.6 |
| Vertex (2,2): | 4,3.6 |
| Vertex (3,0): | 2,4.2 |
| Vertex (3,1): | 3.1,4.4 |
| Vertex (3,2): | 4.1,4.3 |
| Vertex (4,0): | 2.1,5 |
| Vertex (4,1): | 3.2,5.2 |
| Vertex (4,2): | 4.1,5.1 |

When the M and N directions are oriented as illustrated above, and you're using the PEDIT command to edit vertices, the **Left/Right/Up/Down** portion of the prompt works correctly and the vertex marker moves in the indicated direction.

When the M and N directions are oriented differently, you can still move from vertex to vertex successfully with **Left/Right/Up/Down** if you remember that **Up** always moves in the direction of increasing **M**, and **Right** always moves in the direction of increasing **N**.

The above mesh isn't a typical 3D mesh, because it's flat (all the Z coordinates are 0 by default). It's intended only to illustrate the relationship between the order of the vertices (as they appear in the prompts of the 3DMESH command), the M and N directions, and the **Left/Right/Up/Down** directions in the PEDIT command. A more typical mesh, with vertices at varying Z locations, is shown below from a viewpoint of 1,–2,1.

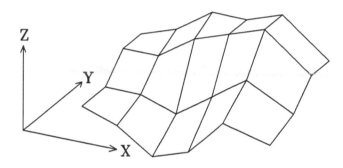

## TABSURF

**Creates a tabulated surface mesh from a path curve and a direction vector**

When prompted, select the path curve, then the direction vector. The path curve (which can be a line, circle, arc or polyline) actually traces out the surface, and is traditionally known as the *generatrix*. The direction vector determines the direction and distance the path curve will move as it traces out the surface, and is traditionally known as the *directrix*.

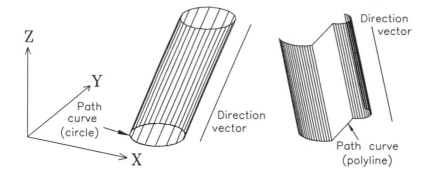

Although the direction vector can be either a line or an open polyline, only its endpoints are important. The beginning of both the path curve and the direction vector are nearest the points at which they are selected, except for a circle (whose beginning is at its zero angle) or a closed polyline (whose beginning is at its first endpoint). Thus, the 0,0 vertex is located at the corner of the mesh that corresponds to the beginning of the path curve and the beginning of the direction vector.

In a tabulated surface mesh, **M** is always **2** and increases in the direction of the direction vector.

**N** increases in the direction of the path curve and is determined by system variable **SURFTAB1**. If SURFTAB1 is set at 12 and the path curve is a line, arc, circle or spline-fit polyline, there will be 12 equally spaced vertices in the N direction. If SURFTAB1 is set at 12 and the path curve is a 2D polyline with both line segments and arc segments, vertices will occur at the ends of each line segment and each arc segment will be divided into 12 equally spaced vertices.

## RULESURF

### Creates a ruled surface mesh
### between two entities

When prompted, select the two entities that will define the mesh. The entities can be points, lines, circles, arcs or polylines. If one of the entities is closed (a circle or a closed polyline), then the other entity must also be closed. A point can be used with either an open or closed entity, but not with another point.

The 0,0 vertex is located at the beginning of the entity you select first. The **M** direction increases from the first entity to the second, and therefore is always **2**. The **N** direction increases from the beginning to the end of the first entity (if it's an open entity) and is determined by system variable **SURFTAB1**.

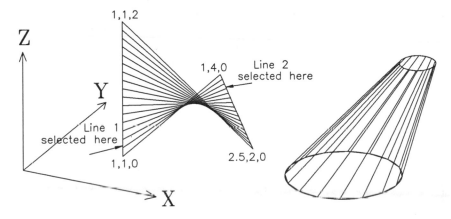

For circles, the N direction starts at the circle's zero-angle point. If a rulesurf is created between two circles, the edge lines joining vertices will usually not cross each other as long as the construction plane for one circle is parallel to the construction plane for the other. However, if the second circle is drawn on a construction plane that is tilted or rotated in relation to the first construction plane, the edge lines may cross each other or give an hourglass effect.

For closed polylines, the N direction starts at the polyline's last vertex. Suppose your two entities are a circle and a polyline and the ruled surface crosses over itself. To correct this you may need to reconstruct the polyline in reverse order, or use two polyarcs in place of the circle, or reconstruct the circle in the same location but on a flipped construction plane.

## REVSURF

**Creates a surface-of-revolution mesh from a path curve and an axis of revolution**

When prompted, select the path curve (generatrix), then the axis of revolution, then enter the start angle, then the included angle. The direction of the axis of revolution runs from the end nearest its pick point to the opposite end. In turn, this direction and the right-hand rule determine the direction of rotation for the two angles, as illustrated below.

The path curve can be a line, circle, arc or polyline. The axis of revolution can be a line or an open polyline (in which case only the endpoints are important). The path curve doesn't need to lie in the same plane as the axis of revolution. The **M** direction revolves around the axis of revolution and the number of vertices is determined by system variable **SURFTAB1**. The **N** direction runs along the path curve, and the number of vertices is determined by system variable **SURFTAB2** in a manner similar to the TABSURF command.

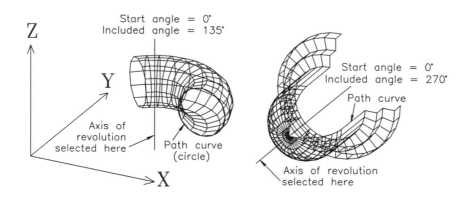

## EDGESURF

**Creates a Coons surface mesh with four connected entities as defining edges.**

When prompted, select the entities that will be the four defining edges. These entities can be any combination of lines, arcs or open polylines. The endpoint of each entity must coincide with the startpoint of the next entity, forming a complete circuit. The first edge you select will determine the **M** direction, running from the endpoint nearest the pick point to the opposite end.

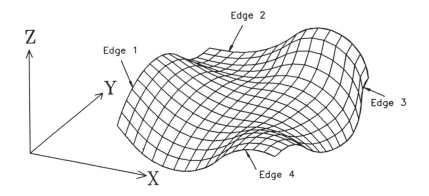

SURFTAB1 determines the number of vertices in the **M** direction, **SURFTAB2** in the **N** direction.

## SURFTAB1 SURFTAB2 SYSTEM VARIABLES

### Control the number of surface elements in the M and N directions of a mesh

In the **TABSURF** and **RULESURF** commands, SURFTAB1 determines the number of surface elements in the **N** direction (**M** is always **2** for these types of meshes). In the **REVSURF** and **EDGESURF** commands, **SURFTAB1** determines the number of surface elements in the **M** direction, while **SURFTAB2** determines the number in the **N** direction.

When a mesh is closed in a given direction, the number of surface elements and the number of vertices in that direction will be equal. When a mesh is open in a given direction, the number of vertices will be one more than the number of surface elements.

The smallest possible value for either variable is **2**.

## SMOOTH SURFACES

You can smooth a mesh by editing it with the **PEDIT** command and selecting the **S** option (see PEDIT in Chapter 29). The level of smoothness is determined by system variable SURFTYPE, while the number of vertices is determined by system variables SURFU and SURFV.

System variable **SURFTYPE** controls the level of smoothness. A setting of 5 produces a quadratic surface with a low level of smoothness, 6 produces a cubic surface with a medium level of smoothness, and 8 produces a Bezier surface with a high level of smoothness (see the illustrations below). Notice that smoothness and conformity are inversely related—the smoother the surface, the less it conforms to the defining mesh.

System variables **SURFU** and **SURFV** control the number of elements in the smoothed surface. **SURFU** controls the number of elements in the **M** direction of the mesh, **SURFV** in the **N** direction. High values in SURFU and SURFV produce a fine, smoothed mesh, but they also take longer to regenerate on the screen.

Don't confuse SURFU and SURFV with SURFTAB1 and SURFTAB2, which control the number of vertices in the original (unsmoothed) mesh. SURFU and SUFRV apply only to smoothed surfaces.

When system variable **SPLFRAME = 0**, the smoothed surface is displayed. When **SPLFRAME** is non-zero, only the defining mesh is displayed.

# SMOOTHED SURFACES

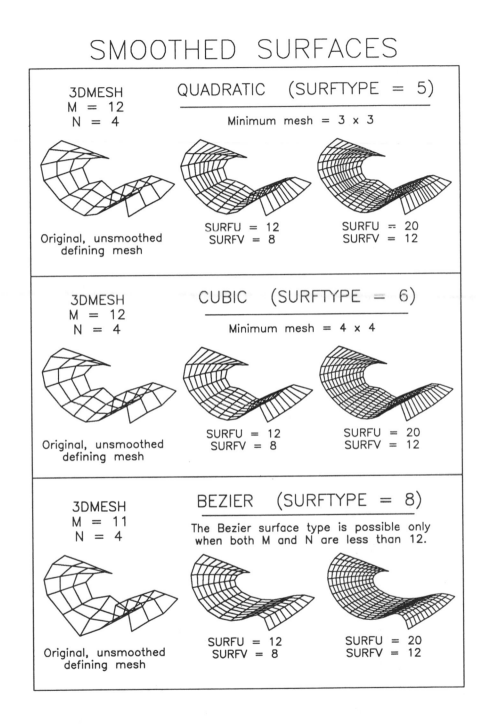

**3DMESH**
M = 12
N = 4

### QUADRATIC (SURFTYPE = 5)

Minimum mesh = 3 x 3

Original, unsmoothed defining mesh

SURFU = 12
SURFV = 8

SURFU = 20
SURFV = 12

**3DMESH**
M = 12
N = 4

### CUBIC (SURFTYPE = 6)

Minimum mesh = 4 x 4

Original, unsmoothed defining mesh

SURFU = 12
SURFV = 8

SURFU = 20
SURFV = 12

**3DMESH**
M = 11
N = 4

### BEZIER (SURFTYPE = 8)

The Bezier surface type is possible only when both M and N are less than 12.

Original, unsmoothed defining mesh

SURFU = 12
SURFV = 8

SURFU = 20
SURFV = 12

# 35 ATTRIBUTES

## ATTDEF

**Defines attributes**

An attribute is simply information in the form of text assigned to a block. This text can be predetermined or entered at the time a block is inserted.

See Appendix C for a sample drawing with attributes, as well as a sample extract file and the programs that produce a parts list file and place it in a drawing.

ATTDEF displays four modes, with their default settings:

| Mode | | Default Settings |
|------|---|------------------|
| Invisible | N | (Attributes will appear on screen and be plotted.) |
| Constant | N | (You'll be prompted to enter a value each time the block with this attribute is inserted. If **Constant** is changed to **Y**, each insertion of the block will have the same value, which cannot be edited later.) |
| Verify | N | (No opportunity to verify a constant value.) |
| Preset | N | (Value will be requested during block insertion. If **Preset** is changed to **Y**, the value is not requested, but is assigned the default value or assigned null if there is no default value. Dialogue boxes used to assign attribute values operate the same whether **Preset** is **N** or **Y**.) |

Enter **I** to change Invisible mode, **C** to change Constant mode, **V** to change Verify mode and/or **P** to change Preset mode. Press **<RETURN>** to accept the settings as currently displayed.

Then enter the attribute tag (the name of the attribute).

Then enter the prompt that you want to appear when the block is inserted, and the default value in response to that prompt, if any. (If **Constant** mode is **Y**, you'll be asked for the value instead of the default value.)

Then locate the starting point of the text (or **A** for aligned, **C** for centered, **R** for right-justified or **S** for style), then enter the height and angle (similar to the TEXT command). To place an attribute tag immediately below the previous tag, press <**RETURN**> when asked for a starting point.

Upon completion, the attribute tag will appear on the drawing in ALL CAPS.

To make this attribute part of a block, select it along with the other entities making up the block.

When the block is subsequently inserted, the prompt you entered earlier will ask you for the value (text) to be associated with this attribute. The value you enter will be displayed in place of the tag (assuming Invisible mode is N).

Attributes can also be entered with the Entering Attributes dialogue box if you use the pull-down menu Draw/INSERT, or if you first set system variable **ATTDIA** to non-zero, then use the regular **INSERT** command.

Several different attributes can be included in one block. An attribute can be the only entity in a block.

Attributes can be used in dimensions and notations as well as with actual parts of the drawing's geometry. For example, you could define a block called TOL (for tolerance) with two attribute tags, PLUS and MINUS, which prompt for plus and minus tolerances at the time of block insertion. The height of the text would be smaller than the usual text height so that when placed in the drawing the dimension with its tolerance would be proportioned more like a typical hand-lettered dimension. Or, you could create a block called FR (for fraction) with two attribute tags, NUMERATOR and DENOMINATOR. After prompting for numerator and denominator this block would place a true fraction in the drawing with the numerator above, rather than in line with, the denominator.

You can avoid entering any attribute values while inserting blocks by setting the system variable **ATTREQ** to **0**.

Blocks with attributes can be moved, copied, rotated, scaled and arrayed like any other blocks. However, if the blocks are exploded, the attributes revert to tags and lose their values.

## ATTDISP
**Determines visibility of attributes**

When prompted, enter:

**N** for normal display mode. Whether or not attributes are displayed depends on whether invisible mode was N or Y when the attribute was created with the ATTDEF command.

**ON** to display all attributes.

**OFF** to suppress all attributes.

## ATTEDIT
**Edits attributes associated with inserted blocks**

When prompted, enter:

**Y** to edit attributes individually.

**N** to edit attributes globally (replacing one specified text string with another in a specified group of attributes).

You'll then be prompted for block name specification, tag specification and value specification. You can limit the group of attributes selected for editing by entering specific block names, tag names or values in response to the above prompts. Or you can use the wild card default to edit all blocks, tags and values.

Then indicate whether you want your editing limited to on-screen attributes. On-screen editing can be further limited to a window.

If you're doing global editing, enter the old text string and the new text string.

If you're doing individual editing, the first attribute will be marked with an X.

Now enter:

**N** to select the next attribute.

**V** to change the value of the marked attribute. Then enter **C** to change a few characters, or enter **R** to replace the entire value.

**P** to change the position of the marked attribute.

**H** to change the height of the marked attribute.

**A** to change the angle of the marked attribute.

**S** to change the text style of the marked attribute.

**L** to change the layer of the marked attribute.

Editing of attribute values in single blocks can also be done with a dialogue box. To call up the dialogue box, enter **DDATTE**.

## ATTEXT

**Extracts attributes and places them in an ASCII text file for use by other programs**

Before you can use ATTEXT to extract a CDF or SDF file, you must create a Template File. See "Creating a Template File" below.

When prompted, enter:

**C** for a CDF (comma delimited format) file. This is a sequential file that can be processed by another program.

**S** for an SDF (standard data, or size delimited format) file. This is a random access file that can be processed by another program.

**D** for a DXF file. This is similar in format to AutoCAD's drawing interchange files.

**E** to select entities from which you want to extract attribute information. Select E first if you want to extract information from only part of your drawing. AutoCAD will prompt you again for **C**, **S** or **D**.

For CDF and SDF files, then enter the name of the template file, then the name of the extract file. AutoCAD gives CDF and SDF files the extension .TXT and gives DXF files the extension .DXX. The AutoCAD program files include some sample BASIC programs that post-process these files. Also see Appendix C for a sample extracted file, post-processed files, etc.

## CREATING A TEMPLATE FILE

Template files determine the structure of CDF and SDF extract files. They have the extension .TXT and can be created with EDLIN or a word processor in programming mode. Each line in the template file specifies one type of column to be included in the extract file. The number of lines of values under these headings in the extract file is determined by the number of blocks from which the attribute values are extracted.

The sample template file below would produce an extract file having the headings NAME, X(coordinate), Y(coordinate), PART-NO. and VENDOR. The heading name (such as VENDOR) in the template file must be exactly the same as the tag name for the attribute in the drawing. The headings below that start with BL will pick up the indicated information from the various blocks.

```
BL:NAME       C015000
BL:X          N008004
BL:Y          N008004
BL:Z          N008004
PART-NO.      C018000
VENDOR        C025000
```

— Number of decimal places if field is numeric
— Width of field (number of characters)
— C for a character field (left justified) or
  N for a numeric field (right justified)

Besides using BL:NAME to extract the block's name, and BL:X, BL:Y, and BL:Z to extract the block's location, you can also extract the block's nesting level, number, handle, layer of insertion, rotation, scaling factors and extrusion. See the *AutoCAD Reference Manual.*

# CHAPTER 36

# SHAPES

## SHAPE

**Places a predefined shape in a drawing**

The shape file containing the desired shape must already have been loaded into the drawing.

When prompted, enter:

**?** to get a list of available shapes.

The name of the shape, then the starting point, height, and rotation.

When DRAGMODE is on, you must enter **DRAG** to drag the starting point, height or rotation angle of the shape.

See also "Creating Shape and Text Font Files" in Chapter 37.

## LOAD

**Loads a shape file into a drawing**

*Note:* Text fonts, although they are created in a manner similar to shape files, are loaded automatically, as needed, with the STYLE command.

When prompted, enter:

**?** to get a list of shape files already loaded into the drawing.

The name of the shape file. Don't include the extension .SHX.

# CUSTOMIZING AUTOCAD

## THE CONFIGURATION MENUS

The Configuration menu and its submenu, the Operating Parameters menu, are shown under "Main Menu Organization" in Chapter 2. Some elementary customization is possible by using these two configuration menus.

While a number of the items on the Configuration menu are predetermined by your system's hardware, other items will let you set up the system to suit yourself. A few possibilities are mentioned below.

By default, AutoCAD will normally use the first serial port (COM1) for digitizer input, and the first parallel port (LPT1) for output to a printer-plotter or other raster-based printer (such as a dot-matrix printer or a laser printer).

If you have more than one serial port and/or more than one parallel port, and especially if you use other software that favors a particular serial or parallel port, you may want to use item **2** on the Configuration menu, "Allow detailed configuration." After you've indicated that you want to configure the I/O ports, AutoCAD will let you select the desired I/O port while you're configuring digitizer, plotter or printer-plotter.

You may want AutoCAD to beep at you when you make an input mistake. Or, you may want it to shut up and let you make your mistakes in silence. Item **1** on the Operating Parameters menu, "Alarm on error," will let you decide.

You can install any drawing as the default prototype drawing. To do so, use item **2** on the Operating Parameters menu, "Initial drawing setup," and enter the name of the desired drawing.

If you're not using AutoLISP (or any third-party programs that use AutoLISP), you may want to free up some of the memory that AutoLISP normally uses so AutoCAD will have more room to work. To do so, use item **7** on the Operating Parameters menu, "AutoLISP feature." This same menu item lets you enable Extended AutoLISP.

# LINETYPE

**Loads or defines line types**

When prompted, enter the following:

**?** to list the line types that can be loaded, then enter the name of the file containing the line-type definitions.

**L** to load one or more line types into your drawing, then enter the name of the line-type (or **\*** to load all line types), then the name of the file containing the line-type definition. After a line type has been loaded into the drawing, it can be assigned to a layer using the **LAYER** command or one of these dialogue boxes: SETTINGS—Entity Creation or SETTINGS—Modify Layer. (If the line type definition resides in the ACAD.LIN file, it will be loaded automatically when needed by the LAYER command or the LINETYPE Set command.)

**C** to create a line type. When a line type is created, it's merely written to a file on disk. It isn't associated with the current drawing until it's loaded in the drawing, as described above.

Then enter the name of the new line type, then the name of the file that will contain the new line type.

Then enter the descriptive text (up to 47 characters). Or, you can type in a visual representation of the new line using a series of underlines, spaces and periods.

Then **A,** will appear on the screen. Follow the **A,** with your definition of the line type by entering the lengths of the pen-down segments (positive numbers) and pen-up segments (negative numbers). A length of 0 (zero) is allowed for a pen-down segment, which produces a dot. Enter only one pattern. Begin the pattern with the longest pen-down segment and end it with a pen-up segment.

For example, a line type that appears roughly like this:

———— — — — ———— — — — ————

would be defined like this:

```
A,1,-.12,.1,-.05,.1,-.05,.1,-.12
```

To revise a line type, enter **C,** then the name of the line type. AutoCAD will display the line type's current definition and ask if you want to redefine it.

Line types can also be created and edited using EDLIN or a word processor in programming mode. A line type file is simply a text file with the extension

.LIN, containing a pair of lines (an identifying line and a defining line) for each line type. The file ACAD.LIN contains several different AutoCAD line types, which you can examine with the TYPE command or edit. Make a copy of the file before you edit it.

If the line type defined above were called TRACER, it would look like this in a text file that was created with EDLIN (EDLIN line numbers omitted):

(Identifying line)   `*TRACER,` _____ \_\_ \_\_ \_\_ _____

(Defining line)     `A,1,-.12,.1,-.05,.1,-.05,.1,-.12`

## CREATING SHAPE AND TEXT FONT FILES

This section describes how to create shape files and text font files. These two kinds of files are similar in many ways, but text font files have certain unique features, which are mentioned where appropriate.

Shape files and text font files are first created as regular text files with the extension .SHP. They can be created using EDLIN or a word processor in programming mode.

For use by AutoCAD, these files are then compiled using "Compile shape/font file" on the main menu. When they are compiled, a new file is created and given the same name but with extension .SHX. To edit a shape file, edit the .SHP file, then recompile it.

Some sample shape files are supplied with AutoCAD. PC.SHX is for printed circuit layout. ES.SHX is for electronics schematics. The corresponding .SHP files can be examined with the TYPE command or edited with EDLIN, etc. Make a copy of these files before you edit them.

Each shape in a file is assigned a number from 1 to 255. The shapes (letters, etc.) in a text font file are assigned their ASCII numbers (for example, **A** is ASCII #65, **a** is #97, **1** is #49, etc.). See Appendix B in the *AutoCAD Reference Manual.*

Each shape is created in two lines in the file (see the sample below). The first line (the identifying line) contains an asterisk, then the assigned number, then the number of bytes used in the second line to define the shape, then the name of the shape (in uppercase letters for shape files, preferably in lowercase letters for text font files).

When a text font file that has the shape names in lowercase is compiled, the names are not loaded, which saves space in memory. (The names of text font shapes aren't needed by AutoCAD because the shapes are accessed by ASCII number instead of name.)

The second line (the defining line) contains a series of numbers. Some of these numbers define vectors in the shape; other numbers are special codes, which are explained later.

Some of the numbers in the defining line are hexadecimal numbers (base 16) rather than decimal numbers (base 10).

Decimal notation:          0  1  2  3  4  5  6  7  8  9  10  11  12  13  14  15

Hexadecimal notation:   0  1  2  3  4  5  6  7  8  9  A  B   C   D   E   F

Sample: These two lines define the uppercase A pictured below.

(Identifying line) *65,12,uca

(Defining line)   063,2,04B,1,040,2,045,1,06D,2,020,0

Each three-digit number is a hexadecimal number. The leading zero identifies the next two digits as hexadecimal digits. In these three-digit numbers, the middle digit gives the length of the vector, while the final digit gives the direction of the vector. Notice that the number of bytes in the identifying line (12) includes the terminating zero.

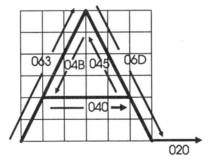

Vector directions are given in the diagram below. Even though the vectors have slightly different lengths, they are all considered to be one vector-length long for purposes of defining shapes.

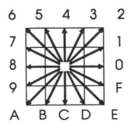

Shape and font definitions can include nonstandard vectors, which are simply X,Y displacements if codes 8 and/or 9 are used (see codes below). You can also use octant arcs and bulge arcs (see the *AutoCAD Reference Manual* ).

Besides the three-digit numbers in the defining line that give the length and direction of vectors, one- and two-digit numbers are used to encode special instructions, as follows:

0    End of shape definition

1    Pen down

2    Pen up

3    Divide vector lengths by next byte

4    Multiply vector lengths by next byte

5    Push current location onto stack

6    Pop current location from stack

7    Draw sub-shape number given by next byte

8    X,Y displacement given in next two bytes

9    Multiple X,Y displacements, terminated by (0,0)

10    Octant arc defined by next two bytes

11    Fractional arc defined by next five bytes

12    Arc defined by X,Y displacement and bulge

13    Multiple bulge-specified arcs

14    Process next command only if vertical text style (used in dual-orientation fonts)

Although it isn't necessary, readability is improved if these code numbers are in decimal notation (without leading zeros) and vector indicators are in hexadecimal notation (with leading zeros), as illustrated in the earlier sample.

The pen is assumed to be down at the start of each shape.

For several lines of text to be written by a text font file, that file must also contain a pair of lines that will allow for a line feed (ASCII #10).

    Line feed: *10,3,1f

        2,0AC,0

In the illustration given earlier, capital letters are six vector-lengths high, so a suitable line feed is 10 vector-lengths down. Thus, the defining line for the line feed gives the following instructions: Raise the pen, move A vector-lengths, move in direction C.

One more pair of lines is needed to complete a text font file. These two lines must be the very first two lines in the text font file, since they contain the name of the font and certain governing statistics about the font, as shown below.

Name of font:  `*0,4,name-of-font`
               `6,2,0,0`

─0 for normal (horizontal) font, 2 for dual-orientation (horizontal and vertical) font
─Number of vector-lengths lowercase letters extend below the baseline
── Number of vector-lengths uppercase letters extend above the baseline

## MENU

### Loads a specified menu

When prompted, enter the name of the menu file. Do not include the extension .MNU or .MNX. If the file hasn't been compiled, AutoCAD will compile the .MNU file and create a new file with the same name but with extension .MNX.

When you save a drawing, the name of the most recently used menu file is saved with that drawing. The next time the drawing is edited, that menu file is loaded automatically (assuming it resides in the default directory or the directory with the AutoCAD program files).

## CREATING A CUSTOM MENU

See Appendix B for a sample custom menu.

A menu file is a text file that contains AutoCAD commands and/or command strings. (Command strings include both commands and responses to prompts.) A menu file has the extension .MNU. The standard AutoCAD menu files are called ACAD.MNU (source file) and ACAD.MNX (compiled file). ACAD.MNU is found in the SOURCE subdirectory on the Support 2 release disk.

You can create a custom menu file using EDLIN or a word processor in programming mode.

AutoCAD can use up to 18 sections in one menu file:

Screen menu—One section, SCREEN

Pointer button menu—One section, BUTTONS

Digitizer tablet areas—Four sections, TABLET1 through TABLET4

Auxiliary function box menu—One section, AUX1

Pull-down menus—Ten sections, POP1 through POP10

Icon menus—One section, ICON

Each section must be headed with a section label. The section label includes the section name preceded by three asterisks, such as ***SCREEN, or ***TABLET1 or ***POP7.

For the screen menu, only eight or fewer characters can be displayed. The on-screen portion is placed in square brackets ([]) with the actual command or command string immediately following the closing bracket.

On some monitors, there's room for only 21 lines of a screen menu to be displayed at once. If you try to display more, AutoCAD will split the list and display NEXT at the bottom of the display. This provides one way to get to the rest of your list of commands.

Here's a short sample menu file. It has only two sections, a screen root menu and a tablet menu.

On-screen portion (can be upper- or lowercase). → 

```
***SCREEN                          Command portion
[STATUS]status                     (can be upper- or
[LOCATION]id                       lowercase).
[DISTANCE]dist
[DESCRIBE]list
[ZOOM IN] zoom 1.3333x
[ZOOM OUT] zoom .75x
[ZOOM ALL] zoom a
[SAVE]save ;                       A semicolon causes a
[END]end                           carriage return.
[QUIT]quit
[*CANCEL*]^C^C                      (= CTRL-C CTRL-C)
***TABLET1
line
circle
arc                                A backslash allows for user input,
text                               either from the keyboard or from
layer s \;                         the pointer.
```

Notice the semicolons in lines 9 and 18. In a menu file, AutoCAD interprets a semicolon as a carriage return (<**RETURN**>). Since AutoCAD also interprets a space as a carriage return, lines 9 and 18 function as follows:

Line 9—Keys in **SAVE**. The space acts like a carriage return and enters the command. (AutoCAD responds by displaying the drawing name as the default response).

Then the semicolon causes a carriage return, which accepts the default response.

Line 18—Keys in **LAYER**. The first space acts like a carriage return and enters the command. (AutoCAD responds with its usual LAYER prompt.)

Keys in **s**. The second space acts like a carriage return and enters the S (this selects "Set" from the LAYER prompt). AutoCAD responds by asking for the layer number or name.

Then the backslash lets you key in and enter the number or name of the desired layer.

AutoCAD responds by redisplaying the usual LAYER prompt. Then the semi-colon causes a carriage return, which exits the LAYER command and returns to command mode.

If you tried to use the above sample menu, you'd discover that the pointer buttons (all but the pick button) had adopted new functions from the screen menu. Button 2 adopts the STATUS command, 3 adopts the ID command, etc. If any of the seven sections of a menu file is missing, the commands from the first section are automatically assigned to that section.

The following section of a menu file will assign <RETURN> to the second button and REDRAW to the third button. (The first button is always the pick button.)

```
***BUTTONS
;
redraw
```

A screen menu can have submenus and sub-submenus, etc. Any submenu will have a heading in the following form:

```
**NAME-OF-SUBMENU (up to 31 characters, no spaces)
```

To display a submenu from an item in the root menu (or parent menu), the command portion should have the following form:

```
$S=NAME-OF-SUBMENU
```

Let's suppose that we want to expand the three zoom commands in the sample screen menu given earlier, and we want to set up a submenu with six zoom options. We'd replace the three zoom commands in the root menu with the following line:

```
[ZOOM]$S=ZOOM-OPTIONS
```

Then we'd add the following lines at the end of the screen section of the menu file:

```
**ZOOM-OPTIONS
    [1/2 size]zoom .5
    [2X size]zoom 2
    [ZOOM IN]zoom 1.3333x
    [ZOOM OUT]zoom .75x
    [ZOOM ALL]zoom a
    [ZOOM #]zoom
    [--root--]$S=SCREEN
```

Notice that the last line above lets you return to the root section of the screen menu. If you had created the above six zoom options as a sub-submenu, and you wanted to be able to return to the submenu from which these options were called, then the last line would read as follows:

```
    [--root--]$S=
```

The above examples assume that AutoCAD is in command mode when each command is entered. However, it's better to make sure that AutoCAD is in command mode by placing two CTRL-C's at the beginning of the command portion, as follows:

```
    [STATUS]^C^Cstatus
```

Type a CTRL-C into a menu file by typing a caret (above the 6) and a C rather than using a regular CTRL-C.

If you place an asterisk in front of the two CTRL-C's (*^C^C) in the command portion, the command with its options will be repeated automatically until you use CTRL-C to cancel the repetition.

Pull-down menu sections (POP1 through POP10) should have as their first line just the on-screen portion; that is, just the text that will appear in the menu bar at the top of the screen—up to 14 characters. Each following line will have both an on-screen portion and a command portion. For example,

```
    ***POP1
    [DISPLAY]
    [ZOOM IN]^C^Czoom 1.3333x
    [ZOOM OUT]^C^Czoom .75x
```

Items in pull-down menus can call submenus just like submenus in the screen section. For example, this line would install a submenu called P3B in place of the present POP3 menu.

```
    $P3=P3B $P3=*
```

The last part of the above line ($P3=*) forces the newly installed P3B submenu to be displayed.

If a submenu is shorter than the one it's replacing, use a single blank line at the end of the shorter menu to make it overwrite the longer menu entirely.

The ICON section of the menu displays slides that represent certain choices. It can be divided into any number of subsections. This lets icon displays be called from any other menu item. It also permits icon nesting or branching.

The first line of any icon menu section is centered at the top of the icon page as a title. Each of the following lines in the section includes a slide portion and a command portion. You can use up to 15 slides in any one icon menu (reserve one slide for an EXIT option).

```
***ICON
**IPATTERNS
[AVAILABLE PATTERNS]
[slide1](patt1)
[slide2](patt2)
[slide3](patt3)
[ EXIT]^C
```

When the above subsection (**IPATTERNS) is called from another menu item, AutoCAD assembles an icon menu on the screen with the heading AVAILABLE PATTERNS as the title, and with each of the slides displayed. Each line that displays a slide also includes a command that calls an AutoLISP function. Notice that the last line includes a space before the word EXIT. The space displays the word instead of a slide.

Suppose you want a menu to access a certain subdirectory. For example, the menu item might call for a certain line type to be loaded from the C:\LINETYPES\SET3.LIN file. Since menu items use the backslash for user input, you must specify the file path with forward slashes like so: **C:/LINETYPES/SET3.LIN.**

See Appendix B for a sample menu that includes an icon section as well as tablet, button and pull-down sections.

## TABLET MENU OVERLAYS

To create and install a tablet menu overlay, you must:

1. design and draw the tablet areas for the overlay, and

2. write a custom menu file that includes the commands that will correspond to each box in the overlay.

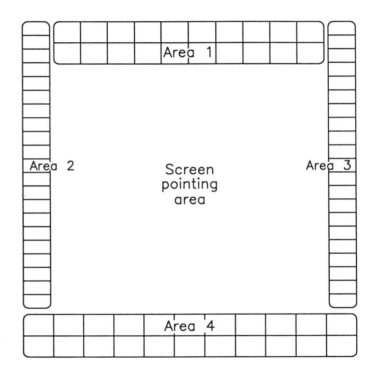

The Summagraphics 1201 digitizing tablet will take an overlay with an active area of up to 11" x 11." The tablet overlay can have up to four areas. The blank overlay shown above illustrates only one of many ways to arrange these areas.

Within each tablet area, the individual boxes are numbered from left to right, then from top to bottom, to correspond to the commands or command strings in that section of the menu file.

After you have created both the overlay and the menu file, you must install them and configure AutoCAD accordingly. Follow these steps:

1. If you want to use the tablet menu overlay exclusively and want to eliminate the screen menu area, go to AutoCAD's configuration menu, select "configure video display," and enter **N** when asked if you want a screen menu area.

2. Start a new drawing. When you're in the drawing editor, enter **MENU**, then enter the name of your menu file (without the extension).

3. Place your tablet overlay on the digitizing tablet. Then enter **TABLET**. When prompted,

> Enter **CFG** to configure menu areas on the tablet, then enter the number of tablet areas.

> Then, for each tablet area, locate the upper left, lower left, and lower right corners and enter the number of columns and rows within that tablet area.

> Then enter the lower left and upper right corners of the screen pointing area.

After the tablet is configured, AutoCAD will assume this configuration for the tablet each time AutoCAD is started. The drawings that have been edited with the menu written for this tablet configuration will automatically call for the same menu when they are edited again. This menu must reside in the current directory or in the directory with the AutoCAD program files.

See the sample custom tablet overlay and menu in Appendix B.

## USING TWO MENU CONFIGURATIONS

You can switch between two or more configurations of AutoCAD without having to repeat all the steps to set up each configuration.

When AutoCAD is started, it uses the ACAD.CFG file and other configuration files (in the same directory where its other program files reside) to determine its present configuration. However, AutoCAD can be instructed to use different configuration files.

Suppose that you want to use two different configurations at different times, as follows:

Configuration 1—Using the standard screen menu and the standard tablet overlay supplied by AutoCAD

Configuration 2—Using a custom tablet menu overlay and no screen menu

Configuration 1 can be used in the normal way (assuming AutoCAD was initially configured using the standard screen menu and standard tablet overlay). When you start AutoCAD, follow the same steps as usual. Configuration 2 can be established in the following manner:

1. Under DOS, use the **MD** command to make a subdirectory under the root directory called TMO (for tablet menu overlay).

2. Establish this subdirectory in the environment by using the **SET** command as follows:

```
SET ACADCFG=\TMO
```

(When AutoCAD starts, it checks for any value that has been assigned to ACADCFG. When it finds \TMO, it searches for configuration files in that subdirectory instead of defaulting to its usual configuration files.)

3. Copy the following files, which reside with the AutoCAD program files, into the \TMO subdirectory:

ACADDS.OVL

ACADDG.OVL

ACADPL.OVL

ACADPP.OVL

ACAD.CFG

4. Start a new drawing. When you're in the drawing editor, use the **TABLET** command to configure the tablet. Now all the necessary configuration files should be present in subdirectory \TMO.

Configuration 2 can now be used by including Step 5 of the start-up procedure. See "AutoCAD Startup" in Chapter 2.

Each time you start a new drawing under this configuration, use the **MENU** command to load your custom menu if needed. It will be loaded automatically if you use a prototype drawing that was created or edited with your custom menu.

## CHANGING THE ACAD.PGP FILE

The ACAD.PGP file lets you access DOS commands and other programs directly from the command prompt. The generic file supplied with AutoCAD is listed below.

```
CATALOG,DIR /W,30000,*Files: ,0
DEL,DEL,30000,File to delete: ,0
DIR,DIR,30000,File specification: ,0
EDIT,EDLIN,42000,File to edit: ,0
SH,,30000,*DOS Command: ,0
SHELL,,127000,*DOS Command: ,0
TYPE,TYPE,30000,File to list: ,0
```

In each line, the first field is the command you'd enter while in command mode. The second field is the command that's sent to DOS. The third field specifies the amount of memory that must be released in order to execute the command or program. This number should be at least 4K greater than the program and never less than 24K for DOS Version 3.3 or earlier. The fourth field is an optional prompt. The fifth field is optional and specifies special codes for specific software (see Appendix B in the *AutoCAD Reference Manual*).

In order to add, for example, the ability to access WordStar from the command prompt, use EDLIN to add this line to the ACAD.PGP file. (The exact amount of memory released may depend on the version of WordStar you're using.)

```
WS,WS,116000
```

Assuming your current directory and/or path are set up appropriately, this would let you move directly from the drawing editor to WordStar and directly back to the drawing editor again.

If you've changed the ACAD.PGP file from within the drawing editor (using SHELL), you must re-enter the drawing editor for the new file to take effect.

## UNDEFINE/REDEFINE

AutoCAD commands can be UNDEFINEd and replaced by AutoLISP commands of the same name. Naturally, they can also be REDEFINEd to recapture their original definitions.

# IMPORTING/EXPORTING

## POST-PROCESSING

"Post-processing" is a general term referring to any use of an AutoCAD drawing file, or files created from or extracted from a drawing file outside of AutoCAD.

Various types of post-processing include:

> Material lists generated from attribute extract files (see Appendix C)
>
> Area and energy calculations for architectural drawings
>
> Generation of tool-path programs for CAM applications
>
> Conversions to files usable by mainframe systems
>
> Finite element analysis
>
> Solids modeling
>
> AutoSHADE

Post-processing can be performed either on drawing interchange files created with the DXFOUT or IGESOUT commands, or on CDF, SDF or DXF format extract files created with the ATTEXT command.

The *AutoCAD Reference Manual* contains a detailed description of the structure of a drawing interchange file, as well as sample BASIC programs that extract information from drawing interchange files. Also see Appendix C in this guide for sample BASIC and AutoLISP programs that post-process attribute files.

The AutoCAD program files also contain some sample BASIC programs that you can run to compile information from extract files. These programs contain documentation that can be listed from within BASICA. The programs include ATTEXT.BAS and BILLMAT.BAS. To load a BASIC program from DOS,

> Enter **BASICA** (loads the Advanced BASIC language).
>
> Enter **LOAD XXXXXX** (loads the BASIC program XXXXXX).
>
> To read the documentation, enter **LIST**, then use **CTRL-NUMLOCK** to stop the scrolling (see "DOS Commands" in Chapter 1).
>
> To run the program, enter **RUN**.

# HANDLES

**Enables or disables entity handles**

A handle is a hexadecimal number assigned to an entity in a drawing. To see an entity's handle, simply **LIST** that entity while handles are enabled. Since handles are output to DXF and IGES files and are available to AutoLISP, you can use them in both internal and external programs, including database programs.

When you start a new drawing, handles are disabled unless you've used a prototype drawing in which the handles are enabled.

Usually, each entity in a drawing keeps its handle for the life of the drawing. That is, handles are saved with the drawing so that any given entity has the same handle during all editing sessions. If you're using handles to link your drawing entities to an external database, it's important for each entity to retain its original handle.

*Warning:* if you disable handles and then re-enable them, each entity in the drawing is assigned a new handle—one that's different from its old handle.

The HANDLES command begins by indicating whether handles are disabled or enabled, and (if enabled) what the next hex number will be. When prompted,

> Enter **ON** to enable handles. When handles are enabled, all existing entities in the drawing (including blocks, attributes, and polyline vertices) are automatically given a unique hex number as a handle. The numbers start with 1 (hex). Then, whether you create an entity directly with one of the drawing commands or indirectly with one of the editing commands, each new entity added to the drawing also receives a handle.

> Enter **DESTROY** to remove all present handles and stop adding handles to new entities. The entire word DESTROY must be entered. The warning that appears contains a phrase that you must enter to complete the process.

> To make it less likely for you to accidentally destroy your handles, the phrase is randomly selected from six possible phrases, including I AGREE, GO AHEAD, DESTROY HANDLES, PRETTY PLEASE, MAKE MY DATA and UNHANDLE THAT DATABASE.

> When handles are disabled, the hex number is removed from every entity in the drawing. Be careful with the **U** and **UNDO** commands, which

will destroy handles without a warning if you undo a HANDLES ON sequence.

The system variable HANDLES holds **0** if handles are disabled, **1** if they are enabled, and is a read-only variable.

All of the drawing commands affect handles as they create entities. The following editing commands also affect handles because they also create entities: ARRAY, CHAMFER, FILLET, MIRROR and retain old entity, and OFFSET. The following editing commands do not affect handles: MOVE, MIRROR and delete old entity, SCALE, ROTATE, CHANGE, EXTEND and STRETCH. BREAK and TRIM affect handles only when they create new entities by separating one entity into two.

When an entity is erased, its handle is discarded and not reused. When a block is exploded, the block's handle is discarded and the individual parts of the block are assigned new handles.

The **WBLOCK** command discards handles and sets the HANDLES system variable to 0 in the WBLOCK output file. If you use the **INSERT** command or the **DXFIN** command to add entities to your drawing, those entities are assigned new handles in the present drawing (assuming handles are enabled in the present drawing).

If the **DXFIN** command is used to create a new drawing from scratch, then handles are enabled if they weren't already, and the handles in the DXF file are adopted in the current drawing. If the **IGESIN** command is used to create a new drawing, new handles are assigned.

The handle is associated with group code **5** both in a DXF file and in the association list obtained from the AutoLISP entget function. You can't use the AutoLISP entmod function to change an entity handle.

## DXFOUT

**Creates a drawing interchange file (ASCII text file) from an existing drawing**

Drawing interchange files can be used by other post-processing programs for a wide range of applications (see "Post-processing" above).

Files created by the DXFOUT command have the extension .DXF.

When prompted, enter the name of the intended interchange file (without the .DXF extension). Or, press <RETURN> to accept the default (drawing name) as the interchange file name.

Then enter the precision (**0 to 16**) for floating point numbers. Or, enter **E** to select entities to be written to the DXF file. When finished selecting entities, you'll be prompted again to enter the precision.

## DXFIN

**Creates an AutoCAD drawing file
from a drawing interchange file**

If you use the DXFIN command as the very first command in the drawing editor, the drawing interchange file will be converted into an AutoCAD drawing. If you use the DXFIN command after you've already created part of a drawing, the entities from the drawing interchange file will be added to the drawing.

When prompted, enter the name of the drawing interchange file (without the .DXF extension).

## IGESOUT

**Creates an IGES file from an
AutoCAD drawing**

When prompted, enter the name for the intended IGES (Initial Graphics Exchange Standard) file. AutoCAD will give this file the extension .IGS.

## IGESIN

**Converts an IGES file into an
AutoCAD drawing**

When prompted, enter the name of the IGES file (without the .IGS extension).

# CHAPTER 39

# AUTOLISP PROGRAMS

## AUTOLISP PROGRAMS

Several AutoLISP program files are supplied with AutoCAD on the release disks. These programs are useful enhancements to the regular drawing and editing commands.

First, load the programs with the AutoLISP **load** function. Let's assume you want to load the CL program (in the CL.LSP file), which has been copied onto the \ACAD directory. (You're currently logged into a different directory and you're in the drawing editor.) Enter:

```
(load "\\acad\\cl")
```

Then, to run the program, enter **CL**.

Here are some of the AutoLISP programs found on the release disks:

**REF.LSP**—You can enter (**ref**) in response to a prompt for a point. Then use relative coordinates to indicate a desired point.

**CL.LSP**—Draws horizontal and vertical center lines through the center of a circle.

**SPIRAL.LSP**—Creates a 2D spiral.

**SLOT.LSP**—Creates holes or slots for 3D surface models, including invisible corner patches.

**SSX.LSP**—Lets you select entities by their common property. You can enter (**ssx**) at the command prompt to create a selection set for later use, or enter (**ssx**) in response to the **Select objects:** prompt. You can select all entities that are a certain type, a certain color or line type, on a certain layer, use a certain text style, have a certain block name or a certain thickness. Will not find colors or line types determined by layer assignments (the color or line type must be explicitly assigned to the entity).

**CHGTEXT.LSP**—Lets you select one or more lines of text, then enter an existing string and a replacement string. Will replace strings embedded in longer words unless you place a space before and/or after the string.

**ASCTEXT.LSP**—Places a text file in the drawing, allowing various modifications including varying the line spacing, including only selected lines from the file, and creating columns. (Lines in the file must be shorter than the distance between columns; the program won't break lines that are too long.)

**DELLAYER.LSP**—Deletes all entities on a specified layer. The layer remains; just the entities are deleted.

**LEXPLODE.LSP**—This is an adaptation of the regular EXPLODE command. When you use EXPLODE to explode dimensions or hatching, the entities are placed on layer 0. In contrast, LEXPLODE places the entities on the same layer that the block or hatching was originally placed on.

**CHFACE.LSP**—Moves the vertex of a 3DFACE.

**EDGE.LSP**—Lets you select edges on 3DFACES and change them from visible to invisible, or vice versa. Lets you highlight invisible edges so they can be selected.

**AXROT.LSP**—Rotates selected objects around any basepoint. The axis of rotation can be parallel to the X, Y or Z axis.

**3DARRAY.LSP**—Makes 3D arrays "rectangular," or polar. A rectangular array has rows, columns and levels. A polar array can revolve around any axis, even one that's oblique to the current X, Y and Z axes.

**3D.LSP**—Lets you construct the following 3D objects: box, cone, spherical dome, spherical dish, full sphere, mesh, pyramid, torus or wedge. Available under "3D" on the screen menu.

**FPLOT.LSP**—Plots the function of two variables. See the *AutoLISP Programmers Reference.*

# AUTOSHADE

## AutoSHADE

Even though AutoSHADE is listed in one of the pull-down menus, it's a separate software package that must be installed before it can be used. See the AutoSHADE manual for information on installing and using AutoSHADE.

AutoSHADE is designed to post-process a 3D AutoCAD drawing and produce a shaded rendering. Its normal input is an AutoCAD drawing in the form of a "filmroll" file (.FLM), in which camera and light source locations have been established.

The shaded renderings can be saved in rendering files (.RND). Various adjustments can be made to all of the typical photographic factors including camera location, focal length, light intensity, interplay between direct and ambient lighting, reflectivity of surfaces, clipping, etc. In addition, stereo pair generation is provided—this takes advantage of depth perception.

However, if you want to use AutoSHADE for a quick, nonperspective rendering of a 3D AutoCAD drawing without bothering with camera locations, light sources, etc., use the procedure below. This procedure assumes that AutoSHADE has been installed in the same directory as AutoCAD.

While in AutoCAD,

> Draw any 3D objects.
>
> Select a viewpoint.
>
> Enter **(load "ashade")**. If your current directory is different than the directory holding the file ASHADE.LSP, you'll need to include the path; for example: (load "\\acad\\ashade").
>
> Enter **FILMROLL**, then enter the filmroll file name.
>
> Exit AutoCAD.

At the DOS prompt, enter **SHADE** to start AutoSHADE.

While in AutoSHADE,

> Pick **File**, then **Open**, then enter the file name.
>
> Pick **Display**, then **Fast Shade** or **Full Shade**.

## TABLE OF CONTENTS

## GENERAL INSTRUCTIONS AND KEYSTROKE INSTRUCTIONS

Several of the exercises in this appendix are organized into two columns: general instructions and keystroke instructions. If possible, you should try to do as much of each exercise as you can by following the general instructions only. If you get stuck, or if you want to examine one way to carry out the general instructions, then look at the keystroke instructions.

The keystroke instructions are written as though you were entering every command and locating every point from the keyboard. Naturally, you may find it easier to enter the commands by using the screen menu, the pull-down menus, or the tablet overlay. Also, since you'll usually set SNAP to an appropriate spacing, you may want to enter most locations with the pointer.

As usual, when entering DOS commands or AutoCAD commands from the keyboard, you need to press <RETURN> after typing each command, each pair of coordinates, etc. A carriage return is indicated in the keystroke instructions as <CR>. Most lines in the keystroke instructions have one <CR>, but in the drawing exercises some lines have two <CR>s and a few have none.

## DOS EXERCISE: FILE MANAGEMENT

This exercise shows how to use certain DOS commands to manage AutoCAD files. Each of these commands is explained under "DOS Commands" in Chapter 1.

You'll need a floppy diskette that's either unformatted or newly formatted.

This exercise is organized into general instructions and keystroke instructions (see the explanation above). The <RETURN> key is indicated in the keystroke instructions as <CR>.

Take time to think about what's happening as you use each of these DOS commands. Mastering these basic commands will form a good foundation for learning variations on these and other commands later.

We're assuming that your system is set up and ready to run, with the necessary DOS program files loaded onto the hard disk (drive C:) and a path installed that includes the directory holding the DOS files.

Naturally, we don't want to change any of the AutoCAD program files or any of the drawing files you might already have on your computer. So, we'll work in a newly created subdirectory, and on a newly formatted floppy diskette.

If your computer is turned off, make sure the floppy disk drive (**drive A:**) is empty, then turn it on. With drive A: empty, the system will boot from the hard disk (**drive C:**), which is what we want it to do.

Soon after your system is turned on, it should display a DOS prompt. The prompt may look something like this: C> or it may look something like this: C:\DRAWINGS>. If a DOS prompt appears, then you're ready to begin at instruction number 1 below.

If a menu appears (and a DOS prompt doesn't appear) then you'll need to access DOS. Look for a menu item that reads **Return to DOS** or **System** or **DOS prompt** and select it. If no such item is listed on the menu, you'll have to escape from the menu a different way. Press the **ESC** key, or hold down the **CTRL** key and tap the **BREAK** key.

Remember that all DOS command lines have the same basic syntax (structure):

COMMANDspaceARGUMENT1spaceARGUMENT2

First, the DOS command itself.

Then a space and the first argument (if there is one).

Then a space and the second argument (if there is one).

There must be at least one space between the command and each argument, but no spaces within arguments. Some commands don't need any arguments, and some commands need only one argument. All DOS commands and file names can be typed in either upper- or lowercase letters.

## SETUP

**General Instructions:**

1. Establish a prompt that will display the current drive letter and the current directory (path).

**Keystroke Instructions:**

```
PROMPT $P$G <CR>
```

2. Look at the DOS prompt to see what directory you're currently in. If you aren't already in the root directory on drive C:, go there. In other words, make C:\ the current (default) directory. The backslash stands for the root directory.

If the DOS prompt says C:\> (and nothing else), you're already in the root directory on drive C:. If not, enter CD \ <CR>.

3. Create a new directory called PRACTICE immediately under the root directory. If the computer says it can't create this directory, use a different name.

MD \PRACTICE <CR>
If needed, substitute a different name for PRACTICE.

4. Move to your new PRACTICE directory.

CD \PRACTICE <CR>
The prompt will indicate that you're in the \PRACTICE directory.

5. Get a listing of the files in this directory. There should be only two housekeeping files, the "." file and the ". ." file. This is considered an empty directory.

DIR <CR>
Look at the top of the listing. The second line tells you what drive or directory the listing is from.

6. Enter the current date.

DATE <CR>
The computer's current date will be displayed. If it's correct, simply press <CR> when prompted for the new date. If the date is incorrect, enter the current date in the same format that the date appears in the system's display. For example, enter 2-14-89 <CR>.

7. Enter the current time.

TIME <CR>
The computer's current time will be displayed. If it's correct, simply press <CR> when prompted for the new time. If the time is incorrect, enter the current time in the same

format that the time appears in the system's display, remembering to use 24-hour (military) format. For example, enter `14:25 <CR>`.

Remember that the syntax (structure) of the COPY command normally in-cludes two arguments after the COPY command. The first argument is the "from" part of the command line—the source file(s). The second argument is the "to" part of the command line—the target.

8. Use the COPY command to create a file called X that con-tains one line of 10 X's.

```
COPY CON X <CR>
XXXXXXXXXX <CR>
^Z  <CR>
```
You can get the ^Z with F6 or CTRL-Z.

9. Get a directory listing to make sure this file exists.

```
DIR <CR>
```

10. Display the contents of this file.

```
TYPE X <CR>
```

11. Use the COPY command to create a file called Y that con-tains one line of 10 Y's.

```
COPY CON Y <CR>
YYYYYYYYYY <CR>
^Z  <CR>
```
You can get the ^Z with F6 or CTRL-Z.

12. Get a directory listing to make sure this file exists. The listing should include the files X and Y.

```
DIR <CR>
```

13. Display the contents of this file.

```
TYPE Y <CR>
```

14. Change the name of X to XLINE.

```
RENAME X XLINE <CR>
```

15. Change the name of Y to YLINE.

```
RENAME Y YLINE <CR>
```

16. Get a directory listing to make sure both files have been renamed. The listing should include the files XLINE and YLINE.

```
DIR <CR>
```

17. Use the COPY command to duplicate the contents of file XLINE under the name X.DOC.

```
COPY XLINE X.DOC <CR>
```

18. Use the COPY command to duplicate the contents of file YLINE under the name Y.DOC.

```
COPY YLINE Y.DOC <CR>
```

19. Get a directory listing to make sure all four files are there. The listing should include XLINE, YLINE, X.DOC and Y.DOC.

```
DIR <CR>
```

20. Display the contents of each file.

```
TYPE XLINE <CR>
TYPE YLINE <CR>
TYPE X.DOC <CR>
TYPE Y.DOC <CR>
```

## COPYING AND RENAMING FILES ON VARIOUS DRIVES

For this section of the exercise you'll need an empty, formatted, floppy diskette in drive A:.

To tell whether a floppy diskette is formatted, place it in drive A: and enter `DIR A: <CR>`.

> If you get an error message such as **Not ready reading drive A:**, the diskette is probably not formatted.

> If you get the message **File not found,** the diskette is formatted, but empty.

> If you get a listing of one or more files, the diskette is not only formatted, but also has files on it that you probably don't want to destroy by formatting it.

If you need to format the diskette, place it in drive A: and then enter FORMAT A: <CR>. The **A:** in the previous command line is very important because it tells the computer which disk to format. *Remember:* if you format a diskette that already has files on it, you destroy all those files.

21. While you're still in the C:\PRACTICE directory, copy XLINE to the diskette in drive A:.

    COPY XLINE A: <CR>

22. While you're still in the C:\PRACTICE directory, copy YLINE to the diskette in drive A:.

    COPY YLINE A: <CR>

23. Get a listing of the files on the diskette in drive A:. The listing should include the files XLINE and YLINE.

    DIR A: <CR>

24. Move over to drive A: (make drive A: the current drive).

    A: <CR>
    The prompt will indicate that you are now on drive A:.

25. While you're on drive A:, copy file X.DOC to drive A:.

    COPY  C:\PRACTICE\X.DOC <CR>

26. Also copy file Y.DOC to drive A:.

    COPY  C:\PRACTICE\Y.DOC <CR>

27. Get a listing of the files on the diskette in drive A:. The listing should include the four files XLINE, YLINE, X.DOC and Y.DOC.

    DIR <CR>

28. Get a listing of all the files with the extension .DOC.

    DIR *.DOC <CR>

29. Rename all four files as follows:
    XLINE becomes FILE1
    YLINE becomes FILE2
    X.DOC becomes FILE3
    Y.DOC becomes FILE4
    Then get a directory listing.

```
RENAME XLINE FILE1 <CR>
RENAME YLINE FILE2 <CR>
RENAME X.DOC FILE3 <CR>
RENAME Y.DOC FILE4 <CR>
DIR <CR>
```

30. Copy FILE1 to C:\PRACTICE.

```
COPY FILE1 C:\PRACTICE <CR>
```

31. Erase FILE2, then get a directory listing. The listing should include FILE1, FILE3 and FILE4.

```
ERASE FILE2 <CR>
```
You can use DEL instead of ERASE.
```
DIR <CR>
```

32. Move back to C:\PRACTICE and then get a directory listing of C:\PRACTICE. The listing should include XLINE, YLINE, X.DOC, Y.DOC and FILE1.

```
C: <CR>
DIR <CR>
```

33. Erase FILE1 from drive A:, then get a directory listing of drive A:. The listing should include FILE3 and FILE4.

```
ERASE A:FILE1 <CR>
DIR A: <CR>
```

34. Using wild cards, copy FILE3 and FILE4 from drive A: to C:\PRACTICE, then get a directory listing of C:\PRAC-TICE. The listing should include XLINE, YLINE, X.DOC, Y.DOC, FILE1, FILE3 and FILE4.

```
COPY A:*.* <CR>
DIR <CR>
```

35. Get a wide listing of all the files.

```
DIR /W <CR>
```

36. Get a listing of files beginning with the letter F.

```
DIR F*.* <CR>
```

37. Get a listing of just the file X.DOC. (Listing just one file can be handy when a directory holds too many files to scan visually.)

```
DIR X.DOC <CR>
```

38. Get a sorted listing of all the     `DIR | SORT <CR>`
    files.

39. Using wild cards, erase all the     `ERASE Y*.* <CR>`
    files that begin with Y, then get    `DIR <CR>`
    a directory listing. (The listing
    should include XLINE, X.DOC,
    FILE1, FILE3 and FILE4.)

## CLEANUP

40. Erase all files on C:\PRACTICE.      `ERASE *.* <CR>`
                                         When the computer asks if you are
                                         sure, check the prompt to make
                                         sure you're in the \PRACTICE direc-
                                         tory, then enter
                                         `Y <CR>.`

41. Move to C:\ (the root direc-         `CD \ <CR>`
    tory).

42. Remove the \PRACTICE direc-          `RD \PRACTICE <CR>`
    tory.

## SETUP EXERCISE

Drawing setup in AutoCAD can be simple or complex. The simplest setup involves using the default sheet that appears when you first enter the drawing
editor. This sheet is 12x9 inches, uses decimal units with GRID and SNAP both
set to 1, and has one layer and one text style. Naturally, this setup is suitable
for only certain types of drawings.

In this exercise you'll use LIMITS, GRID, SNAP and other commands, and in
the process you'll create four separate drawings that you can use as prototype
drawings. Three of these drawings use inches and the fourth uses millimeters.
Each one will have a simple border drawn around the edge of the limits.

| Sheet | Size | Format size | Orientation |
|-------|------|-------------|-------------|
| SHEETA.DWG | Size A | 10 x 7.5 inches | Horizontal |
| SHEETV.DWG | Size A | 7.5 x 10 inches | Vertical |
| SHEETB.DWG | Size B | 16 x 10 inches | Horizontal |
| SHEETBM.DWG | Size B | 406 x 254 mm | Horizontal |

These four sheets will come in handy as prototype drawings for many of the other drawing exercises in this guide. For example, when you're starting a new drawing (you selected 1 at the main menu), and you want to use one of the prototype drawings, simply place the name of the prototype drawing after an equal sign when you enter the name of the new drawing, using the format XXXXXXXX=SHEETA. See "Starting a New Drawing" in Chapter 2.

If you need to set up prototype drawings for scales other than 1=1, see the chart in "Setting Limits" in Chapter 17.

Prototype drawings let you avoid repeating the same setup procedure every time you begin a new drawing. A prototype drawing might include the settings listed below. All of the settings, which you normally establish at the beginning of a drawing, can also be changed any time during the drawing/editing process. You can also edit a prototype drawing at any time.

You should avoid using "Setup" on the root screen menu for the following reasons. First, as a general rule your drawing limits should correspond with the format size (sheet size minus borders), but "Setup" sets limits at the sheet size. Second, two of the options in "Setup," decimal units and scientific units, produce incorrect limits whenever you choose a scale other than full scale. Third, "Setup" doesn't go far enough; for example, it doesn't adjust the grid or snap for drawing to various scales.

A full-blown prototype drawing might include all of the following settings:

1. Type of linear unit and accuracy of readout, type of angular unit and accuracy of readout, direction of zero angle and positive rotation

2. Limits—lower left corner and upper right corner

3. Grid spacing

4. Snap style and spacing

5. Axis spacing

6. Layers and associated line types and colors

7. Dimensioning variables as determined by the final plotting scale

8. Line-type scale as determined by the final plotting scale

9.   Default text height as determined by the final plotting scale

10.  Text styles as needed

11.  Predefined blocks as needed

Since this is a beginning exercise, we're assuming that you haven't yet learned to use layers, dimensioning variables, text styles or blocks. Thus, the prototype drawings created here won't include any of these items. Later, when you learn to use them, you can edit your prototype drawing to suit your needs.

Our approach will be as follows: We'll start a "junk" drawing and establish various settings for Sheet A, then save the drawing under the name SHEETA. Then we'll change the settings for each of the next sheets and save the drawing under the appropriate name.

Each plotter and printer is different. If your plotter or printer has maximum drawing limits that differ from the format sizes listed above, you'll want to substitute the appropriate numbers as you go through this exercise.

This exercise is organized into general instructions and keystroke instructions (see the explanation at the beginning of this appendix).

## Creating Sheet A (Size A, horizontal orientation, inches)

| General instructions: | Keystroke instructions: |
|---|---|
| 1.   Start a new drawing called JUNK. | At the main menu<br>1 <CR><br>JUNK <CR> |
| 2.   Set units as follows:<br>      Linear units—decimal units<br>          with four-place readout<br>      Angular units—decimal<br>          angles with four-place<br>          readout<br>      Zero angle—East (3 o'clock),<br>          with positive angles<br>          rotating counterclockwise | UNITS <CR><br>2 <CR><br>4 <CR><br>1 <CR><br>4 <CR><br>0 <CR><br>N <CR><br>Press F1 to return to the graphics<br>screen. |
| 3.   Set the limits at 10 x 7.5 (leave lower left corner at 0,0 and set upper right corner at 10,7.5). | LIMITS <CR><br>0,0 <CR><br>10,7.5 <CR> |

4.  Do a ZOOM All.

```
ZOOM <CR>
A <CR>
```

5.  Set grid at .5.

```
GRID <CR>
.5 <CR>
```

6.  Set snap at .0625.

```
SNAP <CR>
.0625 <CR>
```

As you move the cursor around the screen, the coordinate readout in the status line will jump in increments of .0625. Press **F6** if your coordinate readout is frozen.

7.  Set AXIS at 2.

```
AXIS <CR>
2 <CR>
```

8.  Draw a line around the limits.

```
LINE <CR>
0,0 <CR>
10,0 <CR>
10,7.5 <CR>
0,7.5 <CR>
C <CR>
```

28. Save this drawing under the name SHEETA.

```
SAVE <CR>
SHEETA <CR>
```

## Creating Sheet V (Size A, vertical orientation, inches)

10. Erase the border line.

```
ERASE <CR>
Pick the four lines
<CR>
```

11. Change limits to 7.5 x 10 and do a ZOOM All.

```
LIMITS <CR>
0,0 <CR>
7.5,10 <CR>
ZOOM <CR>
A <CR>
```

12. Draw a line around the border.

```
LINE <CR>
0,0 <CR>
7.5,0 <CR>
7.5,10 <CR>
```

```
                                    0,10 <CR>
                                    C <CR>
```

13. Save this drawing under the      SAVE <CR>
    name SHEETV.                      SHEETV <CR>

## Creating Sheet B (Size B, horizontal orientation, inches)

14. Erase the border line.            ERASE <CR>
                                      Pick the four lines
                                      <CR>

15. Change limits to 16 x 10 and      LIMITS <CR>
    do a ZOOM All.                    0,0 <CR>
                                      16,10 <CR>
                                      ZOOM <CR>
                                      A <CR>

16. Change GRID to 1 and SNAP         GRID <CR>
    to .125.                          1 <CR>
                                      SNAP <CR>
                                      .125 <CR>

17. Draw a line around the border.    LINE <CR>
                                      0,0 <CR>
                                      16,0 <CR>
                                      16,10 <CR>
                                      0,10 <CR>
                                      C <CR>

18. Save this drawing under the       SAVE <CR>
    name SHEETB.                      SHEETB <CR>

## Creating Sheet BM (Size B, horizontal orientation, millimeters)

19. Erase the border line.            ERASE <CR>
                                      Pick the four lines
                                      <CR>

20. Change grid to 10, axis to 50, and snap to 1.

```
GRID <CR>
10 <CR>
AXIS <CR>
50 <CR>
SNAP <CR>
1 <CR>
```

21. Change limits to 406 x 254 and do a ZOOM ALL.

```
LIMITS <CR>
0,0 <CR>
406,254 <CR>
ZOOM <CR>
A <CR>
```

22. Change units to three-place readout for linear units.

```
UNITS <CR>
2 <CR>
3 <CR>
<CR> <CR> <CR> <CR>
```
Press F1 to return to graphics screen

23. Draw a line around the border.

```
LINE <CR>
0,0 <CR>
406,0 <CR>
406,254 <CR>
0,254 <CR>
C <CR>
```

24. Save this drawing under the name SHEETBM.

```
SAVE <CR>
SHEETBM <CR>
```

25. Get out of the JUNK drawing.

```
QUIT <CR>
Y <CR>
```

## Listing the drawings

26. Get a listing of the four drawings you've just created while you're still in AutoCAD (they'll have a .DWG extension).

At the main menu
```
6 <CR>
1 <CR> <CR>
```
<CR> to return to File Utility menu
0 <CR> to return to main menu

27. Exit AutoCAD and get another listing of your drawing files.

At the main menu
0 <CR>
at the DOS prompt
DIR *.DWG <CR>

# LINES

## LINE EXERCISE 1

In this exercise, you'll draw the two picture frames shown below. The exercise uses two methods of point entry—absolute, and relative (both relative rectangular and relative polar). Use the keyboard to type in all commands and coordinates.

This exercise is organized into general instructions and keystroke instructions (see the explanation at the beginning of this appendix). The **<RETURN>** key is indicated in the keystroke instructions as **<CR>**.

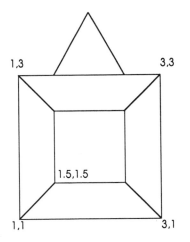
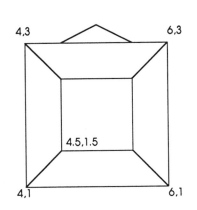

**General instructions:**

1. Start a new drawing called LINEX1.

**Keystroke instructions:**

At the main menu
1 <CR>
LINEX1 <CR>

2. Draw a two-inch square for the outside of the left frame, with lower left corner at 1,1. Use absolute coordinates.

```
LINE <CR>
1,1 <CR>
3,1 <CR>
3,3 <CR>
1,3 <CR>
1,1 <CR><CR>
```

3. Draw a one-inch square for the inside of the left frame, with lower left corner at 1.5,1.5. Again, use absolute coordinates.

```
LINE <CR>
1.5,1.5 <CR>
2.5,1.5 <CR>
2.5,2.5 <CR>
1.5,2.5 <CR>
C <CR>
```

4. Redraw the screen.

```
REDRAW <CR>
or press F7 twice
```

5. Draw a two-inch square for the outside of the right frame, with lower left corner at 4,1. Use relative rectangular coordinates.

```
LINE <CR>
4,1 <CR>
@2,0 <CR>
@0,2 <CR>
@-2,0 <CR>
@0,-2 <CR><CR>
```

6. Draw a one-inch square for the inside of the right frame, with lower left corner at 4.5,1.5. Use relative rectangular coordinates.

```
LINE <CR>
4.5,1.5 <CR>
@1,0 <CR>
@0,1 <CR>
@-1,0 <CR>
C <CR>
```

7. Redraw the screen.

```
REDRAW <CR>
or press F7 twice
```

8. On the left frame, draw the four diagonal lines connecting the corners of the larger square to the corners of the smaller square. Use relative rectangular coordinates. Each line extends .5 inch in both the X and the Y directions.

```
LINE <CR>
1,1 <CR>
@.5,.5 <CR><CR>
LINE <CR>
3,1 <CR>
@-.5,.5 <CR><CR>
LINE <CR>
3,3 <CR>
@-.5,-.5 <CR><CR>
```

```
LINE <CR>
1,3 <CR>
@.5,-.5 <CR><CR>
```

9.  On the right frame, draw the four diagonal lines connecting the corners of the larger square to the corners of the smaller square. Use relative polar coordinates. The length of each line is .7071.

```
LINE <CR>
4,1 <CR>
@.7071<45 <CR><CR>
LINE <CR>
6,1 <CR>
@.7071<135 <CR><CR>
LINE <CR>
6,3 <CR>
@.7071<-135 <CR><CR>
LINE <CR>
4,3 <CR>
@.7071<-45 <CR><CR>
```

10. Redraw the screen.

```
REDRAW <CR>
```
or press F7 twice

11. Draw the string holding the left frame. Both sides of the string meet the top of the frame .5 inch from the edge, are 1 inch long, and are 60° from horizontal. Use relative polar coordinates.

```
LINE <CR>
1.5,3 <CR>
@1<60 <CR>
@1<-60 <CR><CR>
```

12. Draw the string holding the right frame. Both sides of the string meet the top of the frame .5 inch from the edge, and extend .25 inch above the frame. Use relative rectangular coordinates.

```
LINE <CR>
4.5,3 <CR>
@.5,.25 <CR>
@.5,-.25 <CR><CR>
```

13. Redraw the screen.

```
REDRAW <CR>
```
or press F7 twice

14. Save your drawing and return to the main menu.

```
END <CR>
```

## LINE EXERCISE 2

This exercise emphasizes the use of the pointer, along with three drawing aids—snap, ortho, and the coordinate readout on the status line. You'll want to use the default limits of **0,0** (lower left corner) to **12,9** (upper right corner).

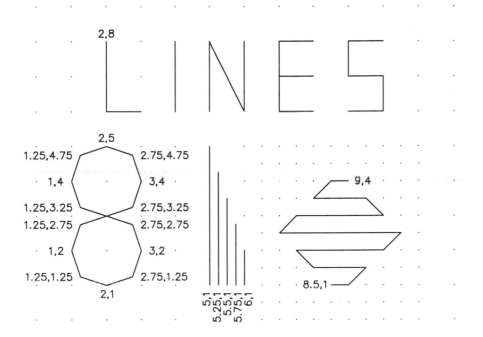

### Drawing the "LINES"

Set **GRID** at **1**. The grid will appear on the screen automatically when you enter **GRID** and then enter the spacing. (If you use the Settings—Drawing Aids dialogue box, the grid will appear on the screen only if you turn it on in the dialogue box.) Later you can turn it on and off using **F7**.

Set **SNAP** at **1**. The snap will be turned on automatically when you enter **SNAP** and then enter the spacing. (If you use the Settings—Drawing Aids dialogue box, SNAP will be turned on only if you turn it on in the dialogue box.) Later you can turn it on and off using **F9**.

**ORTHO (F8)** can be on or off.

Start by entering the **LINE** command, then move the pointer to the appropriate location so the coordinate readout displays 2.0000,8.0000. You may need to press **F6** once or twice to get the coordinate readout to display absolute coordinates. As you draw the lines, use the grid points to guide you in locating each endpoint.

### Drawing the figure eight

Keep **GRID** at **1**, turned on. Set **SNAP** at **.25**. Turn **ORTHO (F8)** off.

As you draw the lines that make up the figure eight, watch the coordinate readout in the status line to make sure your pointer is at the right location.

### Drawing the vertical lines

The lengths of the lines are **4, 3.25, 2.5, 1.75** and **1**.

Keep **GRID** at **1**. Keep **SNAP** at **.25**. Use **F8** to turn **ORTHO** on.

Start at the bottom of each line and watch the coordinate readout to see when your line is the proper length. You may need to press **F6** once or twice to get the coordinate readout to display distance and angle. As you move the pointer up, the vertical distance must be exact, but the pointer (crosshair) can be somewhat left or right of the desired endpoint, since you have ORTHO turned on.

### Drawing the zig-zag

Set **GRID** at **.5**. Set **SNAP** at **.5**. Turn **ORTHO (F8)** on and off as needed.

## SHEET A

If you've already made the Sheet A prototype drawing in the setup exercise, simply edit that drawing (use item 2 at the main menu) and skip to the section below entitled "Draw the left . . . ."

If you're starting from scratch, begin at "Setup" below.

- If you have already created SHEETA in the Setup exercise, you can simply add the title-block to that prototype drawing.
- After this sheet is drawn, it can be used as a prototype drawing.
- If you need help drawing the lines in this border and title-block, see "One Way to Draw the Lines in Sheet A."
- If you know how to use layers, you may want to draw this on layer 4 (see chart under LAYER command).
- If you know how to create text styles: The text in the title-block is a compressed style (.7 width factor), .100 high, using the TXT font.
- Suggested height of letters when filling in title-block: Drawing title .2 inch (5mm), All other lines in title-block .12 inch (3mm).

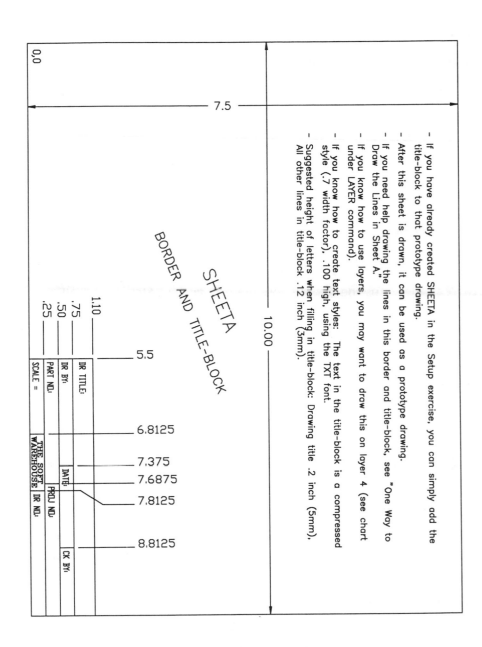

SHEETA
BORDER AND TITLE-BLOCK

### Setup

Start a new drawing and call it **SHEETA**.

Set **GRID** at **.5**.

Set **AXIS** at **2**.

Set **SNAP** at **.0625**. This will let you snap to most of the endpoints.

Set **LIMITS** with lower left corner at **0,0** and upper right corner at **10,7.5**.

Do a **ZOOM All**.

### Draw the border

Use **F8** to turn **ORTHO** on. Then enter the **LINE** command and use the pointer to draw the bottom border line from **0,0** to **10,0**. (You can press **F6** once or twice so the status line displays absolute coordinates.) Stay in the LINE command and draw the right and top lines. Watch the coordinate readout in the status line as you draw. Then enter **C** to close the border. Redraw the screen (press **F7** twice).

### Draw the left and top edges of the title block

Leave **ORTHO** on. Enter the **LINE** command and use the pointer to locate **5.5,0**. Then enter relative coordinates **@0,1.1**. Then use the pointer to draw the top edge of the title block extending to the right border. Then exit the LINE command. Redraw the screen.

### Draw the remaining lines

With **ORTHO** and **SNAP** still on, use the pointer to draw the three remaining horizontal lines and the short vertical lines in the title block. Redraw the screen.

### Save your drawing

Enter **END**.

## LINE EXERCISE 3

Although the POLYGON command provides an easier way to draw each of the polygons below, this exercise will give you practice in using the LINE command with relative polar coordinates.

For each figure below, start with a horizontal line from left to right of the specified length. Then use relative polar coordinates to locate each following point.

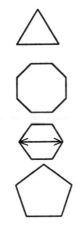

1. Draw an equilateral triangle **1"** on each side. (Enter any point, then enter @1<0, then **@1<120**, then **"C."**)

2. Draw an octagon **.75"** on each side.

3. Draw a hexagon **2"** across corners.

4. Draw a pentagon **1.5"** across sides.

5. Draw an equilateral triangle **1"** tall. Length of side = **1.1547**

6. Draw a hexagon **2"** across flats.

7. Draw an octagon **4"** across flats. Length of side = **1.6569**

8. Draw a **1"** square rotated **45˚**, then draw its diagonals. Length of diagonal = 1.4142

9. Draw a five-pointed star using **2"** lines. Point angle = **36˚**

# 2D FIGURES

## Circle Exercise

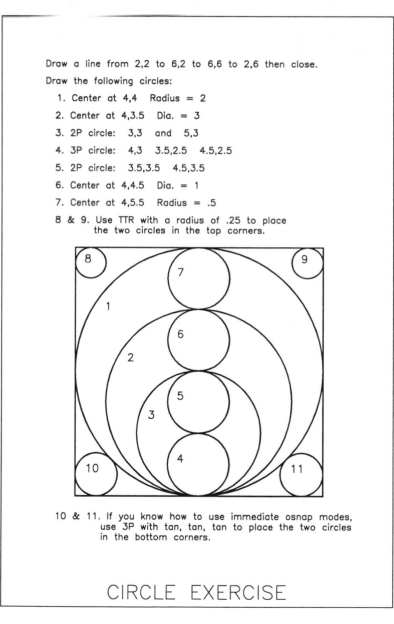

Draw a line from 2,2 to 6,2 to 6,6 to 2,6 then close.

Draw the following circles:

1. Center at 4,4    Radius = 2
2. Center at 4,3.5    Dia. = 3
3. 2P circle:    3,3    and    5,3
4. 3P circle:    4,3    3.5,2.5    4.5,2.5
5. 2P circle:    3.5,3.5    4.5,3.5
6. Center at 4,4.5    Dia. = 1
7. Center at 4,5.5    Radius = .5

8 & 9. Use TTR with a radius of .25 to place the two circles in the top corners.

10 & 11. If you know how to use immediate osnap modes, use 3P with tan, tan, tan to place the two circles in the bottom corners.

CIRCLE EXERCISE

## Plate Profile

If you've already created Sheet A, you can use it as a prototype for this plate drawing. To do so, at the main menu enter **1** to begin a new drawing, then when you're prompted for the name of the drawing, enter **PLATE=SHEETA**. If you use Sheet A as a prototype, you can skip the setup section below (except SNAP).

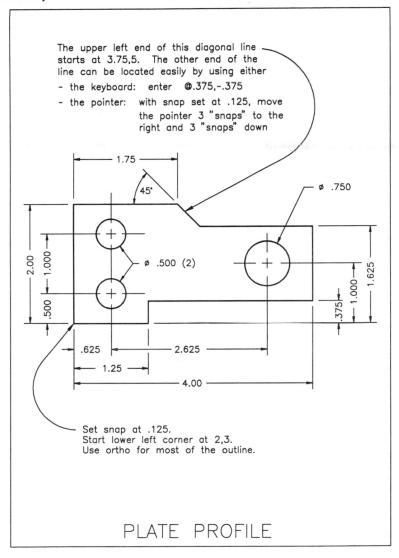

The upper left end of this diagonal line starts at 3.75,5. The other end of the line can be located easily by using either

- the keyboard:   enter   @.375,-.375
- the pointer:   with snap set at .125, move the pointer 3 "snaps" to the right and 3 "snaps" down

Set snap at .125.
Start lower left corner at 2,3.
Use ortho for most of the outline.

PLATE  PROFILE

### Setup

Set **GRID** at **.5.**

Set **AXIS** at **2.**

Set **SNAP** at **.125.** This lets you snap to all points.

Set the **LIMITS** with lower left corner at **0,0** and upper right corner at **10,7.5.**

Do a **ZOOM All.**

### Draw the outline

Start a line at **2,3.** **ORTHO** and **SNAP** should be on. Use **F6** to place the coordinate readout in polar mode (displaying distance and angle). From **2,3** draw a line **1.25** to the right, then **.375** up, then **2.75** to the right, then **1.25** up, then exit the **LINE** command.

Start another line at **2,3** that goes **2.00** up, then **1.75** to the right. Stay in the **LINE** command, but turn **ORTHO** off (use **F8**), so you can draw the line at the 45-degree angle. (This line moves .375 vertically and, since it's at 45 degrees, moves .375 horizontally as well.)

Since SNAP is set at .125, you can draw this line easily by moving your crosshair three snaps down and three snaps over. Or you can use relative rectangular coordinates—**@.375,−.375.** Redraw the screen.

## Draw the circles

Draw the lower left circle first. Start the **CIRCLE** command. With **SNAP** on, use the pointer to locate the center of the circle. Use the grid to help you find the point that's **.625** over and **.500** up from the lower left corner of the plate. After you pick the center, enter **D,** then enter the diameter (**.5**). Use the grid to help you locate the next circle 1" above this circle.

To locate the center of the large circle, place the crosshair at **5.25,4.** After you've drawn this circle, redraw the screen.

Save your drawing.

## ARC EXERCISE

You can enter the coordinates given below by using the keyboard or by setting **SNAP** at **.25** and using the pointer.

| | | | | |
|---|---|---|---|---|
| 1. | (3 POINT) | Start point 4.25,4 | Second point 4,4.25 | End point 3.75,4 |
| 2. | SCE | Start point 3.75,4 | Center 4.25,4 | End point 8,4 |
| 3. | SCA | Start point 4.75,4 | Center 4,4 | Angle 180 |
| 4. | SCL | Start point 3.25,4 | Center 4.25,4 | Length of chord 2 |
| 5. | SEC* | Start point 5.25,4 | End point 2.75,4 | Center 4,4 |
| 6. | SER | Start point 2.75,4 | End point 5.75,4 | Radius 1.5 |
| 7. | SEA | Start point 5.75,4 | End point 2.25,4 | Included angle 180 |
| 8. | SED | Start point 2.25,4 | End point 6.25,4 | Direction 270 |
| 9. | CSE | Center 4,4 | Start point 6.25,4 | End point 0,4 |
| 10. | CSA | Center 4.25,4 | Start point 1.75,4 | Included angle 180 |
| 11. | CSL | Center 4,4 | Start point 6.75,4 | Length of chord 5.5 |
| 12. | Continue | End point 7.25,4 | | |

*Not on screen menu

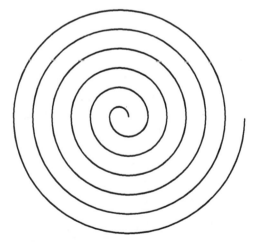

Also experiment using positive and negative included angle, radius and length of chord.

## QUARTER-PANEL DRAWING

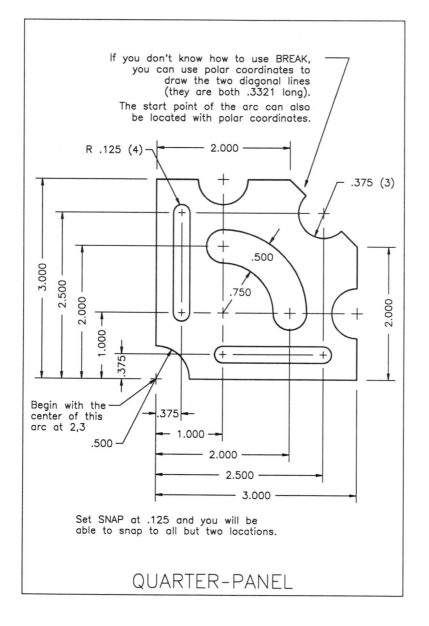

If you don't know how to use BREAK,
you can use polar coordinates to
draw the two diagonal lines
(they are both .3321 long).

The start point of the arc can also
be located with polar coordinates.

R .125 (4)

2.000

.375 (3)

.500

.750

3.000

2.500

2.000

1.000

.375

2.000

Begin with the
center of this
arc at 2,3

.375

.500

1.000

2.000

2.500

3.000

Set SNAP at .125 and you will be
able to snap to all but two locations.

QUARTER-PANEL

## PLAT DRAWING

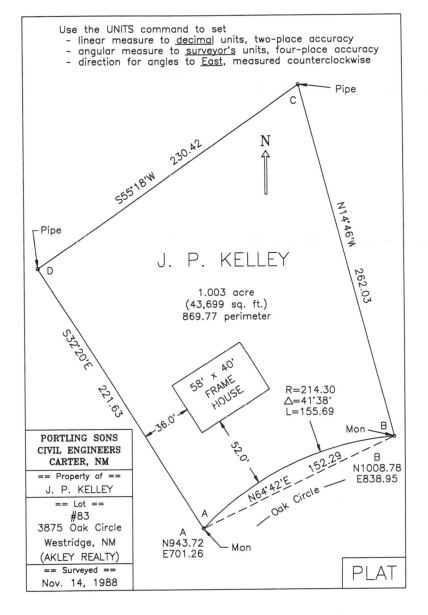

Use the UNITS command to set
- linear measure to <u>decimal</u> units, two-place accuracy
- angular measure to <u>surveyor's</u> units, four-place accuracy
- direction for angles to <u>East</u>, measured counterclockwise

Pipe

C

N

S55°18'W    230.42

N14°46'W    262.03

Pipe

D

J. P. KELLEY

1.003 acre
(43,699 sq. ft.)
869.77 perimeter

S32°20'E    221.63

58' × 40'
FRAME
HOUSE

R=214.30
△=41°38'
L=155.69

Mon    B

36.0'

52.0'

B
N1008.78
E838.95

N64°42'E    152.29

Oak Circle

A

A
N943.72
E701.26

Mon

**PORTLING SONS
CIVIL ENGINEERS
CARTER, NM**

== Property of ==
J. P. KELLEY

== Lot ==
#83
3875 Oak Circle
Westridge, NM
(AKLEY REALTY)

== Surveyed ==
Nov. 14, 1988

PLAT

## DISPLAY EXERCISE

This exercise uses several commands related to the display, including ZOOM, PAN, VIEW, RENAME, VIEWRES and REGEN.

The exercise is organized into general instructions and keystroke instructions (see the explanation at the beginning of this appendix). The <RETURN> key is indicated in the keystroke instructions as <CR>.

## SETUP

**General instructions:**

**Keystroke instructions:**

1. Start a new drawing called **DISPLAY**. You can use AutoCAD's default drawing area of 12 x 9, or you can use the **SHEETA** prototype drawing you created in the Setup exercise. (If you change the limits after you enter the drawing editor, do a **ZOOM All**.)

2. Set **GRID** at **1** and **SNAP** at **.25**.

3. Draw the circles, lines and square as shown below. When you're done, leave the grid on the screen. Turn **SNAP** off.

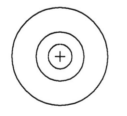

3 circles
centered at 2,4
R = .25
R = .50
R = 1.00

4 lines
3" long
.5" apart

5,4

2" square
Lower left
corner at
7,1

## USING ZOOM AND PAN

4.  Zoom out by a factor of 3 (make the objects on the screen appear one-third their original size).

    ZOOM <CR>
    .33 <CR>

5.  Return to the previous screen.

    ZOOM <CR>
    A <CR>

6.  Zoom in by a factor of 2 (make the objects appear twice as large on the screen).

    ZOOM <CR>
    2 <CR>

7.  Zoom in again by a factor of 2 (entities should be twice the size of the current display).

    ZOOM <CR>
    2x <CR>

8.  Zoom out to the limits.

    ZOOM <CR>
    A <CR>

9.  Zoom in on the circles.

    ZOOM <CR>
    W <CR>
    Pick two opposite corners forming a window around the circles, approx. .5″ larger than the circles on all sides.

10. Pan over to the lines. (Make sure **ORTHO** is off.) You may need to pan twice to get a full view of the lines.

    PAN <CR>
    Pick a point near the right edge of the screen, then a point near the left edge. If needed, do another pan.

11. Pan down to the square. (Make sure **ORTHO** is off.) You may need to pan twice to get a full view of the square.

    PAN <CR>
    Pick a point near the bottom of the screen, then a point near the top. If needed, do another pan.

12. Return to a view of the lines.

    ZOOM <CR>
    P <CR>
    If needed, repeat.

13. Zoom out to the limits.

```
ZOOM <CR>
A <CR>
```

14. Zoom in tightly on the lower left corner of the square.

```
ZOOM <CR>
W <CR>
```
Pick two opposite corners forming a small window around the lower left corner of the square.

15. Zoom out so that you have the largest possible display of all the objects in the drawing.

```
ZOOM <CR>
E <CR>
```

16. Zoom out from this current display so you have a small blank area around the objects.

```
ZOOM <CR>
.9x <CR>
```

17. Zoom in on the lines.

```
ZOOM <CR>
W <CR>
```
Pick two opposite corners forming a window around the lines.

## DYNAMIC ZOOM

18. Use **ZOOM** Dynamic to zoom in on the square.

```
ZOOM <CR>
D <CR>
```
Move the cursor so the window surrounds the square. <CR>

19. Use **ZOOM** Dynamic to zoom in on the circles.

```
ZOOM <CR>
D <CR>
```
Move the cursor so the window surrounds the circles. <CR>

20. Use **ZOOM** Dynamic to include both the lines and the square.

```
ZOOM <CR>
D <CR>
```
Move the cursor so the left edge of the window is just to the left of the lines. Press the pick button, then move the cursor to the right so the

window surrounds both the lines and the square. You can also move the cursor up and down.
<CR>

21. Use **ZOOM** Dynamic to zoom in on the smallest circle. If the smallest circle isn't visible after you do a ZOOM D, you may have to approximate its location, then do a second ZOOM D.

    ZOOM <CR>
    D  <CR>
    Move the cursor so the left edge of the window is just to the left of the smallest circle. Press the pick button, then move the cursor to the left so the window surrounds just the smallest circle.
    <CR>

22. Zoom out to the limits.

    ZOOM <CR>
    A <CR>

## USING VIEW NAMES

23. Save a window view of the circles under the name **C**.

    VIEW <CR>
    W  <CR>
    C  <CR>
    Pick the opposite corners forming a window around the circles.

24. Save a window view of the lines under the name **L**.

    VIEW <CR>
    W  <CR>
    L  <CR>
    Pick the opposite corners forming a window around the lines.

25. Zoom in on the square.

    ZOOM <CR>
    W  <CR>
    Pick the opposite corners forming a window around the square.

26. Save the current display under the name **SQ**.

    VIEW <CR>
    S  <CR>
    SQ <CR>

27. Get a listing of the views you've saved, then return to the graphics screen.

```
VIEW <CR>
? <CR>
F1 (function key)
```

28. Restore the view of the lines.

```
VIEW <CR>
R <CR>
L <CR>
```

29. Restore the view of the circles.

```
VIEW <CR>
R <CR>
C <CR>
```

30. Delete the name of the square from the list of saved views.

```
VIEW <CR>
D <CR>
SQ <CR>
```

31. Change the name of the view of the lines from **L** to **LINES**.

```
RENAME <CR>
VI <CR>
L <CR>
LINES <CR>
```

32. Change the name of the view of the circles from **C** to **CIRCLES**.

```
RENAME <CR>
VI <CR>
C <CR>
CIRCLES <CR>
```

33. Get a listing of the views currently saved, then return to the graphics screen.

```
VIEW <CR>
? <CR>
F1 (function key)
```

## CHANGING THE VIEW RESOLUTION

34. Zoom out to the limits.

```
ZOOM <CR>
A <CR>
```

35. Zoom in tightly on the smallest circle. Notice the polygon appearance of the circle. This is a result of AutoCAD's use of its virtual screen.

```
ZOOM <CR>
W <CR>
```
Pick opposite corners forming a small window surrounding just the smallest circle.

36. Regenerate the screen. Notice the effect on the shape of the circle.

```
REGEN <CR>
```

37. Zoom out to the limits.

```
ZOOM <CR>
A  <CR>
```

38. Turn fast zooms off.

```
VIEWRES <CR>
N  <CR><CR>
```

39. Zoom in tightly on the smallest circle. Notice its appearance. When you turn fast zooms off, AutoCAD doesn't use its virtual screen, but regenerates the display for each zoom.

```
ZOOM <CR>
W  <CR>
Pick opposite corners forming a
small window surrounding just the
smallest circle.
```

40. Zoom out to the limits.

```
ZOOM <CR>
A  <CR>
```

41. Turn fast zooms back on and set view resolution at **10000**.

```
VIEWRES <CR>
Y  <CR>
10000 <CR>
```

42. Zoom in tightly on the smallest circle. Notice that the higher resolution setting produces a round circle even though AutoCAD is using its virtual screen. This greater accuracy of the screen representation of circles and arcs takes more time to generate (much more noticeable when you have many circles or arcs in the drawing).

```
ZOOM <CR>
W  <CR>
Pick opposite corners forming a
small window surrounding just the
smallest circle.
```

43. Zoom out to the limits.

```
ZOOM <CR>
A  <CR>
```

44. Leave fast zooms on, but set view resolution at 10. Notice that even without zooming in, circles look like polygons because of the low resolution setting. These approximations of circles generate very quickly. Despite their appearance on the screen, the circles are still round in the database and in a plot.

```
VIEWRES <CR>
Y <CR>
10 <CR>
```

45. Get out of the drawing.

```
QUIT <CR>
Y <CR>
```

Keep in mind that all of these display operations have been within a single viewport. Each of the operations works the same (within a single viewport) when several viewports are active. When you use more than one viewport, you won't need to use ZOOM and PAN quite so often, even though each viewport covers a smaller area on the screen. See VPORTS in Chapter 33.

## OBJECT SNAP/INQUIRY

### Osnap and Inquiry Exercise

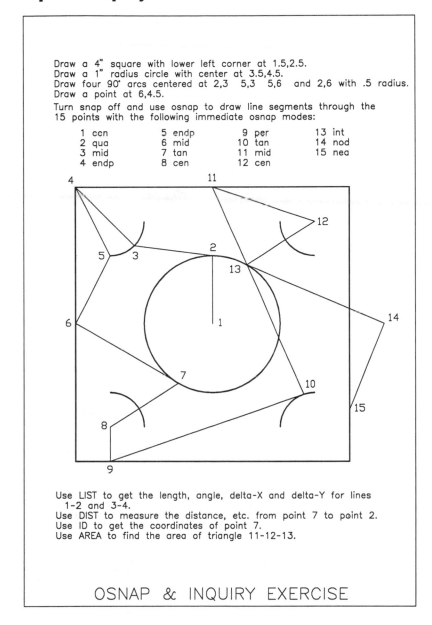

Draw a 4" square with lower left corner at 1.5,2.5.
Draw a 1" radius circle with center at 3.5,4.5.
Draw four 90° arcs centered at 2,3  5,3  5,6  and 2,6 with .5 radius.
Draw a point at 6,4.5.

Turn snap off and use osnap to draw line segments through the
15 points with the following immediate osnap modes:

| | | | |
|---|---|---|---|
| 1 ccn | 5 endp | 9 per | 13 int |
| 2 qua | 6 mid | 10 tan | 14 nod |
| 3 mid | 7 tan | 11 mid | 15 nea |
| 4 endp | 8 cen | 12 cen | |

Use LIST to get the length, angle, delta-X and delta-Y for lines
  1-2 and 3-4.
Use DIST to measure the distance, etc. from point 7 to point 2.
Use ID to get the coordinates of point 7.
Use AREA to find the area of triangle 11-12-13.

OSNAP & INQUIRY EXERCISE

## Area Exercise

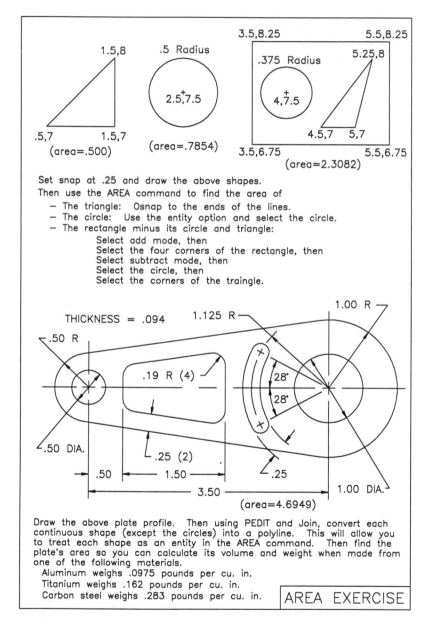

3.5,8.25          5.5,8.25

1.5,8          .5 Radius          5.25,8

.375 Radius

2.5,7.5          4,7.5

.5,7          1.5,7          4.5,7   5,7

(area=.500)          (area=.7854)          3.5,6.75          5.5,6.75

(area=2.3082)

Set snap at .25 and draw the above shapes.
Then use the AREA command to find the area of
— The triangle:  Osnap to the ends of the lines.
— The circle:  Use the entity option and select the circle.
— The rectangle minus its circle and triangle:
          Select add mode, then
          Select the four corners of the rectangle, then
          Select subtract mode, then
          Select the circle, then
          Select the corners of the traingle.

THICKNESS = .094          1.125 R          1.00 R

.50 R

.19 R (4)          28°

28°

.50 DIA.

.25 (2)          .25

.50          1.50          1.00 DIA.

3.50

(area=4.6949)

Draw the above plate profile.  Then using PEDIT and Join, convert each
continuous shape (except the circles) into a polyline.  This will allow you
to treat each shape as an entity in the AREA command.  Then find the
plate's area so you can calculate its volume and weight when made from
one of the following materials.
  Aluminum weighs .0975 pounds per cu. in.
  Titanium weighs .162 pounds per cu. in.
  Carbon steel weighs .283 pounds per cu. in.          AREA EXERCISE

## EDITING—GROUP ONE

### EDITING EXERCISE

This exercise involves several editing commands—MOVE, COPY, MIRROR, ROTATE and SCALE. When you finish, you'll have a drawing like the one below.

The exercise doesn't show you the most efficient way to produce this drawing. Instead, it's designed to illustrate some of the options available for each of the editing commands.

This exercise is organized into general instructions and keystroke instructions (see the explanation at the beginning of this appendix). The <RETURN> key is indicated in the keystroke instructions as <CR>.

## SETUP

1. Start a new drawing called EDIT-EX and set the lower left corner of the limits at **0,0** and the upper right corner at **12,9** (AutoCAD's default). Then enter **ZOOM All**. Also set **GRID** at **1** and **SNAP** at **.25**.

```
LIMITS <CR>
0,0 <CR>
12,9 <CR>
ZOOM <CR>
A <CR>
GRID <CR>
1 <CR>
SNAP <CR>
.25 <CR>
```

## DRAWING THE BORDER LINES

2. Draw a horizontal line from **0,3** to **12,3**.

```
LINE <CR>
0,3 <CR>
12,3 <CR><CR>
```

3. Copy this line **6** units up. Then move the original line **3** units down.

```
COPY <CR>
L <CR><CR>
0,6 <CR><CR>
MOVE <CR>
```
Pick lower line. <CR>
```
0,-3 <CR><CR>
```

4. Draw a vertical line from **2,0** to **2,9**.

```
LINE <CR>
2,0 <CR>
2,9 <CR><CR>
```

5. Copy this line **10** units to the right. Then move the original line **2** units to the left.

```
COPY <CR>
L <CR><CR>
10,0 <CR><CR>
MOVE <CR>
```
Pick original vertical line. <CR>
```
-2,0 <CR><CR>
```

6. Draw four arcs, each with a radius of .75 running from 0 to 90 degrees. The first arc should have its center at 4,5. After drawing one arc, use the Multiple option in the **COPY** command to create the other three arcs. Place the center of the second arc at **5,5,** the third at **6,5** and the fourth at **7,5.**

```
ARC <CR>
C <CR>
4,5 <CR>
@.75,0 <CR>
A <CR>
90 <CR>
COPY <CR>
L <CR><CR>
M <CR>
4,5 <CR>
5,5 <CR>
6,5 <CR>
7,5 <CR><CR>
```
Press F7 twice to clean up the screen.

7. Move the first arc from **4,5** to **11,8.**

```
MOVE <CR>
Pick the first arc. <CR>
4,5 <CR>
11,8 <CR>
```

8. Move the second arc from **5,5** to **1,8.** Then rotate it **90°** counterclockwise around its own center.

```
MOVE <CR>
Pick the second arc.<CR>
5,5 <CR>
1,8 <CR>
ROTATE <CR>
Pick the arc you just moved. <CR>
1,8 <CR>
90 <CR>
```

9. Rotate the third arc **180°** around its own center. Then move it **5** units to the left and **4** units down.

ROTATE <CR>
Pick the third arc. <CR>
6,5 <CR>
180 <CR>
MOVE <CR>
Pick the arc you just rotated.<CR>
0,0 <CR>
-5,-4 <CR>

10. Move the fourth arc **4** units to the right and **4** units down. Then rotate it **90°** clockwise around its own center.

MOVE <CR>
Pick the fourth arc.<CR>
Pick any point.
@4,-4 <CR>
ROTATE <CR>
Pick the arc you just moved.<CR>
11,1 <CR>
-90 <CR>

11. Draw a line that starts at **.25,1** and extends **7** units up. Then copy this line **11.5** units to the right.

LINE <CR>
.25,1 <CR>
@0,7 <CR><CR>
COPY <CR>
L <CR><CR>
11.5,0 <CR><CR>

12. Draw a line that starts at **1,8.75** and extends **10** units to the right. Then copy this line **8.5** units down.

LINE <CR>
1,8.75 <CR>
@10,0 <CR>
COPY <CR>
L <CR><CR>
Pick any point.
@8.5<-90 <CR>
Press F7 twice to clean up the screen.

## Drawing the face

13. Draw a circle centered at **6,5** with a radius of **3** units.

```
CIRCLE <CR>
6,5 <CR>
3 <CR>
```

14. Draw a circle centered at **6,8.5** with a radius of **.5** units.

```
CIRCLE <CR>
6,8.5 <CR>
.5 <CR>
```

15. Scale the small circle, based at its own center, by a factor of **1.5**.

```
SCALE <CR>
L <CR><CR>
6,8.5 <CR>
1.5 <CR>
```

16. Move the small circle up **.25**.

```
MOVE <CR>
L <CR><CR>
0,.25 <CR><CR>
```

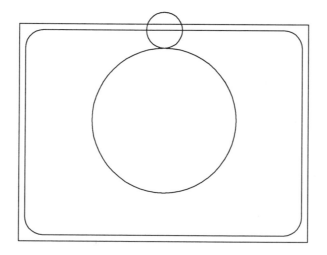

17. Rotate the small circle **90°** clockwise around the center of the large circle.

```
ROTATE <CR>
L <CR><CR>
6,5 <CR>
-90 <CR>
```

18. Copy the small circle **7.5** units
    to the left.

```
COPY <CR>
L <CR><CR>
-7.5,0 <CR><CR>
```

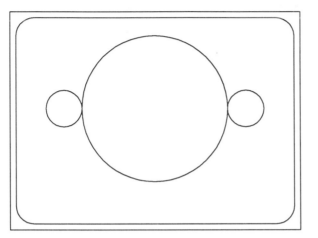

19. Draw an arc through these
    three points: 6.5,6   7.1,6.25
    and 7.7,6.

```
ARC <CR>
6.5,6 <CR>
7.1,6.25 <CR>
7.7,6 <CR>
```

20. Mirror the arc around a mirror
    line from **6,6** to **8,6** and retain
    the original arc.

```
MIRROR <CR>
L <CR><CR>
6,6 <CR>
8,6 <CR><CR>
```

21. Flip (mirror and delete
    original) the upper arc around
    a mirror line from **6,6** to **6,8**.

```
MIRROR <CR>
Pick upper arc. <CR>
6,6 <CR>
6,8 <CR>
Y <CR>
```

22. Flip (mirror and delete original) the left arc around a mirror line from **4,6** to **6,6**.

```
MIRROR <CR>
Pick left arc.<CR>
4,6 <CR>
6,6 <CR>
Y  <CR>
```

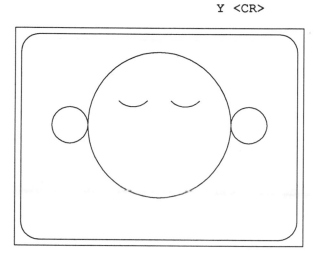

23. Copy the left arc **2.6** units at an angle of **– 65** degrees.

```
COPY <CR>
Pick left arc.<CR>
Pick any point.
@2.6<-65 <CR>
```

24. Mirror this lower arc around a mirror line from **5,4.25** to **7,4.25** and retain the original arc.

```
MIRROR <CR>
L <CR><CR>
5,4.25 <CR>
7,4.25 <CR><CR>
```

25. Scale this last arc around the center of the large circle so that the distance between the ends of the arc becomes **.65** (use the **Reference** option).

```
SCALE <CR>
L <CR><CR>
6,5 <CR>
R <CR>
ENDP <CR>
OSNAP to one end of arc.
ENDP <CR>
OSNAP to other end of arc.
.65 <CR>
```

26. Rotate the entire face around the center of the large circle so that the center of the arc representing the eye on the right side of the picture is directly above the center of the arc representing the mouth (use the **R**eference option).

```
ROTATE <CR>
W <CR>
Pick one corner of window.
Pick other corner.<CR>
6,5 <CR>
R <CR>
CEN <CR>
Pick right arc.
CEN <CR>
Pick bottom arc.
270 <CR>
```

27. Flip (mirror and delete original) both eyes around a diagonal mirror line joining the corners of the eyes.

```
MIRROR <CR>
Pick both eyes.<CR>
ENDP <CR>
Pick corner of one eye.
ENDP <CR>
```

Pick corner of other eye.
Y <CR>

28. Scale the entire face at base point **1,8** so that the distance between the centers of the eyes becomes **1.7** (use the **Reference** option).

SCALE <CR>
W <CR>
Pick corner of window.
Pick other corner. <CR>
1,8 <CR>
R <CR>
CEN <CR>
Pick one eye.
CEN <CR>
Pick other eye.
1.7 <CR>

29. Rotate the entire face around base point **1,1** so that the face is upright again (use the **Reference** option).

ROTATE <CR>
P <CR><CR>
1,1 <CR>
R <CR>
CEN <CR>
Pick ear on left of picture.
CEN <CR>
Pick other ear.
0 <CR>

30. Move the entire face so that it's centered in the drawing (center of large circle is at **6,4.5**).

MOVE &lt;CR&gt;
P &lt;CR&gt;&lt;CR&gt;
CEN &lt;CR&gt;
Pick large circle.
6,4.5 &lt;CR&gt;

# HANGER

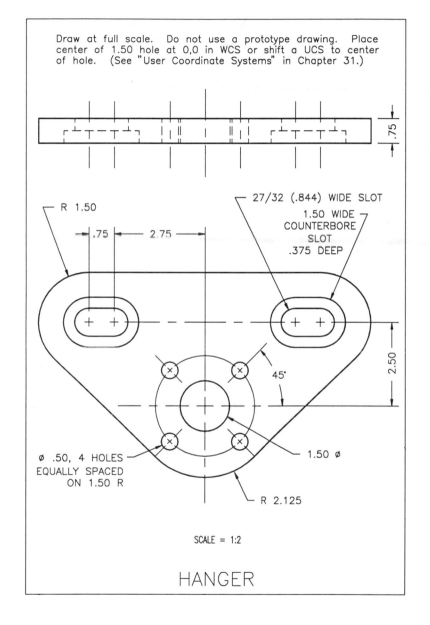

Draw at full scale.  Do not use a prototype drawing.  Place center of 1.50 hole at 0,0 in WCS or shift a UCS to center of hole.  (See "User Coordinate Systems" in Chapter 31.)

.75

27/32 (.844) WIDE SLOT

1.50 WIDE COUNTERBORE SLOT .375 DEEP

R 1.50

.75

2.75

2.50

45°

Ø .50, 4 HOLES EQUALLY SPACED ON 1.50 R

1.50 Ø

R 2.125

SCALE = 1:2

HANGER

## FORK PROFILE

If you've already created Sheet A, you can use it as a prototype for this fork drawing. To do so, at the main menu enter **1**, then when prompted for the name of the drawing enter **FORK=SHEETA**. If you use Sheet A as a prototype, skip the Setup section below (except for SNAP).

The general strategy is to draw the top half of the fork first, then use the **MIRROR** command to create the bottom half.

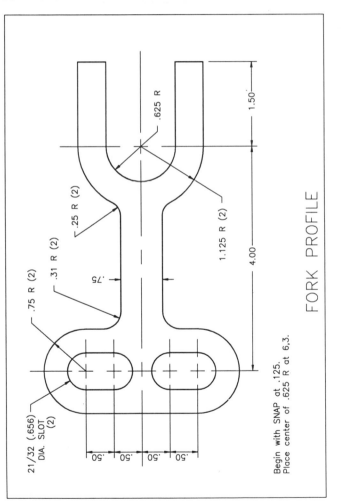

FORK PROFILE

### Setup

Set **GRID** at **.5**.

Set **AXIS** at **2**.

Set **SNAP** at **.125**. This lets you snap to most points.

Set **LIMITS** with lower left corner at **0,0** and upper right corner at **10,7.5**.

Do a **ZOOM All**.

### Drawing the upper right end

Make sure **SNAP** and **GRID** are on. Use the pointer to locate all points.

Draw the small arc (**R .625**) first using the **Center-Start-Angle** option. Place the center at **6,3**. Place the start point **.625** above the center and use **90°**.

Then draw the large arc. Place the start point **1.125** above the center and use **60°**. The exact number of degrees is unimportant because this large arc will be filleted later.

Draw the three remaining lines that are to the right of these arcs. Redraw the screen.

### Drawing the upper left end

Draw the large arc first, using the **Center-Start-Angle** option. Place the center at **2,4**. Place the start point **.75** to the right of the center and use **180°**.

Next draw the small arc at the top of the **21/32 DIA.** slot. After locating the center, use relative coordinates to locate the start point of the arc (**@.328,0** or **@.328<0**). Draw the lower arc in a similar manner.

You can connect vertical lines to the ends of these arcs with immediate osnap. Turn **SNAP** off. Enter the **LINE** command. When prompted for **From point:**, (1) enter **ENDP** from the keyboard or select **ENDPOINT** from the osnap options in the screen menu or pull-down menu, then (2) attach the line to the right end of one of the arcs by capturing the right half of the arc in the aperture that appears on the crosshairs. Repeat (1) and (2) to attach the other end of the line to the right end of the other arc. Use a similar procedure to connect the left ends of the arcs with a vertical line. Redraw the screen.

## Completing the top half

Turn **SNAP** and **ORTHO** on. Start a line at the right end of the **R .75** arc, **.625** down and **2.00** to the right. **FILLET** these two lines with a radius of **.31**.

**FILLET** the horizontal line and the **1.125** arc with a radius of **.25**.

## Creating the bottom half

Start the **MIRROR** command, use a window to select everything, then (with ORTHO on) indicate a mirror line extending to the right or left of **6,3**. Add the vertical line at the extreme left end of the fork. Redraw the screen.

Save your drawing.

# Clip

Start at upper right end of clip, located at 6,6.
Proceed one section at a time toward lower left end of clip.
Make full use of osnap and relative polar coordinates.

Construct one side of the clip first, then offset by .062.

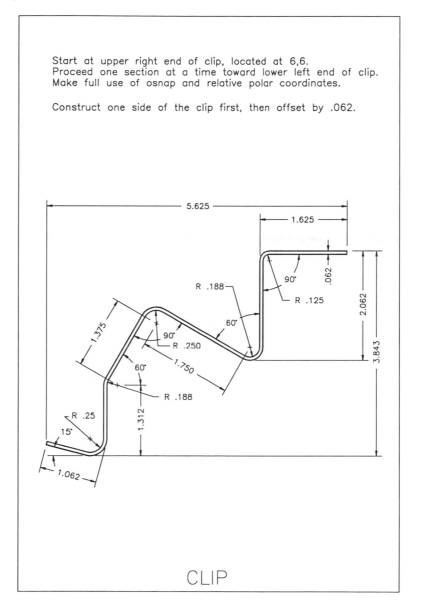

CLIP

## Strip Layout

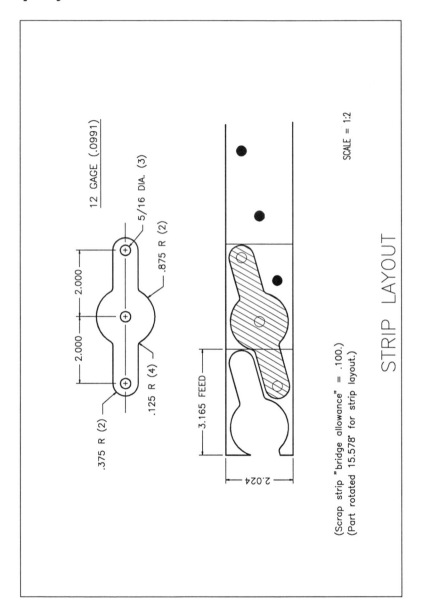

12 GAGE (.0991)

5/16 DIA. (3)

.875 R (2)

.375 R (2)

.125 R (4)

2.000

2.000

3.165 FEED

2.024

(Scrap strip "bridge allowance" = .100.)
(Part rotated 15.578° for strip layout.)

SCALE = 1:2

STRIP LAYOUT

## Text Exercise

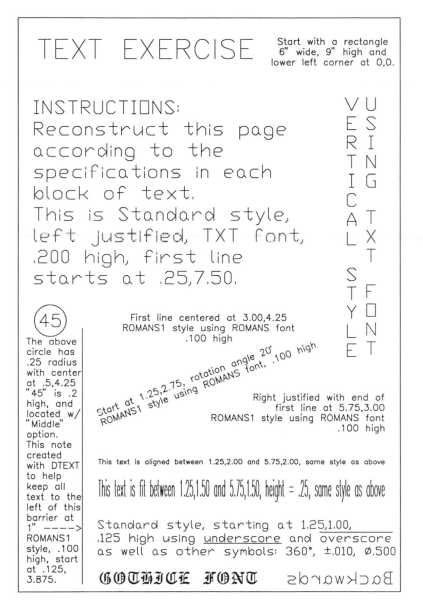

TEXT EXERCISE   Start with a rectangle 6" wide, 9" high and lower left corner at 0,0.

INSTRUCTIONS:
Reconstruct this page according to the specifications in each block of text.
This is Standard style, left justified, TXT font, .200 high, first line starts at .25,7.50.

VERTICAL STYLE

USING TXT FONT

(45)

The above circle has .25 radius with center at .5,4.25 "45" is .2 high, and located w/ "Middle" option.
This note created with DTEXT to help keep all text to the left of this barrier at 1" ----->
ROMANS1 style, .100 high, start at .125, 3.875.

First line centered at 3.00,4.25
ROMANS1 style using ROMANS font
.100 high

Start at 1.25,2.75, rotation angle 20°
ROMANS1 style using ROMANS font, .100 high

Right justified with end of first line at 5.75,3.00
ROMANS1 style using ROMANS font
.100 high

This text is aligned between 1.25,2.00 and 5.75,2.00, same style as above

This text is fit between 1.25,1.50 and 5.75,1.50, height = .25, same style as above

Standard style, starting at 1.25,1.00, .125 high using <u>underscore</u> and overscore as well as other symbols: 360°, ±.010, ⌀.500

GOTHICE FONT   Backwards

# EDITING—GROUP TWO

## Stencil

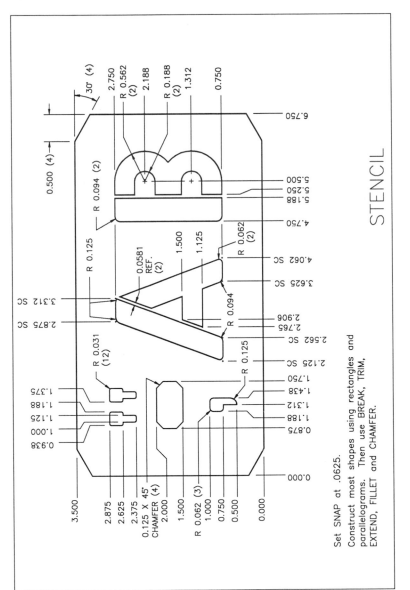

Set SNAP at .0625.

Construct most shapes using rectangles and parallelograms. Then use BREAK, TRIM, EXTEND, FILLET and CHAMFER.

STENCIL

## Leaf Spring Profile

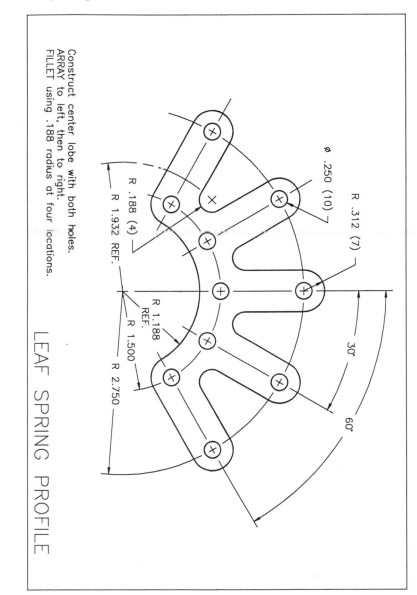

Construct center lobe with both holes.
ARRAY to left, then to right.
FILLET using .188 radius at four locations.

LEAF SPRING PROFILE

## Pivot Arm Profile

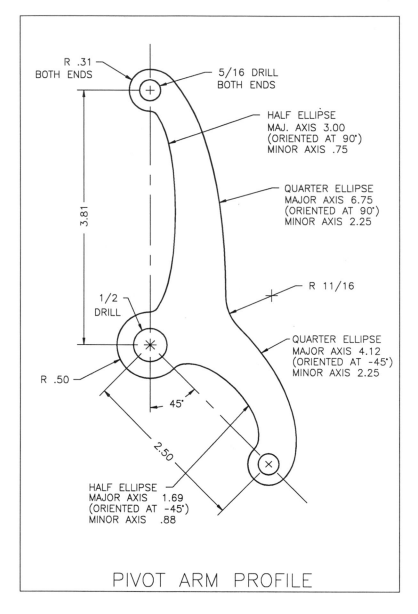

PIVOT ARM PROFILE

# BLOCKS

## Block Exercise

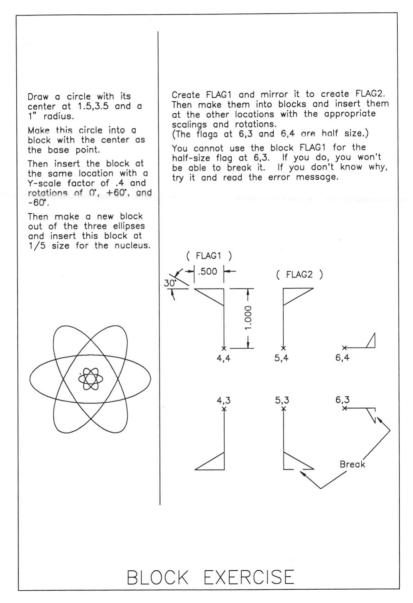

Draw a circle with its center at 1.5,3.5 and a 1" radius.

Make this circle into a block with the center as the base point.

Then insert the block at the same location with a Y-scale factor of .4 and rotations of 0°, +60°, and -60°.

Then make a new block out of the three ellipses and insert this block at 1/5 size for the nucleus.

Create FLAG1 and mirror it to create FLAG2. Then make them into blocks and insert them at the other locations with the appropriate scalings and rotations.
(The flags at 6,3 and 6,4 are half size.)

You cannot use the block FLAG1 for the half-size flag at 6,3. If you do, you won't be able to break it. If you don't know why, try it and read the error message.

( FLAG1 )

.500

( FLAG2 )

30°

1.000

4,4

5,4

6,4

4,3

5,3

6,3

Break

BLOCK EXERCISE

## Cylinder

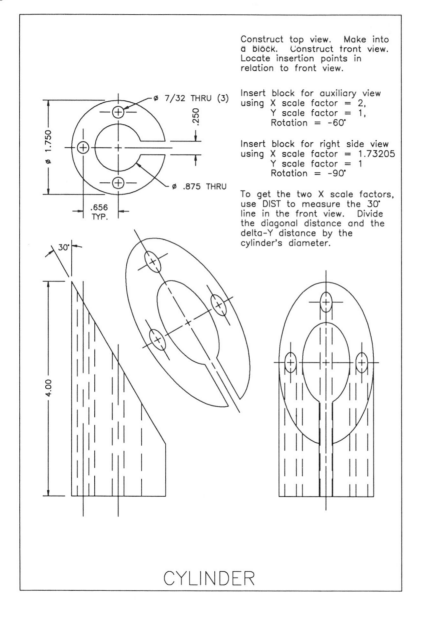

Construct top view.  Make into a block.  Construct front view. Locate insertion points in relation to front view.

Insert block for auxiliary view using X scale factor = 2,
Y scale factor = 1,
Rotation = -60°

Insert block for right side view using X scale factor = 1.73205
Y scale factor = 1
Rotation = -90°

To get the two X scale factors, use DIST to measure the 30° line in the front view.  Divide the diagonal distance and the delta-Y distance by the cylinder's diameter.

ø 7/32 THRU (3)

.250

ø 1.750

ø .875 THRU

.656
TYP.

30°

4.00

CYLINDER

## DIMENSIONS/HATCHING

### Wheel Puller

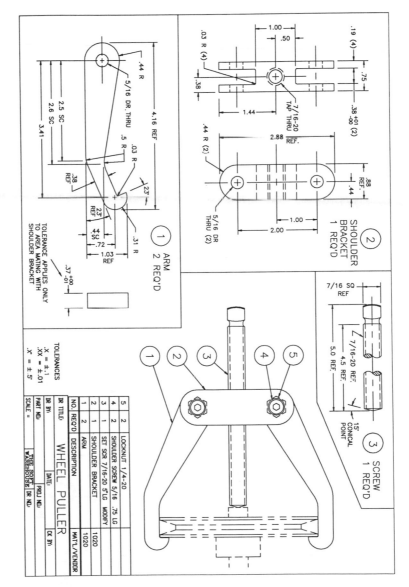

## Surface Gage

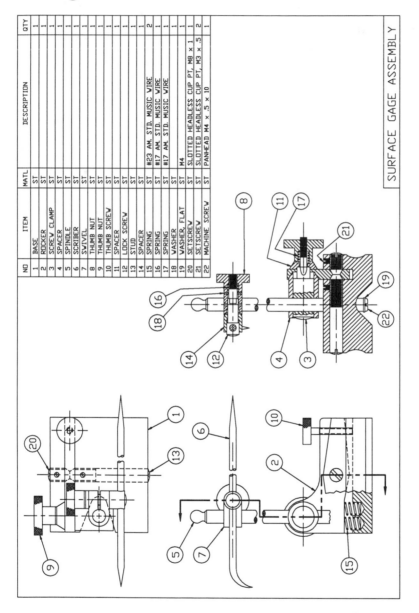

| NO | ITEM | MATL | DESCRIPTION | QTY |
|----|------|------|-------------|-----|
| 1 | BASE | ST | | 1 |
| 2 | ROCKER | ST | | 1 |
| 3 | SCREW CLAMP | ST | | 1 |
| 4 | SPACER | ST | | 1 |
| 5 | SPINDLE | ST | | 1 |
| 6 | SCRIBER | ST | | 1 |
| 7 | SWIVEL | ST | | 1 |
| 8 | THUMB NUT | ST | | 1 |
| 9 | THUMB NUT | ST | | 1 |
| 10 | THUMB SCREW | ST | | 1 |
| 11 | SPACER | ST | | 1 |
| 12 | LOCK SCREW | ST | | 1 |
| 13 | STUD | ST | | 1 |
| 14 | SPACER | ST | | 1 |
| 15 | SPRING | ST | #23 AM. STD. MUSIC WIRE | 2 |
| 16 | SPRING | ST | #17 AM. STD. MUSIC WIRE | 1 |
| 17 | SPRING | ST | #17 AM. STD. MUSIC WIRE | 1 |
| 18 | WASHER | ST | M4 | 1 |
| 19 | WASHER, FLAT | ST | | 1 |
| 20 | SETSCREW | ST | SLOTTED HEADLESS CUP PT, M8 × 1 | 1 |
| 21 | SETSCREW | ST | SLOTTED HEADLESS CUP PT, M3 × .5 | 2 |
| 22 | MACHINE SCREW | ST | PANHEAD M4 × .5 × 10 | 1 |

SURFACE GAGE ASSEMBLY

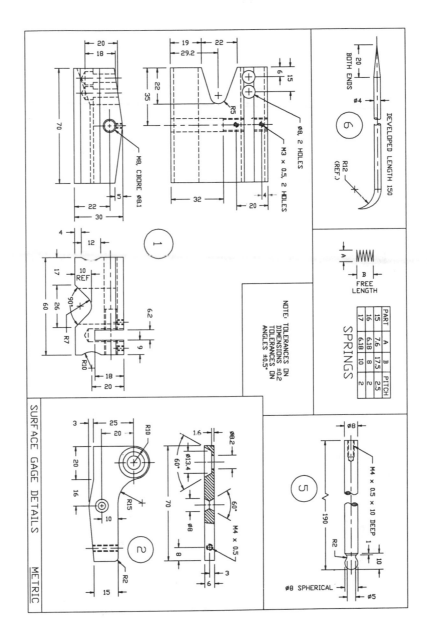

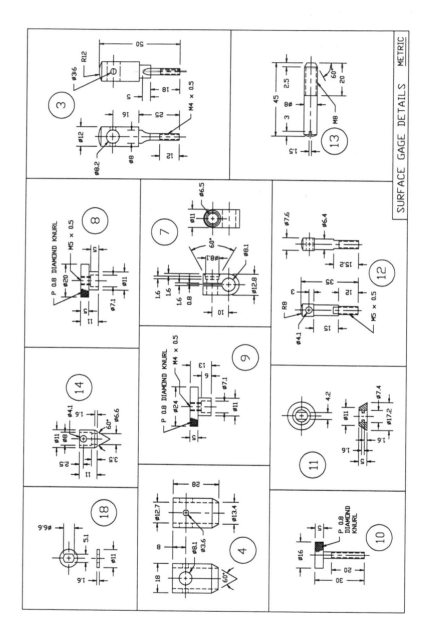

SURFACE GAGE DETAILS    METRIC

# POLYLINE EXERCISE

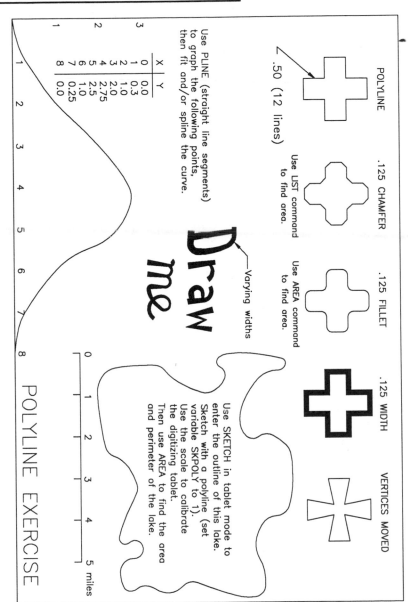

POLYLINE

.125 CHAMFER
Use LIST command
to find area.

.125 FILLET
Use AREA command
to find area.

.125 WIDTH

VERTICES MOVED

.50 (12 lines)

Draw me
—Varying widths

Use PLINE (straight line segments)
to graph the following points,
then fit and/or spline the curve.

| X | Y |
|---|-----|
| 0 | 0.0 |
| 1 | 0.3 |
| 2 | 1.0 |
| 3 | 2.0 |
| 4 | 2.75 |
| 5 | 2.5 |
| 6 | 1.0 |
| 7 | 0.25 |
| 8 | 0.0 |

Use SKETCH in tablet mode to
enter the outline of this lake.
Sketch with a polyline (set
variable SKPOLY to 1).
Use the scale to calibrate
the digitizing tablet.
Then use AREA to find the area
and perimeter of the lake.

0   1   2   3   4   5 miles

POLYLINE EXERCISE

# ISOMETRIC DRAWINGS

## Channel Block

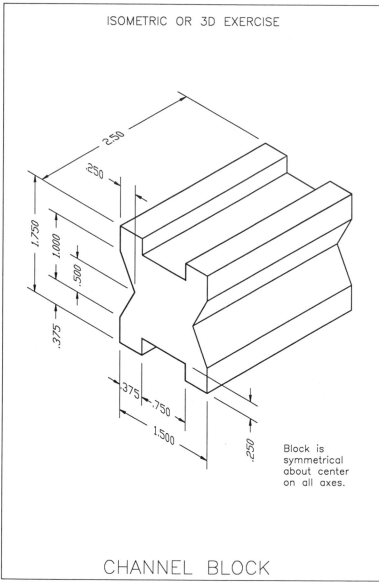

ISOMETRIC OR 3D EXERCISE

2.50
.250
1.750
1.000
.500
.375
.375
.750
1.500
.250

Block is
symmetrical
about center
on all axes.

CHANNEL BLOCK

## Iso-Ellipse Comparison

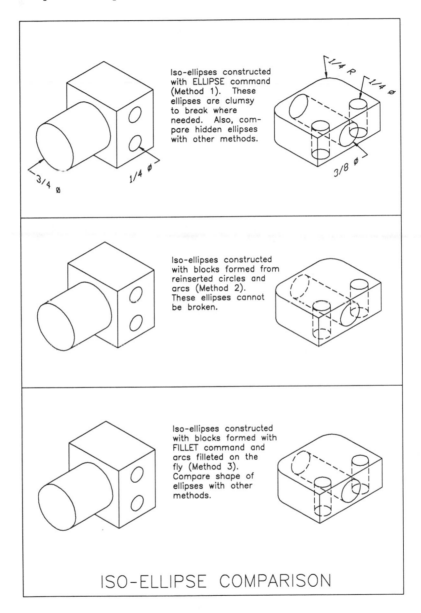

Iso-ellipses constructed with ELLIPSE command (Method 1). These ellipses are clumsy to break where needed. Also, compare hidden ellipses with other methods.

1/4 R   1/4 ∅

3/4 ∅   1/4 ∅   3/8 ∅

Iso-ellipses constructed with blocks formed from reinserted circles and arcs (Method 2). These ellipses cannot be broken.

Iso-ellipses constructed with blocks formed with FILLET command and arcs filleted on the fly (Method 3). Compare shape of ellipses with other methods.

ISO-ELLIPSE COMPARISON

## Linkage Base

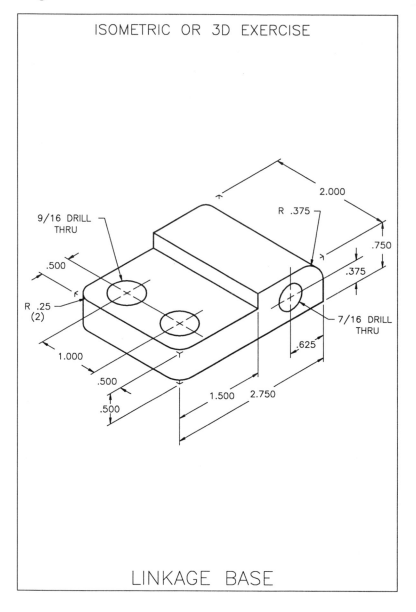

## Swivel Bracket

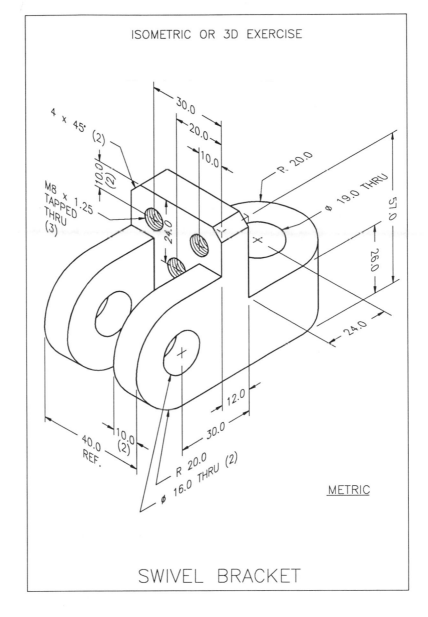

ISOMETRIC OR 3D EXERCISE

SWIVEL BRACKET

## DODECAHEDRON EXERCISE

This exercise will give you practice in establishing, saving and restoring various X-Y construction planes (User Coordinate Systems) as well as combining 3D faces with invisible edges. The exercise will refer to the face numbers and corner numbers shown in the drawing below.

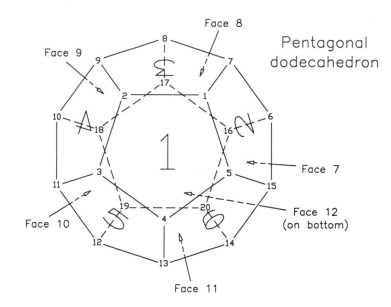

Pentagonal dodecahedron

The overall strategy for drawing the dodecahedron is as follows: First, construct a pentagonal face (from two 3D faces) and make it into a block. Then, for each face of the dodecahedron, create an X-Y construction plane (UCS), insert the pentagonal face and draw the appropriate number.

Be sure to include the numbers on the faces. If you don't, you'll find the dodecahedron much harder to construct.

## Constructing Face 12

Start a new drawing called **DODECA**.

Face **12** (the bottom face) will be created first, then used to construct the other 11 faces.

Set the lower left corner of the **LIMITS** at –3,–3 and the upper right corner at **3,3**. Then do a **ZOOM All**.

If you need to, use the **UCSICON** command to make the UCS icon visible. Refer to this icon often.

Use the **POLYGON** command to create a five-sided polygon, centered at **0,0**, inscribed, with a radius of **1**. Enter the radius from the keyboard so the bottom of the polygon will be horizontal. This polygon is temporary. It serves only to establish points 16, 17, 18, 19 and 20.

Make a **3DFACE** using points **18, 19, 20** and **16**, with the edge between points 16 and 18 invisible. (**OSNAP** to the corners of the polygon.) Then make another 3DFACE using points **16, 17** and **18**, again with the edge between points 16 and 18 invisible.

Make a block called **PENTA** that includes these two 3DFACES, with the insertion point at **19**. When you select the 3DFACES for the block, select them with the pick box rather than with a window, because you don't want the original polygon in the block. After the block has disappeared, redraw the screen so the original polygon reappears. Draw a reference line from point **19** to anywhere, then erase the polygon.

Reinsert **PENTA** at its original location and size (using the end of the reference line for the insertion point). Then erase the reference line.

The rest of the dodecahedron will be constructed on top of this face, in the positive **Z** direction (toward the viewer according to the present viewpoint). You're now looking at what will become the inside of face 12.

To place the number 12 on this surface so it appears correct from the outside of the dodecahedron, create an X-Y construction plane on the flip side of the current construction plane. Use the **UCS** command and the three-point option.

> When prompted for the **0,0,0** point, select point **20**.
>
> When prompted for a point on the positive **X** axis, select point **19**.
>
> When prompted for the point on the positive **Y** plane, select point **17**.

Use **PLAN** to switch to a plan view in this (current) **UCS**. Use the UCS command again to save this UCS under the name **12**.

Place **12** in the middle of the surface. Use lines and arcs to create the numbers for each surface; text may not hide properly. Also, the lines and arcs forming the numbers may occasionally hide as though they were just behind the surface they were drawn on. Solution: Move these lines/arcs a short distance, perhaps **.001**, in the positive **Z** direction.

Return to the World Coordinate System (**WCS**) and establish a **VPOINT** of 3,–5,2.

## Constructing Face 11

To construct face 11, we must create a new UCS that forms the proper dihedral angle with face 12. We'll do this in two steps:

> Shift the origin. Use **UCS**, select **0**, then **OSNAP** to point **19** (the leftmost point on the screen).
>
> Rotate the X-Y construction plane around the X axis of this present construction plane. Use **UCS**, select **X**, and enter an angle of **116.56505118**.

Use the **UCS** command again to save this UCS under the name **11**.

Insert **PENTA** at **0,0**, full scale, unrotated.

Draw number **11** on this face.

To help visualize the objects, you'll want to use **HIDE** frequently throughout the rest of this exercise.

## Constructing Faces 7, 8, 9 and 10

Return to **WCS**. If needed, establish a **VPOINT** of 3,–5, 2.

Make a polar **ARRAY** of face 11 around **0,0** (five items, filling 360° rotating the objects as they are copied).

If needed, do a **ZOOM All**, then use **HIDE**. Then use **REGEN** to prepare for the next step.

Establish and save a **UCS** for each of these four new faces. Then switch to the plan view of each of these UCSs and draw the appropriate numbers on each face.

## Constructing the top half

In **WCS**, establish a viewpoint of **3, –5, 2**. Use **HIDE**.

Begin with face 6. Create a **UCS** using points **13, 14** and **15**.

Insert **PENTA** in this new UCS at **0,0**, full scale, unrotated.

Switch to **WCS** and array the new surface around 0,0 to form surfaces 2, 3, 4 and 5. Do a **ZOOM All**.

Finally, create a **UCS** on the very top and insert **PENTA** one more time for face 1.

Establish and save a **UCS** for each of these five new faces. Then draw the appropriate numbers on each face.

Return to **WCS** and view the dodecahedron from various viewpoints.

# 3D ENTITIES AND MESHES

## 3D Exercises

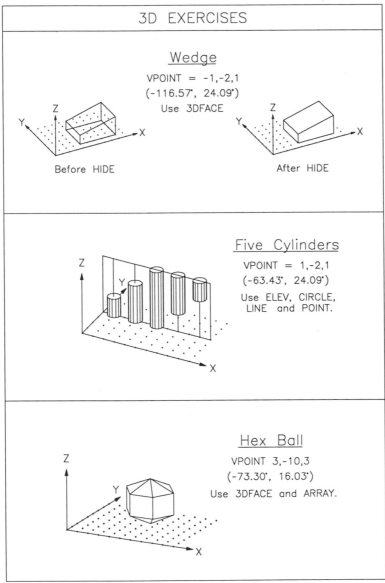

3D EXERCISES

### Wedge

VPOINT = -1,-2,1
(-116.57°, 24.09°)
Use 3DFACE

Before HIDE

After HIDE

### Five Cylinders

VPOINT = 1,-2,1
(-63.43°, 24.09°)

Use ELEV, CIRCLE,
LINE and POINT.

### Hex Ball

VPOINT 3,-10,3
(-73.30°, 16.03°)
Use 3DFACE and ARRAY.

## 3D EXERCISES

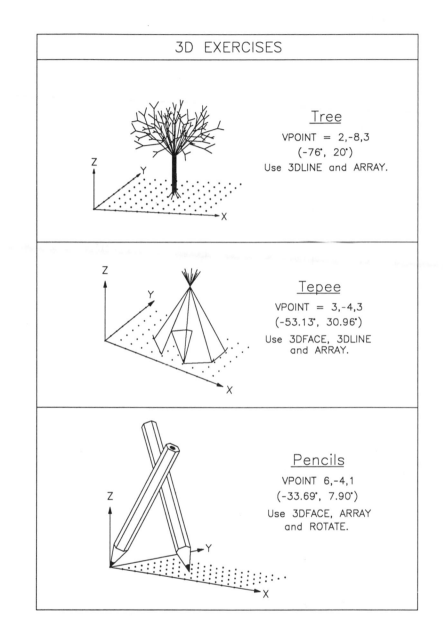

### Tree

VPOINT = 2,-8,3
(-76°, 20°)
Use 3DLINE and ARRAY.

### Tepee

VPOINT = 3,-4,3
(-53.13°, 30.96°)
Use 3DFACE, 3DLINE
and ARRAY.

### Pencils

VPOINT 6,-4,1
(-33.69°, 7.90°)
Use 3DFACE, ARRAY
and ROTATE.

# Right Hand

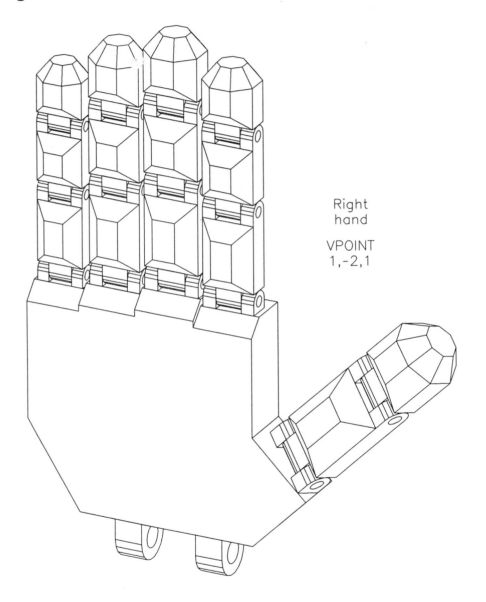

Right
hand

VPOINT
1,-2,1

# B

# CUSTOM MENU AND TABLET OVERLAY

The sample menu and tablet overlay in this appendix are intended for use with a digitizing tablet that has an 11-inch-square active area and a three-button pointer. The menu is at the end of this appendix.

The menu is designed for use without a screen menu area. You can remove the screen menu area by using "Configure video display" on the configuration menu.

The tablet overlay that corresponds to the ***TABLET sections of the menu is illustrated on the next page. The overlay is purposely kept simple and limited to those commands used most frequently. Commands not appearing on the overlay must be entered either from the keyboard or from the pull-down menus, since the menu has no screen menu section. (Of course, it could be combined with the screen menu portion of the standard AutoCAD menu.) By keeping the overlay uncluttered, you can easily spot the command you want and quickly memorize where commands are.

The BELT, XY and XYD commands that appear on the overlay and in the ***TABLET sections of the menu are calls to AutoLISP commands.

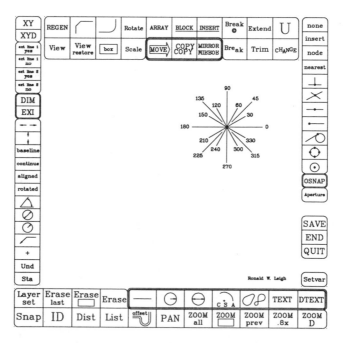

All AutoCAD commands are included, in alphabetical order, within the ***POP (pull-down) sections of the menu. The pull-down menus are illustrated below.

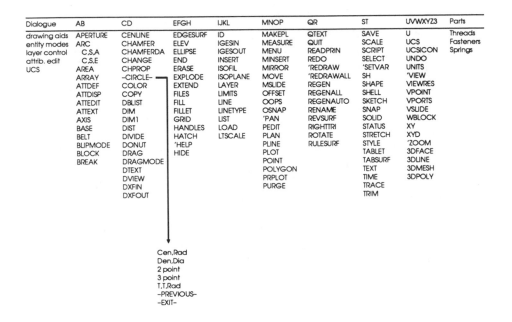

| Dialogue | AB | CD | EFGH | IJKL | MNOP | QR | ST | UVWXYZ3 | Parts |
|---|---|---|---|---|---|---|---|---|---|
| drawing aids | APERTURE | CENLINE | EDGESURF | ID | MAKEPL | QTEXT | SAVE | U | Threads |
| entity modes | ARC | CHAMFER | ELEV | IGESIN | MEASURE | QUIT | SCALE | UCS | Fasteners |
| layer control | C,S,A | CHAMFERDA | ELLIPSE | IGESOUT | MENU | READPRIN | SCRIPT | UCSICON | Springs |
| attrib. edit | C,S,E | CHANGE | END | INSERT | MINSERT | REDO | SELECT | UNDO | |
| UCS | AREA | CHPROP | ERASE | ISOFIL | MIRROR | 'REDRAW | 'SETVAR | UNITS | |
| | ARRAY | –CIRCLE– | EXPLODE | ISOPLANE | MOVE | 'REDRAWALL | SH | 'VIEW | |
| | ATTDEF | COLOR | EXTEND | LAYER | MSLIDE | REGEN | SHAPE | VIEWRES | |
| | ATTDISP | COPY | FILES | LIMITS | OFFSET | REGENALL | SHELL | VPOINT | |
| | ATTEDIT | DBLIST | FILL | LINE | OOPS | REGENAUTO | SKETCH | VPORTS | |
| | ATTEXT | DIM | FILLET | LINETYPE | OSNAP | RENAME | SNAP | VSLIDE | |
| | AXIS | DIM1 | GRID | LIST | 'PAN | REVSURF | SOLID | WBLOCK | |
| | BASE | DIST | HANDLES | LOAD | PEDIT | RIGHTTRI | STATUS | XY | |
| | BELT | DIVIDE | HATCH | LTSCALE | PLAN | ROTATE | STRETCH | XYD | |
| | BLIPMODE | DONUT | 'HELP | | PLINE | RULESURF | STYLE | 'ZOOM | |
| | BLOCK | DRAG | HIDE | | PLOT | | TABLET | 3DFACE | |
| | BREAK | DRAGMODE | | | POINT | | TABSURF | 3DLINE | |
| | | DTEXT | | | POLYGON | | TEXT | 3DMESH | |
| | | DVIEW | | | PRPLOT | | TIME | 3DPOLY | |
| | | DXFIN | | | PURGE | | TRACE | | |
| | | DXFOUT | | | | | TRIM | | |

Cen,Rad
Den,Dia
2 point
3 point
T,T,Rad
–PREVIOUS–
–EXIT–

By comparing the above display with the menu listing at the end of this appendix, you'll notice that the ***POP sections of the menu illustrate the following four features:

First, there are several AutoLISP commands among the other pull-down menu items. When these pull-down menus appear on the screen, the AutoLISP commands are grayed out to remind you that they're available only if they have been loaded during the current editing session. The tilde (~) in front of the command name causes the name to be grayed out. See, for example, the BELT command in the ***POP2 section of the menu.

Second, the ***POP1 section illustrates the use of dialogue boxes, called by three **'dd** commands.

Third, the ***POP3A section illustrates a submenu called by the –CIRCLE– item.

Fourth, the ***POP10 and ***ICON sections illustrate the use of icon menus. In ***POP10, only the Threads item is functional (no command portions are included for Fasteners or Springs). The Threads item makes "ITHREADS" the current icon menu and displays the icon menu shown below. In the **ITHREADS portion of the menu, thdsld1, thdsld2, etc., call slides for display in the icon menu, while (thd1), (thd2), etc., call various AutoLISP functions.

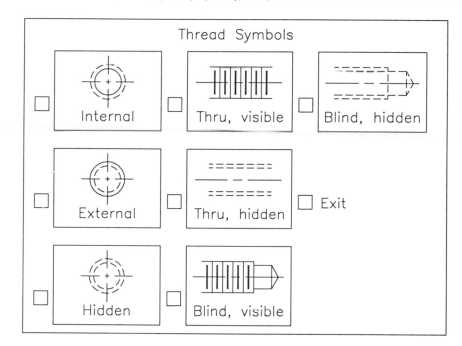

***BUTTONS
;
'redraw
***TABLET1
^C^Cregen
^C^Cchamfer
^C^Cfillet
^C^Crotate
^C^Carray
^C^Cblock
^C^Cinsert

^C^Cbreak \ f \@
^C^Cextend
^C^Cu
^C^Cview
'view r
box
^C^Cscale
^C^Cmove
^C^Ccopy
^C^Cmirror
^C^Cbreak

^C^Ctrim
^C^Cchange
***TABLET2
^C^Cxy
^C^Cxyd
dimse1 off
dimse1 on
dimse2 off
dimse2 on
^C^Cdim
exi
hor
ver
bas
con
ali
rot
ang
dia
rad
lea
cen
und
sta
***TABLET3
non
ins
nod
nea
per
int
mid
endpoint
tan
qua
cen
^C^Cosnap
^C^Caperture
^C^Csave ;
^C^Cend
^C^Cquit
'setvar

***TABLET4
^C^Clayer s \;
^C^Cerase L ;
^C^Cerase box
^C^Cerase
^C^Cline
^C^Ccircle
^C^Ccircle \d
^C^Carc c \\a
^C^Cbelt
^C^Ctext
^C^Cdtext
^C^Csnap
^C^Cid
^C^Cdist
^C^Clist
^C^Coffset
'pan
^C^Czoom a
'zoom w
'zoom p
'zoom .8x
'zoom d
***POP1
[Dialogue]
[Drawing aids]'ddrmodes
[Entity modes]'ddemodes
[Layer control]'ddlmodes
[Attrib. edit]^C^Cddatte
[UCS]^C^Cdducs
***POP2
[AB]
[APERTURE]^C^Caperture
[ARC]^C^Carc
[ C,S,A] ^C^Carc c \\a
[ C,S,E] ^C^Carc c
[AREA]^C^Carea
[ARRAY]^C^Carray
[ATTDEF]^C^Cattdef
[ATTDISP]^C^Cattdisp
[ATTEDIT]^C^Cattedit
[ATTEXT]^C^Cattext

[AXIS]^C^Caxis
[BASE]^C^Cbase
[~BELT]^C^Cbelt
[BLIPMODE]^C^Cblipmode
[BLOCK]^C^Cblock
[BREAK]^C^Cbreak
***POP3
**P3A
[CD]
[~CENLINE]^C^Ccenline
[CHAMFER]^C^Cchamfer
[~CHAMFERDA]^C^Cchamferda
[CHANGE]^C^Cchange
[CHPROP]^C^Cchprop
[–CIRCLE–]$P3=P3B  $P3=*
[COLOR]^C^Ccolor
[COPY]^C^Ccopy
[DBLIST]^C^Cdblist
[DIM]^C^Cdim
[DIM1]^C^Cdim1
[DIST]^C^Cdist
[DIVIDE]^C^Cdivide
[DONUT]^C^Cdonut
[DRAG]drag
[DRAGMODE]^C^Cdragmode
[DTEXT]^C^Cdtext
[DVIEW]^C^Cdview
[DXFIN]^C^Cdxfin
[DXFOUT]^C^Cdxfout


**P3B
[——]
[Cen,Rad]^C^Ccircle  $P3=P3A
[Cen,Dia]^C^Ccircle \d  $P3=P3A
[2 point]^C^Ccircle 2p  $P3=P3A
[3 point]^C^Ccircle 3p  $P3=P3A
[T,T,Rad]^C^Ccircle ttr  $P3=P3A
[–PREVIOUS–]$P3=P3A  $P3=*
[–EXIT–]$P3=P3A


***POP4
[EFGH]

[EDGESURF]^C^Cedgesurf
[ELEV]^C^Celev
[ELLIPSE]^C^Cellipse
[END]^C^Cend
[ERASE]^C^Cerase
[EXPLODE]^C^Cexplode
[EXTEND]^C^Cextend
[FILES]^C^Cfiles
[FILL]^C^Cfill
[FILLET]^C^Cfillet
[GRID]^C^Cgrid
[HANDLES]^C^Chandles
[HATCH]^C^Chatch
['HELP]'help
[HIDE]^C^Chide
***POP5
[IJKL]
[ID]^C^Cid
[IGESIN]^C^Cigesin
[IGESOUT]^C^Cigesout
[INSERT]^C^Cinsert
[~ISOFIL]^C^Cisofil
[ISOPLANE]^C^Cisoplane
[LAYER]^C^Clayer
[LIMITS]^C^Climits
[LINE]^C^Cline
[LINETYPE]^C^Clinetype
[LIST]^C^Clist
[LOAD]^C^Cload
[LTSCALE]^C^Cltscale
***POP6
[MNOP]
[~MAKEPL]^C^Cmakepl
[MEASURE]^C^Cmeasure
[MENU]^C^Cmenu
[MINSERT]^C^Cminsert
[MIRROR]^C^Cmirror
[MOVE]^C^Cmove
[MSLIDE]^C^Cmslide
[OFFSET]^C^Coffset
[OOPS]^C^Coops
[OSNAP]^C^Cosnap

['PAN]'pan
[PEDIT]^C^Cpedit
[PLAN]^C^Cplan
[PLINE]^C^Cpline
[PLOT]^C^Cplot
[POINT]^C^Cpoint
[POLYGON]^C^Cpolygon
[PRPLOT]^C^Cprplot
[PURGE]^C^Cpurge
***POP7
[QR]
[QTEXT]^C^Cqtext
[QUIT]^C^Cquit
[~READPRIN]^C^Creadprin
[REDO]^C^Credo
['REDRAW]'redraw
['REDRAWALL]'redrawall
[REGEN]^C^Cregen
[REGENALL]^C^Cregenall
[REGENAUTO]^C^Cregenauto
[RENAME]^C^Crename
[REVSURF]^C^Crevsurf
[~RIGHTTRI]^C^Crighttri
[ROTATE]^C^Crotate
[RULESURF]^C^Crulesurf
***POP8
[ST]
[SAVE]^C^Csave
[SCALE]^C^Cscale
[SCRIPT]^C^Cscript
[SELECT]^C^Cselect
['SETVAR]'setvar
[SH]^C^Csh
[SHAPE]^C^Cshape
[SHELL]^C^Cshell
[SKETCH]^C^Csketch
[SNAP]^C^Csnap
[SOLID]^C^Csolid
[STATUS]^C^Cstatus
[STRETCH]^C^Cstretch
[STYLE]^C^Cstyle
[TABLET]^C^Ctablet

[TABSURF]^C^Ctabsurf
[TEXT]^C^Ctext
[TIME]^C^Ctime
[TRACE]^C^Ctrace
[TRIM]^C^Ctrim
***POP9
[UVWXYZ3]
[U]^C^Cu
[UCS]^C^Cucs
[UCSICON]^C^Cucsicon
[UNDO]^C^Cundo
[UNITS]^C^Cunits
['VIEW]'view
[VIEWRES]^C^Cviewres
[VPOINT]^C^Cvpoint
[VPORTS]^C^Cvports
[VSLIDE]^C^Cvslide
[WBLOCK]^C^Cwblock
[~XY]^C^Cxy
[~XYD]^C^Cxyd
['ZOOM]'zoom
[3DFACE]^C^C3dface
[3DLINE]^C^C3dline
[3DMESH]^C^C3dmesh
[3DPOLY]^C^C3dpoly
***POP10
[Parts]
[Threads]$I=ITHREADS $I=*
[Fasteners]
[Springs]
***ICON
**ITHREADS
[THREAD SYMBOLS]
[thdsld1]^C^C(thd1)
[thdsld2]^C^C(thd2)
[thdsld3]^C^C(thd3)
[thdsld4]^C^C(thd4)
[thdsld5]^C^C(thd5)
[thdsld6]^C^C(thd6)
[thdsld7]^C^C(thd7)
[ EXIT]^C

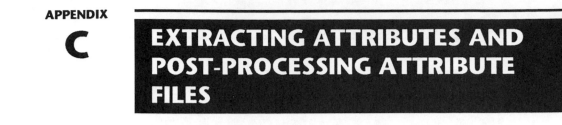

# EXTRACTING ATTRIBUTES AND POST-PROCESSING ATTRIBUTE FILES

This appendix shows how to extract attribute information from a drawing and how to convert an attribute file into a parts list. The process of producing a parts list, or bill of materials, is diagrammed below. See Chapter 35 for a discussion of the ATTDEF, ATTDISP, ATTEDIT and ATTEXT commands.

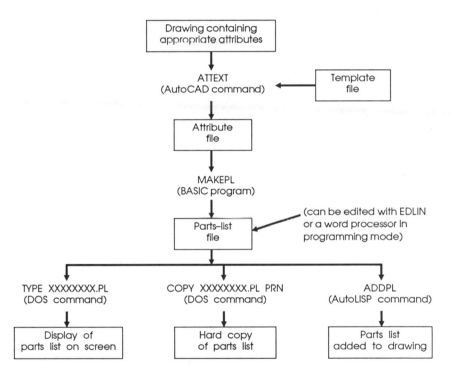

Following these steps can ensure that assembly drawings and parts lists match. It can also speed up producing and revising parts lists, especially if predrawn blocks with the appropriate attributes already exist in a parts library.

On the next two pages are two plottings of an outlet box. The drawing file is named OUTLETBX.DWG. The first plotting shows the drawing with its attributes (ATTDISP is on) ready for extraction and post-processing. When the drawing is at this stage it's represented by the top box in the diagram above. The second plotting shows the completed drawing (ATTDISP is off).

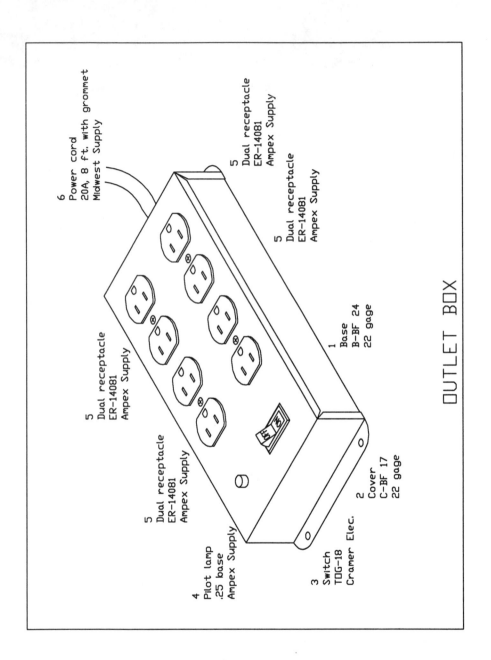

6
Power cord
20A, 8 ft. with grommet
Midwest Supply

5
Dual receptacle
ER-14081
Ampex Supply

5
Dual receptacle
ER-14081
Ampex Supply

5
Dual receptacle
ER-14081
Ampex Supply

5
Dual receptacle
ER-14081
Ampex Supply

4
Pilot lamp
.25 base
Ampex Supply

3
Switch
TOG-18
Cramer Elec.

2
Cover
C-BF 17
22 gage

1
Base
B-BF 24
22 gage

OUTLET BOX

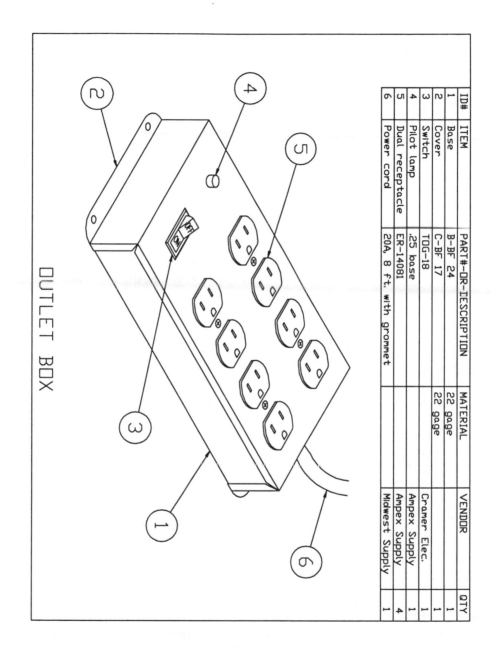

OUTLET BOX

| ID# | ITEM | PART#-OR-DESCRIPTION | MATERIAL | VENDOR | QTY |
|---|---|---|---|---|---|
| 1 | Base | B-BF 24 | 22 gage | Cramer Elec. | 1 |
| 2 | Cover | C-BF 17 | 22 gage | | 1 |
| 3 | Switch | TOG-18 | | Ampex Supply | 1 |
| 4 | Pilot lamp | .25 base | | Ampex Supply | 1 |
| 5 | Dual receptacle | ER-14081 | | Ampex Supply | 4 |
| 6 | Power cord | 20A, 8 ft. with grommet | | Midwest Supply | 1 |

There are six blocks in the drawing: base, cover, switch, pilot, cord and recep ("recep" is the block name of the dual receptacle and appears four times in the drawing). Each block has several attributes (tags). For example, the switch block has these: ID#, ITEM, PART#-OR-DESCRIPTION and VENDOR. The cover block has these: ID#, ITEM, PART#-OR-DESCRIPTION and MATERIAL.

Attributes can be created so that they're large enough to read without zooming in. This often means that they have to extend outside the geometry of the block with which they're associated. There's no problem if they overlap other geometry, even of other attributes, because they can be turned off with the **ATTDISP** command. In the sample drawing, some of the attributes have been moved from their original positions with the ATTEDIT command for the sake of clarity.

Another approach is to make attributes so small that several of them will fit entirely inside the associated geometry. In this case it's usually necessary to zoom in on the block or part of the block to view or edit the attributes.

You extract attribute information with the **ATTEXT** command. In this example, the extract file is in the SDF format. You must create a template file before using the ATTEXT command. The following file, named ATTTEMP.TXT, can be created with EDLIN or a word processor in programming mode. It's designed to extract up to five attributes from each block. A block can have either more or fewer attributes than those listed below.

```
ID#                          C003000
ITEM                         C015000
PART#-OR-DESCRIPTION         C023000
MATERIAL                     C014000
VENDOR                       C014000
```

ID# stands for identification number (balloon number).

Later we'll use a BASIC language program to post-process the attribute file that's extracted using the above template file. In order for that BASIC program to operate correctly, each block must have the ID# attribute (tag).

Notice that the column widths in the file are 3, 15, 23, 14 and 14, a total of 69 characters.

After all the blocks have been inserted in the drawing with the appropriate information in the attributes, and after the template file has been created, we can extract the attribute information and place it in a file. To do so, use the **ATTEXT** command and enter the following information when prompted:

```
CDF, SDF, or DXF?          Enter S (for SDF format file).
Template file:             Enter ATTEMP.
Extract file name:         Enter OUTLETBX.
```

This will produce an SDF format (random access) attribute file named OUT-LETBX.TXT which, when typed on the screen, looks like this (order of the lines may vary):

```
5   Dual receptacle    ER-14081               Ampex Supply

5   Dual receptacle    ER-14081               Ampex Supply

5   Dual receptacle    ER-14081               Ampex Supply

5   Dual receptacle    ER-14081               Ampex Supply

4   Pilot lamp         25 base                Ampex Supply

3   Switch             TOG-18                 Cramer Elec.

6   Power cord         20A, 8 ft.with grommet Midwest Supply

1   Base               B-BF 24  22 gage

2   Cover              C-BF 17  22 gage
```

For this file to become an acceptable parts list file, it must be modified (post-processed) as follows:

    1) Sort lines according to ID number.

    2) Combine identical lines.

    3) Count identical lines so that quantity can be included.

    4) Put spaces between the columns.

    5) Add column headings.

    6) Add a header line to identify the parts list file.

You can use the BASIC program below to make these modifications. It's intentionally written short and simple so you can alter it to suit your needs. This program is designed to work with extract files that are in SDF format and that are created using the ATTTEMP.TXT template file given earlier. If a different format or a different template file is used, you must adjust the BASIC program accordingly. The program will handle an extract file of up to 1,000 lines.

```
100 ' MAKEPL.BAS, written by Ronald W. Leigh, 7-87
110 '  Reads an SDF format attribute file (XXXXXXXX.TXT), sorts the file, com-
120 '  bines identical lines, and creates a new parts list file (XXXXXXXX.PL)
130 ' Variables:
140 '  C counter for identical lines     L$ line of file in buffer
150 '  COMP no. of comparisons           L$(I) array of lines in file
160 '  CR$ carriage return/line feed     MA$ MATERIAL tag info.
170 '  F$ file name                      NLC new line count
180 '  F1$ file name with .TXT           PASS no. of passes
190 '  F2$ file name with .PL            PA$ PART#-OR-DESCRIPTION tag info.
200 '  HL$ header line                   QU$ quantity
210 '  I index                           SF swap flag
220 '  ID$ ID# tag info.                 TEXT$ first 4 lines in parts list file
230 '  IT$ ITEM tag info.                VE$ vendor tag info.
240 '  LC line count
250 '---------- GET ATTRIBUTE FILE ----------
260 SCREEN 0 : WIDTH 80 : KEY OFF : DEFINT C,I,L,N,P,S : DIM L$(1000)
270 INPUT "Name of SDF format attribute file (do not include extension): ",F$
280 PRINT "Header to identify parts list file (up to 78 char., enter below):"
290 LINE INPUT "",HL$
300 F1$ = F$ + ".TXT" : F2$ = F$ + ".PL"
310 OPEN F1$ AS 1 LEN = 71 : FIELD 1, 69 AS L$ : I = 0
320 PRINT "Getting attribute file " F1$
330 I = I + 1 : GET 1
340 IF ASC(L$) > 31 THEN L$(I) = L$ : GOTO 330
350 CLOSE 1 : LC = I - 1
360 '---------- SORT ATTRIBUTE FILE ----------
370 PRINT "Sorting "; : COMP = LC
380 FOR PASS = 1 TO LC - 1
390 COMP = COMP - 1 : SF = 0
400 FOR I = 1 TO COMP
410 IF L$(I) > L$(I+1) THEN SWAP L$(I),L$(I+1) : SF = 1
420 NEXT I : PRINT "*";
430 IF SF = 0 THEN PASS = LC - 1
440 NEXT PASS : PRINT
450 '------- COMBINE & COUNT IDENTICAL LINES, CREATE PARTS LIST FILE -------
460 PRINT "Combining/counting/filing ";
470 OPEN F2$ AS 1 LEN=80 : FIELD 1, 78 AS TEXT$,2 AS CR$
480 LSET TEXT$ = HL$ : LSET CR$ = CHR$(13)+CHR$(10) : PUT 1
490 LSET TEXT$ = "" : PUT 1
500 LSET TEXT$ = "ID# ITEM               PART#-OR-DESCRIPTION    MATERIAL       VEN
DOR           QTY" : PUT 1
510 LSET TEXT$ = STRING$(78,45) : PUT 1
520 FIELD 1, 4 AS ID$,16 AS IT$,24 AS PA$,15 AS MA$,15 AS VE$,4 AS QU$,2 AS CR$
530 C = 1 : NLC = 0
540 FOR I = 1 TO LC
550 IF L$(I) = L$(I+1) THEN C = C + 1 : GOTO 600
560 LSET ID$ = MID$(L$(I),1,3) : LSET IT$ = MID$(L$(I),4,15)
570 LSET PA$ = MID$(L$(I),19,23) : LSET MA$ = MID$(L$(I),42,14)
580 LSET VE$ = MID$(L$(I),56,14) : RSET QU$ = STR$(C)
590 PUT 1 : NLC = NLC + 1 : C = 1 :PRINT "*";
600 NEXT I : CLOSE 1 : PRINT
610 PRINT NLC "lines written to file " F2$
620 END
```

To try the program, enter **BASIC** from the DOS prompt, then enter each line. Lines 100–240 are merely documentation and need not be entered for the program to run. Then save the program by entering **SAVE "MAKEPL"** (short for MAKE PARTS LIST). This saves the program in the file MAKEPL.BAS. To return to DOS, enter **SYSTEM.**

To run MAKEPL.BAS from the DOS prompt, enter **BASIC MAKEPL.** When the program prompts for the name of the attribute extract file, enter **OUTLETBX.** The program will also prompt for a header line to identify the parts list file. The program will produce a file named OUTLETBX.PL, similar to the one shown below. To return to DOS, enter **SYSTEM.**

```
Webber National Products, Job No. 85227B, KRV, 11-88
ID#ITEM            PART#-OR-DESCRIPTION MATERIAL VENDOR         QTY
1 Base             B-BF 24              22 gage                 1
2 Cover            C-BF 17              22 gage                 1
3 Switch           TOG-18                        Cramer Elec.   1
4 Pilot lamp       .25 base                      Ampex Supply   1
5 Dual receptacle  ER-14081                      Ampex Supply   4
6 Power cord       20A, 8 ft. with grommet       Midwest Supply 1
```

You can display this OUTLETBX.PL file on the screen by entering **TYPE OUTLETBX.PL** or send it to the printer by entering **COPY OUTLETBX.PL PRN.** It's a regular ASCII text file, so you can edit it with EDLIN or a word processor in programming mode. If you do edit this file, don't change its basic structure, or the AutoLISP program described below won't work properly.

The AutoLISP program listed below is called ADDPL.LSP and is used inside AutoCAD to add the parts list to the drawing, as illustrated in the second plotting earlier in this appendix. The program is designed to work only with parts list files created by the MAKEPL.BAS program.

The ADDPL program prompts for the name of the parts list file, then the location of the lower right or upper right corner of the parts list box, then the distance between lines. (Text height is automatically set at one-half the distance between lines.) The program then draws the outline of the parts list box and asks if you want to continue, or if you want to specify a new location and line spacing.

The program doesn't use the header line from the file. That information is already in the title block of the drawing. It also ignores the blank line and the line of dashes, since the remaining information is placed in a typical parts list box.

```
; c:addpl—Add parts list. Adds a parts list file
; that was produced by MAKEPL.BAS to a drawing.
; Variables:
; c Y or N for continuation          n Number of lines
; f Filename        p Starting corner
                                     of parts list box
; fr File descriptor                 s Line spacing
; h Height of text   x1-x7,y1,y2 Coords.
                                     of parts list box
; line Line from file
(defun c:addpl (/ c f fr h line n p s x1 x2 x3 x4 x5 x6 x7 y1 y2)
  (princ "\n** This program works only with files created with MAKEPL.BAS **")
  (princ "\n** Current text style should have a variable height. **")
  (pl-sizefile) (setq c "N") (setvar "cmdecho" 0)
  (while (= c "N") (pl-getbox))
  (pl-lines-text)
  (setvar "blipmode" 1) (setvar "cmdecho" 1)
  (princ))

(defun pl-sizefile ()
  (while (= "" (setq f (strcase
    (getstring "\nName of parts list file (w/o extension): ")))))
  (setq f (strcat f ".PL") fr (open f "r") n -3)
  (while (read-line fr) (setq n (1+ n)))
  (close fr) (terpri) (princ n) (princ " lines in ")(princ f))

(defun pl-getbox ()
  (setq p (getpoint "\nUpper right or lower right corner of parts list box: ")
    s (getreal "\nDistance between lines (pos. up, neg. down): ")
    h (abs (/ s 2.0)))
  (setvar "blipmode" 0)
  (setq x7 (car p) x1 ( - x7 (* 84 h)) x2 (+ x1 (* 5 h)) x3 (+ x1 (* 22 h))
  x4 (+ x1 (* 47 h)) x5 (+ x1 (* 63 h)) x6 (+ x1 (* 79 h)))
  (setq y1 (cadr p) y2 (+ y1 (* n s)))
  (command "line" p (list x7 y2) (list x1 y2) (list x1 y1) "c")
  (command "zoom" "c" (list (/ (+ x1 x7) 2.0) (/ (+ y1 y2) 2.0))
    (max (* 1.5 ( -x7 x1)) (* 2.0 (abs ( -y2 y1)))))
  (while (not (member (setq c (strcase
    (getstring "\nContinue? (Y/N): "))) (list "Y" "N"))))
```

```
  (if (= c "N") (progn
    (command "erase" "L" "" "erase" "L" "" "erase" "L" "" "erase" "L" "")
    (setvar "blipmode" 1))))


(defun pl-lines-text ()
  (command    "array" "l" "" "r" n 1 s)
  (command    "line" (list x2 y1) (list x2 y2) ""
              "line" (list x3 y1) (list x3 y2) ""
              "line" (list x4 y1) (list x4 y2) ""
              "line" (list x5 y1) (list x5 y2) ""
              "line" (list x6 y1) (list x6 y2) "")
  (setq x1 (+ x1 h) x2 (+ x2 h) x3 (+ x3 h)
     x4 (+ x4 h) x5 (+ x5 h) x6 (+ x6 h)
     y1 ( -(+ y1 (/ s 2.0)) (/ h 2.0)))
  (setq fr (open f "r"))
  (read-line fr) (read-line fr) (pl-printline) (read-line fr)
  (repeat (1- n) (pl-printline)))
(defun pl-printline ()
  (setq line (read-line fr))
  (command    "text" (list x1 y1) h 0 (substr line 1 3)
              "text" (list x2 y1) h 0 (substr line 5 15)
              "text" (list x3 y1) h 0 (substr line 21 23)
              "text" (list x4 y1) h 0 (substr line 45 14)
              "text" (list x5 y1) h 0 (substr line 60 14)
              "text" (list x6 y1) h 0 (substr line 76 3))
(setq y1 (+ y1 s)))
```

# A SIMPLE SYSTEM MENU AND BATCH FILES

Most designers and drafters use more than one applications program on their computers. Besides AutoCAD, you may be using a word processing package, a database program and other technical software. A system menu can help you organize these programs for your own benefit, as well as making it easier for other users to work with your programs.

A number of system menu programs are available commercially. However, this appendix describes a simple system menu and its associated batch files that you can easily create using EDLIN or a word processor in programming (nondocument) mode.

If you aren't familiar with batch files, EDLIN or making subdirectories, you should review the material on these subjects in Chapters 2 and 26 of this guide or in your DOS manual. We're using DOS version 3.2. This version of DOS differs slightly from other versions; we describe the differences later.

```
════════════════ S Y S T E M   M E N U ═══════════════
 1  Format a diskette in drive A:      13  WordStar
 2                                      14
 3  Directory listing of A:            15  PC-File
 4  Directory listing of C:\WORK        16
 5                                      17
 6  Copy all files from A: to C:\WORK   18  AutoCAD w/o tablet menu overlay
 7  Copy all files from C:\WORK to A:   19  AutoCAD with tablet menu overlay
 8                                      20
 9  Erase all files on C:\WORK          21  Synthesis
10                                      22
11                                      23  AniCAM / Minicam
12                                      24
 └To re-display menu and return to the \WORK directory at any time, enter M ┘

Enter number or DOS command below.
```

The system menu described in this appendix includes the menu display shown above, which appears on the screen automatically when you first boot your system and reappears whenever you enter **M** at the DOS prompt. You can expand and adapt it to suit your needs.

Some of the subdirectories on the hard disk are pictured below, along with the names of selected system files in the root directory and selected batch files in the \BATCH directory that make up this menu system.

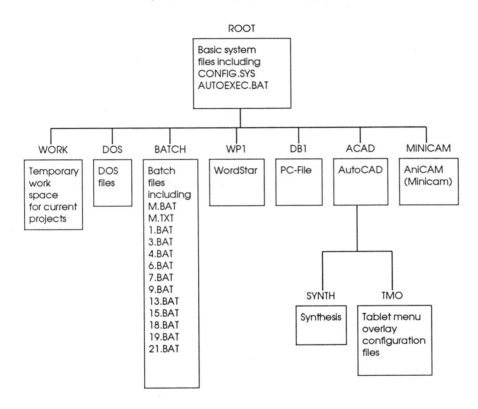

The two files in the root directory contain these lines:

CONFIG.SYS

```
files=20
buffers=20
device=c:\dos\ansi.sys
```

AUTOEXEC.BAT

```
echo off
path c:\;c:\dos;c:\batch
prompt $e[1;33;44m $p $g $e[m
break on
verify on
```

```
cd c:\work
cls
eveclock
echo
type c:\batch\m.txt
```

After the AUTOEXEC.BAT file has executed, the DOS prompt appears near the bottom of the screen. At this point, you have access to the various menu items (batch files) by simply entering the appropriate number, or you can use any DOS command.

Line 3 in the AUTOEXEC.BAT file produces a DOS prompt that has yellow letters on a blue background. This line works only if the CONFIG.SYS file contains a line that installs ANSI.SYS as a device driver, such as line 3 in the CONFIG.SYS file above. If you don't want to deal with a fancy-color DOS prompt, you can simply omit line 3 of the CONFIG.SYS file and change line 3 of the AUTOEXEC.BAT file to read `prompt $p $g`.

Line 8 in the AUTOEXEC.BAT file gets the date and time from the internal battery clock. The exact command line will depend on your clock software.

In line 9 of the AUTOEXEC.BAT file, the **ECHO** command is followed by a space and the character 255. To enter a character 255, hold down the **ALT** key, then enter **255** on the numeric keypad, then release the ALT key. (It will appear as a blank space on the screen when you release the ALT key.) This command line is used here to force the output of the next command (`type ...`) to appear at the beginning of a new line, and may not be needed in your version of this file (depending on how your clock software works). Some earlier versions of DOS use two spaces after the ECHO command to accomplish the same thing.

In subsequent files, you'll find several places where ECHO occurs on a line by itself. As above, it's actually followed by a space and a character 255, but is being used there for its more typical purpose—to place a blank line on the screen.

The M.BAT file, listed below, redisplays the menu and returns you to the \WORK subdirectory. It contains many of the same lines found in the AUTOEXEC.BAT file.

M.BAT

```
echo off
c:
path c:\;c:\dos;c:\batch
prompt $e[1;33;44m $p $g $e[m
```

```
break on
verify on
cd c:\work
cls
type c:\batch\m.txt
```

Both the AUTOEXEC.BAT file and the M.BAT file place the menu on the screen by using the TYPE command to display the contents of the M.TXT file (see the last line of both files). The M.TXT file can be as simple or as fancy as you like.

In the sample display shown on the first page of this appendix, there's a double-line box around the menu options. You can enter the double lines into the M.TXT file (using EDLIN or most line editors/word processors) by holding down the ALT key, entering the ASCII code at the numeric keypad, then releasing the ALT key. The ASCII codes include: 205 for horizontal lines, 186 for vertical lines, and 201, 187, 200 and 188 for the upper left, upper right, lower left, and lower right corners respectively.

The first six options on the menu (items 1, 3, 4, 6, 7 and 9) are general housekeeping utilities. The six batch files that correspond to these options on the menu are given below. The last line in each file runs the M.BAT file which, among other things, redisplays the menu.

1. BAT (formats a diskette in drive A:)

```
echo off
format a:
m
```

3. BAT (gets a directory listing of drive A:)

```
echo off
dir a: /p
pause
m
```

4. BAT (gets a directory listing of C:\WORK)

```
echo off
dir c:\work /p
pause
m
```

6. BAT (copies all files from A: to C:\WORK)

```
echo off
echo Make sure your floppy diskette is in drive A:
pause
copy a:*.* c:\work
m
```

7. BAT (copies all files from C:\WORK to A:)

```
echo off
echo Make sure your floppy diskette is in drive A:
pause
copy c:\work\*.* a:
m
```

9. BAT (erases all files on C:\WORK)

```
echo off
dir c:\work /w
echo ---- You are about to erase the above files ----
erase c:\work\*.*
m
```

The remaining batch files are used to prepare for various applications packages. They log into the proper directory, establish the necessary path and environmental variables, get a directory listing and finally remind you how to start the program (rather than entering the program directly from the batch file). This lets you review, copy and erase files before starting the program.

13. BAT (prepares for WordStar)

```
echo off
c:
cd \wstar
path c:\;c:\dos;c:\batch
dir /w
echo
echo To start WordStar, enter WS
```

15. BAT (prepares for PC-File)

```
echo off
c:
cd \pcfile
path c:\;c:\dos;c:\batch
```

```
dir c:\work /w
echo
echo ---- You are on the \PCFILE subdirectory
echo ---- PC-File is set up to work with databases on
the \DATA subdirectory
echo ---- To start PC-File, enter PCFILE
```

18. BAT (prepares to use AutoCAD without a tablet menu overlay)

```
echo off
c:
path c:\acad;c:\;c:\dos;c:\batch
cd \work
set acadcfg=
set lispstack=4000
set lispheap=41000
set acadfreeram=24
dir /w
echo
echo To start AutoCAD, enter ACAD
```

19. BAT (prepares to use AutoCAD with the standard tablet menu overlay)

```
echo off
c:
path c:\acad;c:\;c:\dos;c:\batch
cd \work
set acadcfg=c:\acad\tmo
set lispstack=4000
set lispheap=41000
set acadfreeram=24
dir /w
echo
echo To start AutoCAD, enter ACAD
```

21. BAT (prepares for Synthesis)

```
echo off
c:
cd \au\synth
path c:\acad;c:\;c:dos;c:\batch
set acadcfg=
set lispstack=4000
```

```
set lispheap=41000
set acadfreeram=24
dir /w
echo
echo To start Synthesis, enter SYNTH
```

23. BAT (prepares for AniCAM/Minicam)

```
echo off
c:
cd \minicam
dir *.in /w
echo
echo To start Minicam, enter MINICAM
```

# METRIC/ENGLISH CONVERSIONS

## If you know the number of British/U.S. units and want to find the number of metric units:

Millimeters = inches x 25.4 (exact)

Centimeters = inches x 2.54 (exact)

Meters = feet x .3048 (exact)

Meters = yards x .9144 (exact)

Kilometers = miles x 1.609344 (exact)

Square centimeters = sq. inches x 6.4516 (exact)

Square meters = sq. feet x .092903

Square meters = sq. yards x .836127

Square kilometers = sq. miles x 2.5900

Hectares = acres x .404686

Cubic centimeters = cubic inches x 16.3871

Cubic meters = cubic feet x .0283168

Cubic meters = cubic yards x .764555

Grams = ounces x 28.3495

Kilograms = pounds x .453592

Metric tons = tons (short tons) x .907185

Milliliters = fluid ounces x 29.5735

Liters = quarts x .946353

Liters = gallons x 3.78541

Meters/second = miles/hour x .44704 (exact)

$$\text{Centigrade} = \frac{5}{9}(\text{Fahrenheit} -32)$$

## If you know the number of metric units and want to find the number of British/U.S. units:

Inches = millimeters x .0393701

Inches = centimeters x .393701

Feet = meters x 3.28084

Yards = meters x 1.09361

Miles = kilometers x .621371

Square inches = sq. centimeters x .15500

Square feet = sq. meters x 10.7639

Square yards = sq. meters x 1.1960

Square miles = sq. kilometers x .38614

Acres = hectares x 2.47105

Cubic inches = cubic centimeters x .06102

Cubic feet = cubic meters x 35.3147

Cubic yards = cubic meters x 1.30795

Ounces = grams x .035274

Pounds = kilograms x 2.20462

Tons (short tons) = metric tons x 1.10231

Fluid ounces = milliliters x .033814

Quarts = liters x 1.05669

Gallons = liters x .264172

Miles/hour = meters/second x 2.23694

$$\text{Fahrenheit} = \frac{5}{9}(\text{Centigrade} + 32)$$

Name _____ Date _____ Latest version _____

Place an X in the box that represents your level for each skill.

## LEVELS

1 **Partial Familiarity Level**—I've tried this skill (or some aspects of it) a few times with fair success.
2 **Mastery Level**—I've used most aspects of this skill many times with good success.
3 **Teacher Level**—I could demonstrate and explain all aspects of this skill.

| SKILLS:                                                          Level: | 1 | 2 | 3 |
|---|---|---|---|
| DOS commands and subdirectories | | | |
| Using the keyboard to enter AutoCAD commands | | | |
| Using the screen menu & pull-down menus to enter commands | | | |
| Using a tablet overlay to enter AutoCAD commands | | | |
| Using dialogue boxes | | | |
| LIMITS | | | |
| GRID, AXIS | | | |
| POINT | | | |
| Relative rectangular & relative polar coordinates | | | |
| SNAP including rotation & style | | | |
| SETVAR command and various system variables (PDMODE, PICKBOX, etc.) | | | |
| LINE | | | |
| Manipulating SNAP, GRID, and ORTHO from function keys | | | |
| SAVE, END, QUIT | | | |
| UNITS | | | |
| Interactive item selection | | | |
| ERASE, OOPS | | | |
| Using the File Utility menu | | | |
| STATUS | | | |
| DRAGMODE | | | |
| ARC | | | |
| ZOOM, PAN, VIEW and VIEWRES | | | |
| OSNAP, APERTURE | | | |

| SKILLS:                                      Level: | 1 | 2 | 3 |
|-----------------------------------------------------|---|---|---|
| ID, DIST, LIST, DBLIST                              |   |   |   |
| AREA                                                |   |   |   |
| MOVE, COPY                                          |   |   |   |
| MIRROR                                              |   |   |   |
| OFFSET                                              |   |   |   |
| FILLET, CHAMFER                                     |   |   |   |
| ROTATE, SCALE                                       |   |   |   |
| U, UNDO, REDO                                       |   |   |   |
| TEXT, DTEXT, QTEXT                                  |   |   |   |
| STYLE using various text fonts                      |   |   |   |
| Using prototype drawings                            |   |   |   |
| PLOT, PRPLOT                                        |   |   |   |
| BREAK, TRIM, EXTEND                                 |   |   |   |
| CHANGE                                              |   |   |   |
| STRETCH                                             |   |   |   |
| DIVIDE, MEASURE                                     |   |   |   |
| TRACE, SOLID, FILL                                  |   |   |   |
| LAYER                                               |   |   |   |
| COLOR, LINETYPE, LTSCALE                            |   |   |   |
| ARRAY                                               |   |   |   |
| POLYGON, ELLIPSE                                    |   |   |   |
| BLOCK, INSERT, EXPLODE, WBLOCK, BASE                |   |   |   |
| PURGE                                               |   |   |   |
| DIM (linear dimensions)                             |   |   |   |
| DIM (all other dimension types and dimensioning variables) |   |   |   |
| Stretching dimensions, HOMETEXT, UPDATE, NEWTEXT    |   |   |   |
| Drawing/plotting at various scales and using metric units |   |   |   |
| HATCH                                               |   |   |   |
| TABLET                                              |   |   |   |
| SKETCH                                              |   |   |   |
| SHELL, Advanced DOS commands, etc.                  |   |   |   |
| MSLIDE, VSLIDE., and using the SLIDELIB program     |   |   |   |
| PLINE, PEDIT, DONUT                                 |   |   |   |
| Isometric drawings                                  |   |   |   |
| User Coordinate Systems                             |   |   |   |
| ELEV, VPOINT, PLAN, HIDE                            |   |   |   |
| 3DLINE, 3DFACE, 3DPOLY                              |   |   |   |

| SKILLS                          Level: | 1 | 2 | 3 |
|----------------------------------------|---|---|---|
| DVIEW                                  |   |   |   |
| Using point filters                    |   |   |   |
| Meshes                                 |   |   |   |
| Attributes, ATTDEF, ATTDISP, ATT-EDIT, ATTEXT using template file |   |   |   |
| Custom linetypes                       |   |   |   |
| LOAD, SHAPE                            |   |   |   |
| Creating custom shapes                 |   |   |   |
| MENU and creating custom screen, tablet and pull-down menus |   |   |   |
| The configuration menus and creating configurations for different users |   |   |   |
| DXFIN, DXFOUT, IGESIN, IGESOUT         |   |   |   |
| Using the ACAD.PGP file                |   |   |   |
| UNDEFINE, REDEFINE                     |   |   |   |
| AutoLISP programming                   |   |   |   |
| Post-processing                        |   |   |   |

# PLOTTER PAPER SIZES

## Sheet Sizes                 Suggested Format Sizes

### For Houston Instruments DMP 40 plotter

| | | |
|---|---|---|
| A | 11 x 8.5 | 9.25 x 6.9  (234 x 175 mm) |
| A | 8.5 x 11  (vertical) | 6.9 x 9.25  (175 x 234 mm) |
| B | 17 x 11 | 14 x 9.25  (355 x 234 mm) |

### For Houston Instruments DMP 42 plotter

| | | |
|---|---|---|
| C | 24 x 18 | 21.5 x 14.5  (546 x 368 mm) |
| D | 36 x 24 | 34 x 21.5  (863 x 546 mm) |

### For JDL-850 EWS printer-plotter

| | | |
|---|---|---|
| A | 11 x 8.5 | 10 x 6.5 (254 x 165 mm)  not rotated when printed<br>9 x 7.5 (229 x 190 mm)  rotated when printed |
| A | 8.5 x 11  (vertical) | 7.5 x 9 (190 x 229 mm)  not rotated when printed<br>6.5 x 10 (165 x 254 mm)  rotated when printed |
| A | 12 x 9 | 11 x 7 (279 x 178 mm)  not rotated when  printed<br>10 x 8 (254 x 203 mm)  rotated when printed |
| A | 9 x 12  (vertical) | 8 x 10 (203 x 254 mm)  not rotated when printed<br>7 x 11 (178 x 279 mm)  rotated when printed |
| B | 17 x 11 | 15.09 x 9 (383 x 229 mm)  not rotated when printed<br>15.00 x 10 (381 x 254 mm)  rotated when printed |
| B | 18 x 12 | 15.09 x 10 (383 x 254 mm)  not rotated when printed<br>16.00 x 11 (406 x 279 mm)  rotated when printed |
| C | 22 x 17 | 20 x 15.09 (508 x 383 mm)  rotated when printed |
| C | 24 x 18 | 22 x 15.09 (559 x 383 mm)  rotated when  printed |

# INDEX

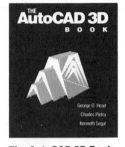

# BECOME EVEN MORE PRODUCTIVE . . .

. . . By ordering the *AutoCAD Concise Guide Diskette*, which allows you to enter the programs and drawings featured throughout the book directly into your computer.

Each 5 1/4" floppy diskette includes the tutorial drawings featured in the forty chapters and six appendices.

Your *AutoCAD Concise Guide Diskette* will run on any 360K IBM-standard format computer and will save hours of tedious errorprone typing. To order your copy, please complete the form below, detach and mail the postage-paid card.

**MAIL TO: Ventana Press, P.O. Box 2468, Chapel Hill, NC 27515. Or, if you'd like it even sooner, call 919/942-0220.**

# BECOME EVEN MORE PRODUCTIVE . . .

. . . By ordering the *AutoCAD Concise Guide Diskette,* which allows you to enter the programs and drawings featured throughout the book directly into your computer.

Each 5 1/4" floppy diskette includes the tutorial drawings featured in the forty chapters and six appendices.

Your *AutoCAD Concise Guide Diskette* will run on any 360K IBM-standard format computer and will save hours of tedious errorprone typing. To order your copy, please complete the form below, detach and mail the postage-paid card.

**MAIL TO: Ventana Press, P.O. Box 2468, Chapel Hill, NC 27515. Or, if you'd like it even sooner, call 919/942-0220.**

Please send me _____ additional copies of *AutoCAD: A Concise Guide to Commands and Features* at $19.95 per book or $39.95 per book with diskette. Add $3.60 per book for normal UPS shipping; $5 for UPS two-day air. North Carolina residents add 5% sales tax. Immediate shipment guaranteed.

**Note: 15% discount for purchases of 5-9 books. 20% discount for purchases of 10 or more books. Resellers please call for wholesale discount information.**

Name: _____ Co: _____

Address (no P.O. Box): _____

City: _____ State: _____ Zip: _____

Telephone: _____

_____ Check or money order enclosed.

Visa or MC Account #: _____

Exp. Date: _____ Signature: _____

**Ventana Press ■ P.O. Box 2468 ■ Chapel Hill, NC 27515 ■ 919/942-0220**

Please send me _____ additional copies of *AutoCAD: A Concise Guide to Commands and Features* at $19.95 per book or $39.95 per book with diskette. Add $3.60 per book for normal UPS shipping; $5 for UPS two-day air. North Carolina residents add 5% sales tax. Immediate shipment guaranteed.

**Note: 15% discount for purchases of 5-9 books. 20% discount for purchases of 10 or more books. Resellers please call for wholesale discount information.**

Name: _____ Co: _____

Address (no P.O. Box): _____

City: _____ State: _____ Zip: _____

Telephone: _____

_____ Check or money order enclosed.

Visa or MC Account #: _____

Exp. Date: _____ Signature: _____

**Ventana Press ■ P.O. Box 2468 ■ Chapel Hill, NC 27515 ■ 919/942-0220**

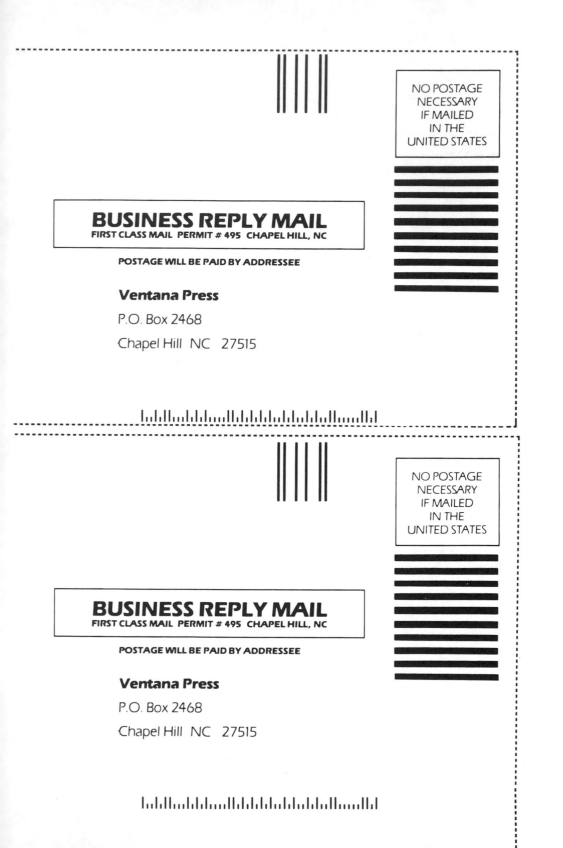

**BUSINESS REPLY MAIL**
FIRST CLASS MAIL  PERMIT # 495  CHAPEL HILL, NC

POSTAGE WILL BE PAID BY ADDRESSEE

**Ventana Press**

P.O. Box 2468

Chapel Hill  NC   27515

NO POSTAGE
NECESSARY
IF MAILED
IN THE
UNITED STATES

**BUSINESS REPLY MAIL**
FIRST CLASS MAIL  PERMIT # 495  CHAPEL HILL, NC

POSTAGE WILL BE PAID BY ADDRESSEE

**Ventana Press**

P.O. Box 2468

Chapel Hill  NC   27515

NO POSTAGE
NECESSARY
IF MAILED
IN THE
UNITED STATES

Please send me _____ additional copies of *AutoCAD: A Concise Guide to Commands and Features* at $19.95 per book or $39.95 per book with diskette. Add $3.60 per book for normal UPS shipping; $5 for UPS two-day air. North Carolina residents add 5% sales tax. Immediate shipment guaranteed.

**Note: 15% discount for purchases of 5-9 books. 20% discount for purchases of 10 or more books. Resellers please call for wholesale discount information.**

Name: _____ Co: _____

Address (no P.O. Box): _____

City: _____ State: _____ Zip: _____

Telephone: _____

_____ Check or money order enclosed.

Visa or MC Account #: _____

Exp. Date: _____ Signature: _____

**Ventana Press ■ P.O. Box 2468 ■ Chapel Hill, NC 27515 ■ 919/942-0220**

---

Please send me _____ additional copies of *AutoCAD: A Concise Guide to Commands and Features* at $19.95 per book or $39.95 per book with diskette. Add $3.60 per book for normal UPS shipping; $5 for UPS two-day air. North Carolina residents add 5% sales tax. Immediate shipment guaranteed.

**Note: 15% discount for purchases of 5-9 books. 20% discount for purchases of 10 or more books. Resellers please call for wholesale discount information.**

Name: _____ Co: _____

Address (no P.O. Box): _____

City: _____ State: _____ Zip: _____

Telephone: _____

_____ Check or money order enclosed.

Visa or MC Account #: _____

Exp. Date: _____ Signature: _____

**Ventana Press ■ P.O. Box 2468 ■ Chapel Hill, NC 27515 ■ 919/942-0220**

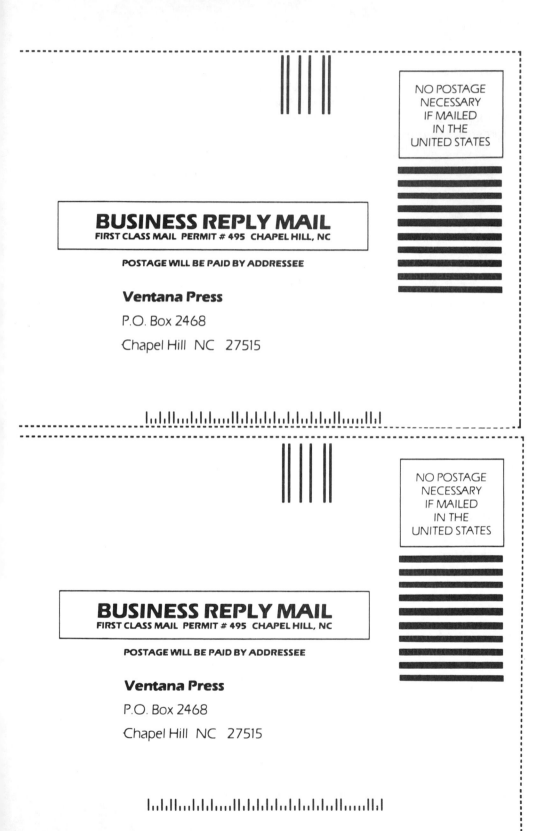

NO POSTAGE
NECESSARY
IF MAILED
IN THE
UNITED STATES

# BUSINESS REPLY MAIL
FIRST CLASS MAIL  PERMIT # 495  CHAPEL HILL, NC

POSTAGE WILL BE PAID BY ADDRESSEE

**Ventana Press**

P.O. Box 2468

Chapel Hill  NC   27515

NO POSTAGE
NECESSARY
IF MAILED
IN THE
UNITED STATES

# BUSINESS REPLY MAIL
FIRST CLASS MAIL  PERMIT # 495  CHAPEL HILL, NC

POSTAGE WILL BE PAID BY ADDRESSEE

**Ventana Press**

P.O. Box 2468

Chapel Hill  NC   27515

19.95